John Brown in New York

John Brown in New York

The Man, His Family, and the Adirondack Landscape

SANDRA WEBER

Cover credit: Photograph of cabin reflection at John Brown homestead by Shelby Bell. Shutterstock.

Published by State University of New York Press, Albany

© 2025 State University of New York

All rights reserved

Printed in the United States of America

No part of this book may be used or reproduced in any manner whatsoever without written permission. No part of this book may be stored in a retrieval system or transmitted in any form or by any means including electronic, electrostatic, magnetic tape, mechanical, photocopying, recording, or otherwise without the prior permission in writing of the publisher.

Links to third-party websites are provided as a convenience and for informational purposes only. They do not constitute an endorsement or an approval of any of the products, services, or opinions of the organization, companies, or individuals. SUNY Press bears no responsibility for the accuracy, legality, or content of a URL, the external website, or for that of subsequent websites.

EU GPSR Authorised Representative:
Logos Europe, 9 rue Nicolas Poussin, 17000, La Rochelle, France
contact@logoseurope.eu

Excelsior Editions is an imprint of State University of New York Press

For information, contact State University of New York Press, Albany, NY
www.sunypress.edu

Library of Congress Cataloging-in-Publication Data

Name: Weber, Sandra, 1961– author.
Title: John Brown in New York : the man, his family, and the Adirondack landscape / Sandra Weber.
Description: Albany : State University of New York Press, [2025]. | Series: Excelsior editions | Includes bibliographical references and index. |
Identifiers: LCCN 2025014362 | ISBN 9798855804638 (hardcover : alk. paper) | ISBN 9798855804652 (ebook) | ISBN 9798855804645 (pbk. : alk. paper)
Subjects: LCSH: Brown, John, 1800–1859. | Brown, John, 1800–1859—Family. | Brown family. | Abolitionists—New York (State)—North Elba (Town)—Biography. | North Elba (N.Y. : Town)—Biography. | Adirondack Mountains Region (N.Y.)—Biography. | United States—Race relations—History—19th century. | John Brown Farm State Historic Site (North Elba, N.Y.). | LCGFT: Biographies.
Classification: LCC F129.N8 W44 2025 | DDC 973.7/116092 [B]—dc23/eng/20250710
LC record available at https://lccn.loc.gov/2025014362

Contents

List of Illustrations	vii
Terminology and Abbreviations	xi
Acknowledgments	xv
Introduction	1
1 A Land of Promise and Hard Toil	9
2 Timbucto	27
3 Cultivators of Soil and Social Justice	43
4 The Genesis of the John Brown Farm and the Demise of Timbucto	59
5 Middling Tuff Times	75
6 High Peaks and Higher Law	89
7 Carrying the War into Africa	99
8 The Anguish of Harpers Ferry	115
9 Vying for John Brown's Body	133

10	Buried Among Kin and Neighbors	153
11	Suffering, Stone Inscriptions, and School	171
12	July Fourth at North Elba	187
13	Wartime in Essex County and Concord	201
14	Truly, the World Moves, and the People Move with It	217

Appendix A: John Brown's Family — 229

Appendix B: Timeline — 233

Notes — 237

Selected Bibliography — 271

Index — 277

List of Illustrations

I.1	Grave of ten Harpers Ferry comrades (two black men and eight white men, including Oliver Brown), Watson Brown's grave, John Brown's grave	3
I.2	Brown farmhouse from graveyard	5
1.1	Map of New York State and western portion of Essex County	10
1.2	John Brown (1800–1859), circa 1850	13
1.3	Mary Ann Day Brown (1816–1884), wife of John, circa 1860	14
1.4	Frederick Douglass, 1845	17
1.5	Willis A. Hodges, Franklin County grantee, founder of Blacksville	20
2.1	"Indian Pass from 'Scotts'"	29
2.2	Gerrit Smith, 1855	39
3.1	David Ruggles (1810–1849)	44
3.2	Mary Brown with Annie and Sarah, 1851	46
3.3	Ruth Brown Thompson, eldest daughter of John Brown	49
3.4	Henry Thompson, husband of Ruth Brown	50
3.5	Lyman Epps (circa 1815–1897)	55
3.6	Major Points of Interest and Residences in North Elba circa 1849–1860	57

4.1	John Brown's House (on Lot 95), North Elba, 1867	64
4.2	John Brown's House (on Lot 95), North Elba, circa 1870–1880	65
5.1	Watson Brown, son of John and Mary	76
5.2	Salmon Brown, son of John and Mary	87
5.3	Abbie Hinckley Brown, wife of Salmon, sister of Alexis Hinckley	88
6.1	"Off Tahawus—East, July 19, 1859"	92
6.2	"Whiteface (Mountain), from Lake Placid"	94
6.3	Philosophers' Camp, from *Frank Leslie's Illustrated Newspaper*, 1858	95
7.1	John Brown, circa 1859	100
7.2	Oliver Brown and wife, Martha Brewster Brown, 1859	103
7.3	Annie Brown, daughter of John and Mary, in her teens	112
8.1	Townspeople and raiders in engine house exchanging rifle fire at Harpers Ferry, Virginia, October 16–17, 1859	120
8.2	"Harpers Ferry Insurrection—Burying the Dead Insurgents"	122
8.3	John Brown's Trial at Charlestown, Virginia, painting by David C. Lithgow, 1923	130
9.1	"Mrs. Brown Escorted from Harper's Ferry to the Jail at Charlestown to Have an Interview with her Husband, the Day Before he was Hanged"	138
9.2	"John Brown's Last Interview with his Wife in the Jail at Charlestown, VA"	139
9.3	"Execution of John Brown" in Charles Town with soldiers surrounding the field, December 2, 1859	142
9.4	Sail Ferry at Barber's Point near Westport, New York	146
9.5	"1858 View of Court House and Clerks Office of Essex County," Elizabethtown, New York	148

9.6	"Arrival of the Body at North Elba. A Moonlight View"	149
9.7	Rev. Joshua Young of Burlington, Vermont	150
10.1	"The Burial of John Brown, North Elba, December 8, 1859"	154
10.2	"The Last View of John Brown's Body"	157
11.1	Abolitionist, suffragist, poet, speaker, and writer Frances Ellen Watkins Harper, circa 1890s	173
11.2	Isabelle (Belle) Thompson Brown, wife of Watson, with their son Freddy, circa 1860	179
11.3	Old Family Tombstone on John Brown's Grave	183
11.4	Osborne Perry Anderson, fought at Harpers Ferry and escaped	185
13.1	Louisa May Alcott, circa 1870	203
13.2	Copy of early version of the "John Brown Song," July 16, 1861	206
14.1	*John Brown's Grave*, painting by William Trost Richards, circa 1864	224
14.2	Home of John Brown, North Elba, New York, circa 1880s	227

Terminology and Abbreviations

In general, this book uses terminology from the antebellum era. Language helps ground the reader in the people and events of that time. The following terms are explained to clarify their usage in this book.

Adirondacks. References to the Adirondacks correspond to the vast region of northern New York known historically as the "Great Wilderness" or "Northern Wilderness," or more recently as the "Adirondack Park." Scholars generally agree that the word *Adirondack* is from the Iroquois word for "bark eater," which they attached to the Algonquin people as an insult. However, the subsequent application of the native nomenclature to the mountain region in 1838 was done with good intentions—of preserving the original culture. A white man, Professor Ebenezer Emmons, wrote: "I propose to call the Adirondack Group, a name by which a well-known tribe of Indians who once hunted here may be commemorated."[1]

Charles Town. The site of Brown's trial and execution was Charlestown, Virginia (now Charles Town, West Virginia) in Jefferson County. It is often confused with Charleston, Virginia (now the capital of West Virginia) in Kanawha County, which was originally Charlestown until 1819. To try to avoid confusion, this book uses Charles Town to refer to the Jefferson County town near Harpers Ferry, except in quoted passages

Names. There are various spellings of the names of early settlers. This book uses Epps (for Eppes). Dickson (for Dickinson, Dixon), Hinckley (for Hinkley), Coppoc (for Coppock, Coppic, and Coppac), and Hasbrook (for Hasbrouck).

North Elba. The Town of North Elba was established in late 1849, and became official in 1850. Prior to that time, it was the western part of the Town of Keene; however, to avoid confusion, this text generally refers to the area as North Elba. (Towns in New York State are denoted as townships in most other states.) In addition to showing the Town boundaries, many historic and modern maps also label a "North Elba" hub on Old Military Road (Route 73) near the Adirondak Loj Road or Ausable River crossing. John Brown often referred to North Elba as "Essex," the name of its county (not to be confused with the village or town of Essex along Lake Champlain). Although North Elba was the popular name for the area in 1850–70, with the growth of tourism around Mirror Lake and Lake Placid in the 1870s, the area became better known as "Lake Placid."

Race. In recent times, it is accepted that race is a socially constructed idea or category of identification, not based on inherent biological differences. However, during the antebellum era, the racial constructs of "black" and "white" were in practice and often used to identify a person. This makes it necessary to refer to people's race in this book. Since there was no single preferred term at that time—African, colored, and black being the most common—this book uses *black*, except in quoted text, to refer to people considered to be of the African or Negro race in the antebellum era.

Timbucto. The name refers to the black community in North Elba, Essex County, New York, presumably named by James Henderson and John Brown in 1848 for the ancient African city of Timbuktu (Timbuctoo, Timbucto, or the French Tombouctou). Henderson, Brown, and Ruth Brown spelled Timbucto with one *o* (an often-used spelling). Many recent accounts refer to the Adirondack community as "Timbuctoo" (with two *o*'s), which belies its historic roots. This text uses Timbucto, except in quoted passages.

Wilderness. This book uses the term *wilderness* as understood from 1849 to 1863, to refer to wild, untamed, unimproved lands. It is not used to imply Wilderness, a later official designation in National Parks and the Adirondack Park.

Abbreviations for Names

AB	Annie Brown
HT	Henry Thompson
JB	John Brown
JBJr	John Brown Jr.
MB	Mary Brown

RBT   Ruth Brown Thompson

SB   Salmon Brown

Abbreviations for Sources

BPL   Boston Public Library, Rare Books and Manuscripts

Cotter   Edwin N. Cotter Jr. Collection, SUNY-Plattsburgh, Special Collections

Gee   Gee-Brown Collection at Hudson Library and Historical Society, Ohio

LOC   Library of Congress

Ohio   Ohio State Historical Society, Cleveland, Ohio

Stutler   Boyd B. Stutler Collection, West Virginia Archives and Online Database

Sykes   Sykes Manuscript Files, Library of Congress

Acknowledgments

This book encompasses thirty-five years of research and writing. I am grateful to a multitude of friends, colleagues, and organizations that inspired, supported, and encouraged this work in many ways. To all of you, my sincerest thank you.

A special thanks to SUNY Editor Richard Carlin for having the wisdom and insight to see what this book could be and for giving me the encouragement to dig deeper. I would like to acknowledge Harpers Ferry National Historical Park for my artist-in-residence in October 2001, which provided an immersion into the John Brown of Harpers Ferry perspective and an opportunity for dedicated research time.

In North Elba, thank you to the late caretaker of the John Brown Farm, Edwin Cotter, for your extraordinary stewardship of the historic site and your pioneering research on John Brown's time in the Adirondacks.

I would like to express my appreciation to the late Dick Gregory for focusing my vision on the significance of "You have John Brown" and to John Brown Lives! for bringing exceptional speakers and programs to the Adirondacks.

As mentors and friends, the late SUNY professor of philosophy and Adirondack historian Warder Cadbury and the late Lake Placid–North Elba historian Mary MacKenzie guided me through the forest of history.

I am also grateful to professor, philosopher, lawyer, and friend Hope Elizabeth May for her stimulating conversations and Memory Parlors, which kept me lucid. Most of all, thank you to my partner, David Hodges. You are my rock.

Introduction

> The *art* of composition is as simple as the discharge of a bullet from a rifle and its masterpieces imply an infinitely greater force behind them. . . . It suggests that the one great rule of composition — and if I were a professor of rhetoric I should insist on this — is, to *speak the truth*. This first, this second, this third; pebbles in your mouth or not.
>
> — Henry David Thoreau, "A Plea for Captain John Brown"

A narrow lane leads from the old military turnpike near Lake Placid through a pine forest to an expansive clearing of high plains. The open fields of the John Brown Farm give way to verdant evergreens that spread southward in waves, dappled in shades of green and garnished with streaks of white birch and red maple, 'til they become engulfed in the towering sentinels of the Adirondack Mountains. The pyramidal profile of Whiteface pervades the view to the north, while Mount Marcy (Tahawus the Cloud-Splitter) rises to the southeast. As I inhale the scene, a sense of untamed nature fills my lungs and heart.

On this blustery day in early May of 2013, I merge with the crowd solemnly milling about under a big white tent near John Brown's grave. We are not gathered for a funeral but for the birthday remembrance known as John Brown Day. The guest of honor, comedian Dick Gregory, greets the enthusiastic crowd and then recalls his three-hour ride from Albany. Upon entering the Adirondack Park near Lake George, his driver started pointing out the profusion of trees of all varieties. Balsam, sugar maple, white pine . . . .

"Damn that's all they told me," says Gregory, "look at the trees."

As he tells the tale, he chuckles and shakes his head and mumbles something about the "vast forest." The audience smiles and giggles a little, not wanting to offend the guest, but not sure what point he is trying to make. Gregory waits, motionless, until the crowd falls silent.

"You want to talk about the damn trees. They got trees all over the world." He takes a long pause before slowly releasing his verdict.

"What they do not have that you have here is John Brown."

I know we have John Brown. I have been studying him and his family and Adirondack history for decades. You won't find John Brown's body in Torrington, Connecticut, the place of his birth, nor in Ohio where he grew up, nor in Kansas where he battled to make it a Free State. His remains are not buried in Harpers Ferry, Virginia (now West Virginia), where he fought against slavery, nor in Charles Town, where he was hanged. John Brown's body rests placidly in the rural Town of North Elba, Essex County, in the Adirondack Park of northern New York State.

"I wonder," says Gregory as he looks through the audience, "do you all really know what this is about, who this person was, and how evil this country was then."

Every year on his birthday (October 12), Gregory visits Harpers Ferry, and every December 2, he goes to Charles Town and hugs the tree next to where John Brown was hung. "I hug the tree," he says, "for the white man who gave up his life for a black man."

Today, Gregory is here, at John Brown's grave, to say "thank you." Because Brown did more than liberate slaves, he "changed the whole world." Gregory adds, "If I had to write on the most important people on this planet, he would be number one."

I am dazed and dazzled all intertwined in a jazz chord. My sureness crumples. I feel taken captive, transported to Gregory's reality. Has the natural scenery made me unable to see the lush significance of the human landscape?

"Right here. You have John Brown."

Gregory seems certain that the audience does not grasp the magnitude of the grave a few feet over his left shoulder. "This man is real," he affirms, "and you have him."

The words decimate the nebulous cloud hanging over the historic site. They clear away the haziness and blurredness. Other places have forests, mountains, and wilderness. Other historic sites have cabins and buildings where "John Brown slept here," but North Elba has John Brown. All that remains of his mortal body is here.

Figure I.1. Left to right: Grave of ten Harpers Ferry comrades (two black men and eight white men, including Oliver Brown), Watson Brown's grave, John Brown's grave. John Brown Farm State Historic Site in Town of North Elba, near Village of Lake Placid, 2021. *Source:* Photo by the author.

> They may hang him on the gibbet; they may raise the victor's cry
> When they see him darkly swinging like a speck against the sky;
> Ah! the dying of a hero that the right may win its way
> Is but sowing seed for harvest in a warm and mellow May!²

On this not-so-warm day in May, standing on the ground that Brown and his family once owned and lived on, I hear the fields echo the whack of the axe, hoe, and scythe. Dragonflies skim across the pond, leading my gaze toward the timber frame barn. It is easy to imagine the pioneer life of the Brown family—milking cows, digging potatoes, and carding sheep's wool on this hardscrabble farm. Here, far from Southern plantations and Boston abolitionists, they affirmed their roles in the fight against injustice and girded themselves for duty and sacrifice. Some served the cause at home, while others fought with weapons and lost their lives.

From the doorway of this humble homestead, John Brown and his sons and neighbors said goodbye to their loved ones and left for far-off battles in Kansas and Harpers Ferry. Those scenes of violence feel continents apart from the John Brown Farm, but the results of those distant events brought grief and suffering to these mountain plains. I feel it still as I gaze through the tall fence of iron pikes at the three burial mounds holding the mortal remains of John Brown, his sons Watson and Oliver, neighbors William and Dauphin Thompson, and seven other men, black and white, who went to Harpers Ferry to liberate enslaved people.

Dick Gregory is correct: the beauty of the trees can overshadow the human landscape. When the shadow is lifted, something unexpected happens. I still see the lush forests and wild mountain scenery surrounding the farm, but now I comprehend them fused into John Brown's persona. Frederick Douglass perceived Brown as "a figure straight and symmetrical as a mountain pine."[3] One admirer believed Brown's conscience was "a Lake Placid, and his resolution to follow it firm as Marcy, firm as Whiteface."[4] Another wrote, "In these wilds, there is something consonant with his own untamable spirit. He is the very air of freedom."[5]

Yes, John Brown marches on, and we have him. The historic site has been, and still is, a gathering place for solemn thoughts and a rallying spot for lovers of human rights. Here, John Brown is alive, still inspiring and still agitating our mind, chafing our conviction, and gnawing at our conscience.

I often recall John Brown saying: "Providence will lead us all more properly to appreciate the amazing unforeseen, untold, consequences; that hang upon the right or wrong doing of things seemingly of trifling account. Who can tell or comprehend the vast results for good, or for evil; that are to follow the saying of one little word." The four little words spoken by Dick Gregory, "You have John Brown," kept festering in my brain. Those words of seemingly trifling account led me to more fully comprehend the significance of North Elba in the lives of the man and his family. The result is this book, *John Brown in New York*.

A North Elba, New York, Perspective

American history is longer, larger, more various, more beautiful, and more terrible than anything anyone has ever said about it.

—James Baldwin, "A Talk to Teachers"

Figure I.2. Brown farmhouse from graveyard. John Brown Farm State Historic Site, 2021. *Source:* Photo by the author.

John Brown is one the most renowned and contentious figures in American history. Each generation grapples with understanding and interpreting his story, yet a part remains incomplete and misrepresented. *John Brown in New York* presents his connection to North Elba, Essex County, New York—a vital piece of John Brown history more intimate, more heartbreaking, and more consequential than has been told.

Off and on from 1849 to 1863, the John Brown family lived in North Elba as common, hardworking pioneer farmers in community with black neighbors, encircled by the Adirondack Mountains. It is an intertwining story of sublime scenery and human rights, of a family who preached and practiced equalitarianism and believed in two doctrines: the Golden Rule and the Declaration of Independence. Their story did not end with Brown's hanging and subsequent burial at his New York home. In the 1860s, abolitionists gathered in North Elba to proclaim their faith in the truths of the Declaration of Independence. Friends of freedom made pilgrimages to their "Calvary," and Civil War veterans placed tributes there.

John Brown in New York focuses on the home front (rather than battlefields) and provides a new perspective on John Brown's inner self, moral fiber, and principles. It serves as a conduit through which to reconcile the poor pioneer farmer, family patriarch, and devoted friend of blacks with his public persona as madman, murderer, or martyr. As one of John Brown's closest brethren in the Adirondacks and beyond, Willis Hodges, declared: "The character displayed by the old man in Kansas and Virginia . . . was in strict keeping with his life in Northern New York." Who John Brown is in the Adirondacks is who he is.

Plenty of books document the saga of John Brown's early life, Kansas years, and Harpers Ferry raid. James Redpath published the first biography immediately after Brown's death, and others followed, written by Franklin Sanborn (1891), Richard J. Hinton (1894), W. E. B. Du Bois (1909), and Oswald Garrison Villard (1910). More recent books include David Reynolds's *John Brown, Abolitionist*, Stephen Oates's *To Purge This Land with Blood*, Louis DeCaro Jr.'s *Fire From the Midst*, H. W. Brands's *The Zealot and the Emancipator*, and John Stauffer's *Black Hearts of Men*. However, North Elba generally plays a minor part in these volumes.

Why the disregard for North Elba? First, its relevance is not as obvious or sensational as Kansas or Virginia. North Elba is the site of the family home, not a rendezvous place or an arms cache. Nor is it the site of abolition conventions or a hotbed of civil conflict, like Boston or New York City or Philadelphia. It is a remote, sparsely populated place known for its natural setting more than its human history. Putting the John Brown story in its proper context in North Elba requires an intimate knowledge of both Adirondack geography and history.

Second, Brown travels quite frequently to tend to his wool business, lawsuits, and antislavery activities, so he is not physically in North Elba for very long. But time does not measure significance. North Elba (or "Essex" as he often calls it) becomes John Brown's favorite place, where he feels in tune with nature and close to God. He has "Essex fever" and, no matter where he travels, he yearns to return to North Elba. It is his *home*, where his wife, children, and grandchildren have a safe refuge and can live cheerfully though in the midst of poverty and anxieties. It is the place he sends letters, money, and provisions to his family—where he longs to lay his head at night.

Most of the current works on John Brown are well-written and firmly rooted in the context of his times. However, in the sections about the family's life in North Elba, the details remain vague and subjective, as bits and pieces of biased recollections, repeated myths, and misinterpretations. For the first time, the whole of this history has been extracted, examined critically, and compiled into a compelling narrative. *John Brown in New York* pulls from a wide range of sources, relying heavily on primary sources from the antebellum era. It transports the reader to the setting and context through a variety of voices, including those of women as well as men, black as well as white, and poor people as well as the rich, ruling class.

Among the many vantage points from which to consider John Brown and his family, the view from the Adirondack Mountains is the most remote but perhaps the most revealing. Why did they make this spot their home? "With John Brown and his family there is a reason for everything," said abolitionist Thomas Wentworth Higginson, "and it is always the same reason . . . the same prompt answer comes ringing back,—the very motto of the tombstone,—'For adherence to the cause of freedom' . . . The same purpose, nay, the selfsame project that sent John Brown to Harper's Ferry sent him to the Adirondacks."[6]

While John's abolitionist views had formed in Ohio and Pennsylvania, it is during the North Elba years that those views intensified and took greater form and action. Moving to North Elba is a pivotal shift in John Brown's life. At age forty-nine, he makes a strategic decision to disengage from business ventures and dedicate himself wholeheartedly to his Godly mission of ending the sin of American slavery. The change from business to social action is not an intentional move toward extremism, militancy, or zealotry; it is a shift in emphasis, of returning to a farming-homesteading lifestyle, which reduced his financial needs, so he could fully engage in moral work according to the principles of John Brown.

Behind the turbulent scenes of national drama, rage, bloodshed, and political upheaval, the rhythm of *ordinary* routine continues at North Elba. Brown's children marry local sweethearts. Illness takes lives, babies are born, seeds planted, and harvests reaped. The hard work of tilling the soil and cultivating character within oneself, of embracing morality and mortality in the Adirondack wilderness goes on. At the same time, the Browns exhibit *extraordinary* qualities. They demonstrate a fierce hatred of slavery and a brotherhood with blacks, especially their black neighbors of Timbucto. It becomes clear that family members are not following John but embrace a personal duty to confront the sin of slavery and a willingness to forego comfort and safety. Several members of the extended family participate in militant actions in Kansas, Missouri, and Harpers Ferry, for which the Browns and their allies pay a high penalty—death, suffering, and unwelcomed celebrity. And an often contested legacy.

In today's world, it is not easy to comprehend or digest the violence and lawbreaking of John Brown and his comrades in the 1850s. Neither is it comfortable to recall that it was legal to enslave people in the United

States or to acknowledge the brutal, barbaric, and inhumane reality of chattel slavery and the millions of people scarred and traumatized by it. American history is not always beautiful; parts of it are terrible. Nevertheless, historians should strive for a complete and factually accurate narrative of the past. Author and scholar Louis DeCaro Jr. describes the John Brown Farm as being unlike other historic sites that serve the mythology and top-down narrative of America. "The John Brown Farm is truly a site of conscience," he says, "that testifies to the real history of the United States with its gross wrongs and injustices; and perhaps the quintessential story of one family that sacrificed everything for the cause of justice."[7]

Chapter 1

A Land of Promise and Hard Toil

> Nature reigns in this wilderness, in her primeval seclusion and solitudes. The daring hunter penetrates its mazes in pursuit of its only denizens, the moose, the bear, the panther and deer. The fisherman, whose ardor leads him to the deep recesses of the forest, breaks the quiet repose of these lakes and rivers, but within the boundaries of this sequestered region, man has scarcely an abode, in his civilization and improvements.
>
> —Winslow Watson, "Supplement to Survey of Essex County," New York, 1853

"[John Brown] flung away life to come up and freeze on the mountains," according to abolitionist Wendell Phillips. While much of the nation was moving from a subsistence economy to a capitalist economy in the mid-1800s, John Brown returned to a pioneer life. Unlike many of his peers, he did not seek the wide-open prairies of the Midwest or the gold mines of the western frontier. Brown moved to the Adirondack Mountains in northern New York State—not to the settled lands near the St. Lawrence River or Lake Champlain, but to the wild lands of western Essex County, surrounded by almost impenetrable high peaks. Eminent men sneered at the region as the "Siberia" of New York and indulged in sarcasm and ridicule of the character and resources of Essex County.[1]

In the eyes of New Englanders, such as Wendell Phillips, North Elba was a place "where wheat freezes, and where nothing can be cultivated but a few potatoes, where the mountains look down on a home that is almost a shanty." Local farmers immediately posted a rebuke to Phillips. They

Figure 1.1. Map of New York State and western portion of Essex County showing Towns of St. Armand, North Elba, and Keene. Indicates the locations of Lot 95 (John Brown Farm, where Browns lived from 1855 to 63) and Lot 110 (Flanders Farm, where Browns lived from 1849 to 51). *Source:* Map by David Hodges, based on French's 1858 map. Used with permission.

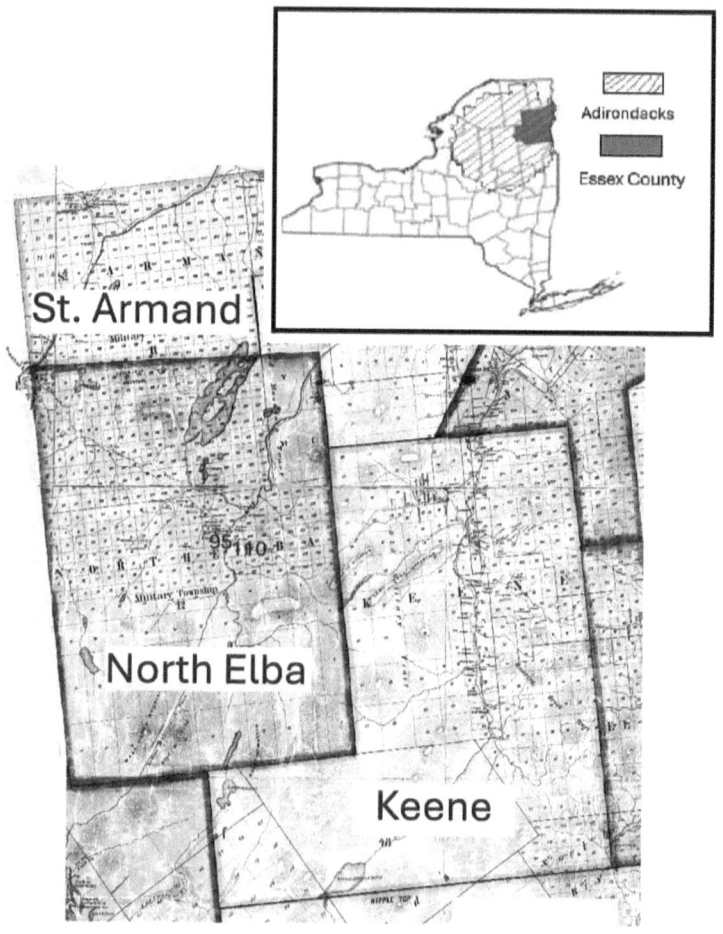

conceded that part of North Elba was mountainous, but "other portions are constituted of beautiful plain, and fine interval, which produce grass, oats, potatoes, rye, wheat, and livestock in great abundance, and often good crops of corn. Thousands of dollars have been paid to the people of North Elba, and the back towns in its immediate vicinity, within the last ten years, by lumbermen, for their surplus grain, hay, pork and beef."[2]

A Burlington, Vermont reporter agreed that Phillips greatly underrated the population, climate, and soil of North Elba. The citizens did not live on "frozen potatoes" and they were "intelligent" people. Proof could be shown by "the single fact that they take not fewer than twenty-five copies of the *N.Y. Weekly Tribune*."[3]

According to Winslow Watson, the reigning agriculturalist and historian of Essex County in the 1850s, those who disparaged the region were unaware that farming and grazing were particularly viable on the "extensive and fertile plains of North Elba." On that table land, the soil was a dark sandy loam, "remarkably rich in organic matter," and free from stones and rocks. However, it was not an easy place to reach (only one road penetrated the barrier of mountains east-to-west), nor was it a place to get rich or partake in swanky affairs (there was no store or tavern). Watson claimed the people displayed the spirit of New Englanders in their farms and "in their general intelligence, their eminent fostering of schools, and their high-toned moral and religious character."[4]

That made it a place well-suited to John Brown and his family. But they could have found other locales with those attributes; what most lured them to North Elba was an opportunity to continue their work for the cause—by living among and advising, encouraging, and aiding the newly arriving black settlers. In this remote mountain town, all could work together in the fight against prejudice, injustice, and slavery. And Mary Ann Day Brown (John's second wife) already had a link to upstate New York and its abolition network.

Mary was born on April 15, 1816, just southeast of the Adirondack Mountains in Granville, Washington County. The area linked transportation lines from New York City, Albany, Boston, and Buffalo with railroads and the Champlain Canal leading to Vermont and Canada, making it a hub for Underground Railroad activity. When Mary was nine years old, her family moved to Crawford County, Pennsylvania, but her half-brother Orson Day stayed in New York and ran a store in nearby Whitehall. This established a long-standing family connection between northeastern New York and northwestern Pennsylvania.

Mary's parents, Charles (a blacksmith) and Mary Ann Little Day (his second wife), settled near their daughter Martha Day Delamater and her husband, Thomas, who ran a tavern in Meadville, Pennsylvania. As abolitionists, the Delamaters were good friends with John Brown and his first wife (Dianthe Lusk), their houses being only four miles apart. They even schooled their children together, at the Browns' house in winter and the

Delamaters' house in the summer. John Brown's older children knew the Delamater children quite well, even before they became cousins.[5]

John Brown was born on May 9, 1800, the son of Owen and Ruth Mills Brown of Torrington, Connecticut. Five years later, the family moved to Hudson, Ohio, in the recently opened Western Reserve. Owen worked as a tanner and became a leader in the establishment of frontier churches and abolitionist activities. During the early years of Oberlin College, he served as a trustee helping to make it one of the first US institutions of higher learning to admit women and black students.

Young John Brown experienced the life of the frontier, learning the practices of farming, breeding, and tanning. He saw the wretched treatment of a slave boy and adopted a hatred of slavery at the age of twelve. A few years later, John felt called to the ministry, but a lack of funds and an eye condition forced him to give up his studies. He returned to Ohio and practiced his father's trade as a tanner and taught himself the art of surveying.

John married Dianthe Lusk in 1820, and they had seven children, five of whom lived to maturity. In 1826, the family moved to Richmond Township in Crawford County, Pennsylvania, where John built a tannery and served as postmaster. Tragedy struck in 1832, when Dianthe died a few days after giving birth to an infant son who also died. The next year, on July 11, 1833, John married Mary Ann Day; he was thirty-three, she was seventeen.[6]

A union between Mary and widower John Brown seemed almost predestined. Mary was no stranger to John or to his five children, and she was already well-versed in abolition and Christian principles before marriage. An old acquaintance of the Day family speculated that John "probably derived much of the inspiration for fighting for a just cause" from Mary.[7] Whether or not she roused his fortitude, John Brown appreciated her as a loving wife and loyal helpmate.

Ten months after marriage, Mary gave birth to the first of thirteen children. In addition to welcoming a baby girl into their household, Mary and John planned to bring "at least one negro boy" into the family and "give him a good English education, learn him what we can about the history of the world, about business, about general subjects, and, above all, try to teach him the fear of God." John believed the endeavor might grow into a school for black students, which might do more toward "breaking their yoke effectually" than any other way. "If the young blacks of our country could once become enlightened," he said, "it would most assuredly operate on slavery like firing powder confined in rock." Then, if Christians in the

Figure 1.2. John Brown (1800–1859), circa 1850. Regarded by the family as the best photo of John. *Source:* Library of Congress. Public domain.

free states would set to work in earnest in teaching the black students, the people of the slaveholding states would find themselves constitutionally driven to set about the work of emancipation immediately.[8]

Although the Browns did not adopt a black child or start a black school in the 1830s, their abhorrence toward slavery was heightened in 1837 by the shooting of white abolitionist publisher Rev. Elijah Lovejoy

A Land of Promise and Hard Toil | 13

Figure 1.3. Mary Ann Day Brown (1816–1884), wife of John, circa 1860. *Source:* Library of Congress. Public domain.

by a proslavery mob in Alton, Illinois. A news report claimed this murder "called forth from every part of the land, a burst of indignation which has not had its parallel in this country since the Battle of Lexington, 1775."[9] The event impelled John Brown to rise at the end of a prayer meeting and publicly pledge that he would devote his life to the overthrow of slavery. Mary and the children made an unflinching commitment to help runaway slaves and to endure sacrifices and hardship for the cause.

The duty to serve the cause of black liberation through education, Underground Railroad activity, and other means was ever-present for John. At the same time, he also had a large family to support: John Jr., Jason, Owen, Ruth, and Frederick (born to Dianthe), along with the younger children born to Mary. In the years between 1835 and 1846, the family moved several times as John pursued a variety of trades and businesses, including farming, tanning, surveying, land speculation, and stock raising. John's situation was not an anomaly among his peers. In "Self-Reliance," Ralph Waldo Emerson described the sturdy New England lad who tried all the professions, "who teams it, farms it, peddles, keeps a school, preaches, edits newspaper, goes to Congress, buys a township, and so forth, in successive years, and always like a cat falls on his feet." Furthermore, Emerson said this man "feels no shame in not 'studying a profession' for he does not postpone his life, but lives already."[10]

John lived a life of action, though he did not always land on his feet. Business debacles, bankruptcy, and children's deaths (four in two weeks in 1843) came his way, and the Brown family drank often from "the bitter cup." John reflected on his life in an 1846 letter to Mary.

My dear Mary,

It is once more Sabbath evening, and nothing so much accords with my feelings as to spend a portion of it in conversing with the partner of my choice, and the sharer of my poverty, trials, discredit, and sore afflictions, as well as of what comfort and seeming prosperity has fallen to my lot for quite a number of years.

   I would you should realize that, notwithstanding I am absent in body, am very much of the time present in spirit. I do not forget the firm attachment of her who has remained my fast and faithful affectionate friend, when others said of me, "Now that he lieth, he shall rise up no more."

   .... I feel considerable regret by turns that I have lived so many years, and have in reality done so little to increase the amount of human happiness. I often regret that my manner is no more kind and affectionate to those I really love and esteem but trust my friends will overlook my harsh, rough ways, when I cease to be in their way as an occasion of pain and unhappiness.[11]

While John expressed his tenderness for Mary, in the latter part of the letter he admitted his not-so-tender ways of disciplining his children. He counseled Mary to be better in his absence. If the older boys committed wrongs, he suggested she appeal to their honor in a kind but powerful manner. "I do not claim that such a theory accords very well with my practice; I frankly confess it does not, but I want your face to shine, even if my own should be dark and cloudy."

John Brown was a stern father. According to biographer Stephen Oates, "He insisted that his young sons learn 'good order and religious habits' and refused to let them play or to have visitors on the Sabbath." John also dealt with lies, disobedience, and other offensives by applying a rod ("a nicely-prepared blue-beech switch"). Though Brown ruled with a strong hand, his children said he never applied it unjustly. In retrospect, John wished he had acted very differently with his children. "I meant to do right, but I can see now where I failed."[12]

By 1847, John had gone into the wool business with Simon Perkins of Ohio and opened an office in Springfield, Massachusetts. Not long after moving his family there, one of the most prominent abolitionists, former slave Frederick Douglass, sought out the white man whom he had heard so much about. Upon seeing him, Douglass quickly sized up this man named John Brown: "under six feet high, less than one hundred and fifty lbs. in weight, aged about fifty" and wearing "plain American woolen" clothes, leather boots, and a cravat of cowhide leather. His smoothly shaved face revealed a strong square mouth and his eyes were grey, "and in conversation they alternated with tears and fire." Douglass concluded that Brown was "built for times of trouble, fitted to grapple with the flintiest hardships."[13]

The Browns did not reside among the businessmen's families in Springfield; they lived in a small wooden house on a back street in a neighborhood of laboring men and mechanics. Douglass observed that the outside of the house was plain and "the inside was plainer." There were "no sofas, no cushions, no curtains, no carpets, no easy rocking chairs." Likewise, there were no hired hands in this house. At teatime, "the mother, daughters and sons did the serving, and did it well . . . as if used to it, untouched by any thought of degradation or impropriety." They did not offer the traditional light meal of tea and toast; they dished out potatoes with cabbage and beef soup. Douglass considered it a meal a man might relish "after following the plough all day" or "after performing a forced march of a dozen miles." When everyone finished eating, the boys helped to clear the table and wash the dishes.

Figure 1.4. Frederick Douglass, 1845. *Source:* Library of Congress. Public domain.

This style of household management seemed a little odd and Douglass felt he needed to comment on it. "A house is more than brick and mortar, wood or paint, this to me at least was. In its plainness," he wrote, "it was a truthful reflection of its inmates: no disguises, no illusions, no make-believes here, but stern truth and solid purpose breathed in all its arrangements." John Brown commanded a strong religious influence "and his family supplied a ready 'Amen.'"

At last, the two men had a private meeting; Douglass listened intently as Brown began to lay out a plan to liberate slaves. On a large map of the United States, he pointed to the Alleghenies. "These mountains are the basis of my plan," he explained. "God has given the strength of these hills to freedom, they were placed here to aid the emancipation of your race."

Brown knew the mountains well and said they were full of natural forts and good hiding places where men could be concealed and elude pursuit for a long time. He planned to start small with twenty-some men who would go to Virginia plantations and liberate slaves. They would avoid fighting and shed no blood except in self-defense. The freed people could retreat to the mountains and form a colony there or follow the mountains north to freedom. Brown reasoned that these invasions would weaken slavery by making slave property insecure and keeping antislavery agitation alive.

Although Douglass was skeptical of the plan, he realized the man was sincere. Brown believed the institution of slavery was "in utter disregard and violation of those eternal and self-evident truths set forth in our Declaration of Independence." Slavery was a war—an "unprovoked, and unjustifiable war" on a portion of citizens of the United States. This view did not belong to an ordinary white man. John Brown was "in sympathy a black man," wrote Douglass, "and is as deeply interested in our cause, as though his own soul had been pierced with the iron of slavery."[14]

Gerrit Smith's Land Experiment

While living in Springfield, John announced to the family that they had a little money to spare. He supported the wishes of Mary and Ruth to purchase furniture for the parlor; then he proposed an alternative. Should the family save the money to buy clothing for the black settlers in the Adirondack Mountains?

"Save the money," was the reply.[15]

A few black men and their families had moved to the North Elba area of Essex County as part of a "scheme of justice and benevolence" initiated in 1846 by Gerrit Smith, a wealthy abolitionist and philanthropist of Peterboro, New York. As one of the largest landholders in the state, he granted 3,000 free black men forty-acre plots of unimproved land he owned, mainly in Essex, Franklin, and Hamilton Counties. His main goal was to encourage black men of New York State to leave "crowded cities and servile employments" and pursue "the manly and dignified labors of agricultural life." Promoters of Smith's plan said, "There is no life like that of the farmer, for overcoming the mere prejudice against color." In a farming community, neighbors assisted neighbors; there was "mutual and equal dependence, mutual sympathy—and labour," which comported to make all citizens equal.[16]

Smith also hoped his scheme would help black men overcome the "mean and wicked exclusion" from voting. Since they were required to own $250 in property in order to vote in New York, "they will become landowners," declared Smith. "Vote they will, cost what it will."[17]

Black men would become property owners—not in Africa or Haiti (as foreign colonization schemes had attempted), but in rural America, in farming communities such as those existing in the Adirondacks. "Be what you should, and can be," Smith told the black grantees, "and the enslavement of your race would no longer be possible." He hypothesized that colonies of black families with thriving farms would demonstrate they could prosper outside of slavery, and slaveholders would be "awe-struck" to realize they had been trampling on good people. Smith imagined that slaveholding hearts would cease beating and "the rod of the oppressor would fall from his relaxed grasp, and the oppressed go free."[18]

Black abolitionists believed that Smith and God had opened to them a "land of promise." The black press praised Smith's benevolence and eagerly promoted his fantastical dream. In his *North Star* newspaper, Frederick Douglass encouraged grantees to form groups of tens or twenties and immediately invade the Adirondack woods. "The Sharp Axe of the sable-armed pioneer should at once be uplifted over the soil of Franklin and Essex Counties and the noise of falling trees proclaim the glorious dawn of civilization within their borders! . . . The spring is near at hand. Seed-time is near; and what a man soweth that shall he reap."[19] A group of grantees responded: "We should like to be among the first to occupy the wilderness, and strike the first blow toward making it blossom like the rose."[20]

The Brooklyn Daily Eagle reported that "40 families of colored people" were leaving New York City for Essex and Franklin County in the spring of 1848.[21]

The *North Star* cheered: "Hurrah for the Smith lands! God speed the plough!"[22]

"Take with you the spirit of freedom," said Rev. Henry Highland Garnet. "Plant the tree of Liberty upon the mountain plains, that it may spread its branches far and wide." (An apt metaphor, but the grantees needed Douglass's "Sharp Axe" to remove trees rather than plant them.)[23]

Willis Hodges of Williamsburg (Brooklyn), editor of the antislavery newspaper *Ram's Horn*, also encouraged grantees to forsake the cities and become "cultivators of the soil." And he decided to take his own advice. Hodges left his grocery business and his newspaper to return to farming, a life he knew as a free-born black man in Virginia. A few others relocated with him near Loon Lake in Franklin County in May of 1848. He bought an additional two hundred acres of land, built a log home, started a farm, and established a settlement called Blacksville. Hodges wrote: "We find ourselves (through the mercy of God and the goodness of the honorable Gerrit Smith) today 'Under our own vine and fig tree,' with none to molest us or make us afraid."[24]

In Essex County, one of the first grantees to arrive was James Henderson. He and his family had lived comfortably in Manhattan where he ran a cobbler's shop by day and taught school in the evenings. Then they moved to Troy, New York, where Henderson became active in black politics. The offer of a land grant compelled the shoemaker to seek land ownership and the possibility of enfranchisement. The family left behind conveniences and comforts and moved even farther north—to the wild woods of Essex County, about as far from Manhattan as one could travel without leaving the state and stepping into Canada.

Figure 1.5. Willis A. Hodges, Franklin County grantee, founder of Blacksville. His autobiography, *Free Man of Color*, was written during his time at Blacksville. *Source:* Wikimedia Commons. Scan from the Afro-American Press. Public domain.

James, age thirty, and his wife Susan, age thirty-two, brought with them five children under the age of ten and James's mother Sally, age sixty-eight. The family began their life in the Adirondacks in the late spring of 1848, and from all indications, the three generations labored and flourished in their new home. "I like the land and the country well," wrote James. "There is no better land for grain." He proudly boasted of growing oats (25 to 50 bushels per acre) and potatoes and turnips (200 to 400 bushels per acre). In addition to his success at farming, he also ran a good business as a shoemaker.[25]

Practical Obstacles

The initial years of the Smith experiment generated plenty of enthusiastic cheers, pledges, and publicity. But Hodges and Henderson are two of the few men who went north and settled on their land in 1846 to 1848. The glitter of idealistic dreams faded when potential grantees heard the details and faced practical realities.

Although reports often claimed that Smith offered free land to *any* black man who would occupy and cultivate it, that was untrue. He restricted the eligibility of grantees, weeding out those who were "in easy circumstances," owners of land, too young or old, or drunkards. (Since Smith was a fervent Temperance man, he preferred grantees who did not drink any "intoxicating liquor.")[26] After setting the rules, Smith was mostly hands-off, assigning the task of finding grantees, distributing deeds, and planning migrations to a group of land agents. These agents included prominent black abolitionists such as Rev. Theodore S. Wright (the first black American graduate of theological seminary), Elder Charles B. Ray (a black minister, newspaper editor, and Underground Railroad activist), Dr. James McCune Smith (the first black graduate of medical school in New York, physician, and antislavery lecturer), and Rev. Henry Highland Garnet (former slave, advocate of slave insurrection, and antislavery speaker). These were highly qualified men, who received no pay for their service—only thank-yous from Gerrit Smith, and perhaps free lots.

When grantees gathered to learn more about their free land, they heard the agents say, "To God be the glory, Who, through this human instrument [Gerrit Smith] has been pleased to open us a 'land of promise.'" Few times before had black men been offered "a chance, for a more practical vindication of our claims to manhood. There is about this, enough of aid to give us the proper impetus—enough of difficulty to try our strength." After heaps of glorious idealism, the land agents had delivered the hard fact: Smith's gift involved hardship. The grantees would soon discover there was *not enough* aid and *more than enough* difficulty.[27]

Families would have to leave their relatives, friends, and community; leave behind their church, school, and social network. They had to quit their jobs as barbers, cooks, housekeepers, waiters, or coachmen and learn the skills of lumberjacks, carpenters, and farmers. Their lots were unimproved; not only was there no house or barn, but in most cases, there was also no water well and no cleared farm field or even a path to their lot. Yet, the agents calmly stated that it was just a jaunt through the woods, "for none of these lands are more than 2 miles from well-travelled roads." Two miles from a road, and then? "You will have to cut down the timber, erect dwellings therefrom, till the land, and undergo the labour and privations incident to pioneer cultivators."

What else did the agents expect of the cash-poor grantees? To get started, settlers would need $100 for furniture, farming tools, horses or oxen, and other items. The agents presumed a grantee could easily gather that amount by avoiding "the expense of balls, parties, and fruit entertainments." After settling on their land, grantees needed to practice economy by planning every expense and practicing self-denial. The "hard and earnest toil" would get them "happy results," declared the agents.

Many grantees may have favored trading city life for farming life, however, their vision of living in the countryside was "a well-mixed country and village life"—not a "consolidated, isolated country life," such as found in the Adirondack wilderness.[28] There was no stagecoach to even reach the vicinity of North Elba in 1846, and once you arrived, there was no store, no post office, no polling location, and no church building. Despite these conditions, the agents predicted 75 percent to 100 percent of the grantees would become successful Adirondack farmers and the people of New York State would "hail our self-emancipation from the drudgery of the cities" and "glory in the prosperity" that the new farms would bring.

Both counts proved to be overenthusiastic. Fewer than 2 percent of the grantees became Adirondack residents and since most lacked experience in homesteading or husbandry, success as a farmer was uncertain. While New Yorkers might "hail" the exodus from cities, the agents did not consider the impact on residents of the Adirondacks. Would the forty or so existing North Elba families "glory" in the prospect of four- or eight-hundred new families moving there?

From the beginning, some of the white residents made efforts to dissuade the black grantees from settling. A land agent reported "a high-handed game" played on grantees trying to locate their land. At a charge of two dollars a day, "pilots" or surveyors sometimes kept the grantees tramping in the woods for several days. A grantee might be shown a very desirable lot, pay the pilot, and then discover the lot did not match his deed. Or he might be shown a spot on a mountain peak or in a swamp, sell it to the pilot for a few dollars, and later discover he sold a deed to fertile land located elsewhere.[29]

Besides scamming grantees, some white people discredited other whites who attempted to help the black settlers. One well-documented case was that of surveyor Wait J. Lewis of the Town of Keene. At a meeting with grantees in 1848, he contracted with several of them to survey their lots. When local citizens learned of Lewis's intention, a group of them sent a letter to Frederick Douglass claiming Lewis was not a trustworthy surveyor. In defense of Lewis, his assistant sent a sworn statement to the *Northern Star and Colored Farmer* saying that the white citizens who opposed Lewis did not want him locating lots for the black grantees. They wanted no more black settlers as it would "ruin the town." These white people believed they could "starve them out" and the lands owned by black men would be resettled by white families. A few even proposed that Wait J. Lewis, Gerrit Smith, and the black residents "ought to be banished to Africa."[30]

The press spread news of the surveying squabble and other difficulties of the grantees. Very few black families gambled on the move to the Adirondacks; most of the grantee parcels remained unoccupied. Henry Highland Garnet told the grantees to cast off the old ways and set an example of independence. "Show the world the falsity of the old doctrine, that we are doomed to be hewers of wood, and drawers of water." It was up to those going to build homes in the wilderness "to say whether that country shall be a Paradise or an abode of sin."[31] Yet, Garnet did not move to his granted lot; he moved to Peterboro in 1848 and soon afterward to Great Britain and Jamaica.

Although Garnet placed responsibility for the outcome on the grantees, it was Gerrit Smith and his agents who created lofty expectations and turned the enterprise into a national stage for the testing of black manhood. The practical needs of the actual settlers went unfulfilled. As Frederick Douglass had observed in early 1848—if the grantees did not take advantage of the Smith lands, the enterprise would become a "curse" rather than a "blessing."

He did not want it proclaimed that free blacks "lack the energy and manly ambition to clear lands for themselves."[32]

When John Brown heard of the obstacles faced by the black settlers in the Adirondacks, particularly the ones in North Elba, Essex County, he wanted to help them. In April of 1848, he went to see Gerrit Smith in Peterboro and offered his assistance. Smith had heard of John Brown and his noble traits—now the man stood before him. "I am something of a pioneer," Brown told Smith. "I grew up among the woods and wild Indians of Ohio, and am used to the climate and the way of life that your colony find so trying." He proposed taking one of the lots among the black settlers, showing them how to clear and plant, surveying their lots, and employing some of them. He would be "a kind of father to them," he said, looking after them as he did his own family "in all needful ways."[33]

Smith accepted Brown's offer but did not give him a farm. Instead, he offered Brown favorable terms on a few desirable lots of land. Upon returning to Springfield, Massachusetts, Brown tried to interest his son John Jr. or his nephew George Delamater in going to the Smith lands. He also urged them to recruit some black men to join the community. Neither John Jr. nor George wanted to go, and John delayed visiting Essex County since Mary was eight months pregnant with her eleventh child. Finally, in October of 1848, he headed to northern New York State.

Mary and five-month-old Ellen traveled with John to Whitehall, New York, where they stayed at the home of Mary's brother, Orson Day. John continued north alone, likely taking the fifty-mile steamboat ride to Westport. From there it was a relatively easy ten-mile wagon ride west to Elizabethtown, followed by a ten-mile stretch past Hurricane Mountain and down into Keene. The last leg was "six miles, six hours" along the Old Mountain Road, through a steep, rocky treacherous pass north of Keene (Pitchoff) Mountain.[34] On the other end of the pass, John Brown enjoyed his first close-up view of the tallest mountains in New York State.

Brown traveled the area, meeting with "a number of good colored families," such as the James Henderson family in Essex County and his old friend Willis Hodges in Franklin County. Brown found the prospect of living there so compelling that he immediately lent a hand. On his way home, he stopped in Troy to buy supplies for the settlers. He sent three barrels of pork and three barrels of flour to Port Kent (for Blacksville, Franklin County) and two barrels of each to "Timbucto" (in Essex County). "I wish you so to divide with the different families as to make all as happy and comfortable as possible," he wrote to Willis Hodges.[35]

Besides sending supplies and encouragement to the settlers, Brown wrote to a convention of prospective grantees in Troy, New York. He told them the lands possessed "many very superior natural advantages" and encouraged them to hold onto their lots "as their most valuable earthly treasure—and sooner suffer nakedness and hunger than part with them."[36]

The grantees already knew John Brown as "the distinguished friend and firm supporter of the colored man, in his efforts to obtain the rights which are his by gift of the Creator of all men," and trusted his word. They passed a resolution to occupy their lands as soon as possible and, "if necessary, even deprive themselves of the necessary comforts of life in order that they may reach their lands." They maintained that it was the duty of every man who held a deed to get to his land, "for in so doing he will be able to attain a respectable position in society—a position that he can never aspire to, so long as he remains lounging about these crowded cities."

In late December, Brown wrote to Willis Hodges again, assuring him that he had not forgotten the settlers and asking how they were getting along. In a postscript, Brown added, "I hope you are all full of courage and good feeling, and doing in earnest." He sent another letter on January 22, 1849, asking Hodges to get word to "his colored friends" that they should be patient about sorting out their building lots. Brown suggested the men should get any job they could find and "busy themselves in cutting plenty of hard wood . . . they need not fear getting too much wood provided."[37] Wise advice, for keeping the woodstove well-fed through the winter was vital.

Brown also had advice beyond practical matters. He wanted the settlers to sustain "the very best character for honesty, truth, industry and faithfulness." They should be determined to not merely conduct themselves as well as white people, "but to set them an example in all things." It pleased Brown to hear that Hodges's nephew had decided to stay at Blacksville and "hang on like a man."

The settlers were getting through the winter "middling well," and Brown was fully committed to moving to Essex County, convinced that he could be of great service to them and to those who might arrive the next year. "I can think of no place where I think I would sooner go than to live with these poor despised Africans to try and encourage them; and show them a little so far as I am capable how to manage."[38] Brown found "no objection" to the Adirondack lands other than the "high Northern Latitude." "They are indeed rather inviting on many accounts." He arranged rental of a nearby farm from Chapin Flanders, intending to move his family there in the early spring of 1849.

A Land of Promise and Hard Toil | 25

In a March 30 letter to Hodges, Brown promised he would settle in North Elba within two weeks. The grantees waited as two weeks passed. Three weeks, four weeks, and still no John Brown. On May 7, he wrote: "Do not get discouraged." He hoped to be on his way that week and would bring "an excellent team" of oxen along with other animals. He blamed his delay on the ill health of his sons, without mentioning the bigger tragedy that had occurred.[39]

Back in the fall, when the Browns arrived home from the trip to Whitehall, the youngest member of the family, baby Ellen, came down with a violent cold. As weeks went by, her illness grew worse and developed into consumption. John helped care for her, even staying up at night to feed the fire and sing to the ill child. On the morning of April 30, 1849, he noticed a change in Ellen and came home several times to see her. A little before noon, he looked at her and said, "She is almost gone."[40]

Ellen heard his voice, opened her eyes, and put up her little hands. John lifted the baby from the cradle and carried her in his arms until she died.

Though John remained calm during Ellen's passing, he broke down and sobbed when she was buried. A few weeks later, when the Brown family headed to the Adirondacks, they could not bear to leave Ellen behind. They brought her body with them and laid her to rest in the North Elba Cemetery. Her tombstone read as follows:[41]

Ellen
Daughter of John & Mary Brown
Born May 20, 1848
Died April 30, 1849

Chapter 2

Timbucto

> Slavery seizes a rational and immortal being . . . [and] makes him a thing, a chattel personal, a machine to be used to all intents and purposes for the benefit of another, without reference to the good, the happiness, or the wishes of the man himself. . . . It abrogates the seventh commandment, by annulling the obligations of marriage, and obliging the slaves to live in a state of promiscuous intercourse, concubinage, and adultery. Nothing will contribute more to break the bondman's fetters, than an example of high moral worth, intellectual culture and religious attainments among the free people of color.
>
> —Angelina Grimke, "Address to the Anti-Slavery Convention of American Women," 1837

"Contempt and scorn [are placed] upon every descendant of Africa," whether enslaved or so-called free, declared antislavery leader William Lloyd Garrison. Willis Hodges, born a free black in Virginia, tried to bring attention to "the wrongs and sufferings [of] the free people of color in the Southern states." But even in a Northern state, he had been pursued by slave catchers. "No free person of color within their reach was safe in person or property," said Hodges, "for these wolves had tasted human blood and liked it too well to let it alone."[1]

Free blacks faced horrific prejudice that limited their access to skilled occupations, higher education, and civil and political power. Black abolitionist Henry Highland Garnet said colorphobia was "the American feeling" but believed prejudice could be destroyed by improving conditions, "elevate any people and sever any chain." He deplored that black people would be divided by party feuds or "would draw a line of blood distinction" and "would form factions upon the shallow basis of complexion." Garnet also found it "unprofitable" for his brethren to spend time debating the question whether to call themselves "*Africans,*" "*Colored Americans,*" "*Africo Americans,*" or "*Blacks.*" Garnet felt the question should be, "*shall we arise and act like men, and cast off this terrible yoke?*"[2]

As with most social movements, activists often disagreed on details and strategies. They proposed various ways to elevate the conditions of free blacks. Gerrit Smith's experiment brought together components of several strategies: land ownership in the country, self-reliance as farmers, and voting rights. It brought hope and enthusiasm to many abolitionists and to grantee-settler James Henderson. When he wrote to Garnet in late January 1849, he referred proudly to his new neighborhood as "West Keene, Timbucto, Essex County."[3]

John Brown first used the word "Timbucto" in a letter to Hodges immediately after visiting the grantees in October 1848. Quite likely, Brown and James Henderson chose the name together, in reference to the city of Timbuktu in Africa. The idiom *from here to Timbuktu* has been used in English vernacular since the 1830s to indicate a remote place, usually far, far away. The roots of the idiom came from the difficulty of Europeans getting to the remote kingdom of Timbuktu in Mali due to resistance from the inhabitants. Timbuktu (Timbuctoo, Timbucto, or the French Tombouctou) was the site of a great African civilization of exceptional wealth, beauty, and learning, circa 1400–1600.

> O child of man, why muse you here alone
> Upon the Mountain, on the dreams of old
> Which fill'd the Earth with passing loveliness,
> Which flung strange music on the howling winds,
> And odours rapt from remote Paradise?
> Thy sense is clogg'd with dull mortality,
> Thy spirit fetter'd with the bond of clay:
> Open thine eye and see.[4]

Timbucto symbolized the dream of Henderson and Brown. Black settlers would create a place of education and prosperity in the naturally beautiful but difficult-to-reach location of western Keene (North Elba). Timbucto referred to this one community conceptually; it never appeared on a map as a physical location. The *North Star* exposed the term to a large audience when it published Henderson's letter on February 16, 1849. No evidence has been found of readers questioning the name or repeating it. The only known written references to Timbucto were the one by Henderson, four by John Brown (in letters to Hodges), one by Ruth Brown in September 1849, and one by John Brown Jr. in October 1849. Though the name was short-lived, it embodied the aspirations of the grantees and the Brown family in 1848–1849.[5]

Helping the settlers of Timbucto attracted Brown to the Adirondack Mountains. Other features also appealed to him and factored into his decision to move there. He felt *at home* amid the wilderness and God-inspiring scenery. North Elba offered a fresh start. It was well-suited to a self-sustaining, pioneer homestead (enabling the family to live frugally so they could use their funds to help others). Its remoteness, surrounded by imposing mountains, made it a safe place for his family during his many absences.

This wasn't the first time Brown connected mountains with refuge and freedom. The Allegheny Mountains were the foundation of his plan

Figure 2.1. "Indian Pass from 'Scotts.'" Artotype, black and white, based on painting by William S. Macy (2017.66.2-.10). View south from Robert Scott's house, near Flanders Farm, North Elba. *Source:* Courtesy of the Adirondack Experience. Used with permission.

to liberate enslaved people. To Brown and others, such as Harriet Tubman, the Allegheny Mountains were a corridor from slavery to liberty, sometimes called the Great Black Way or a Subterranean Passageway. Brown did not view the Adirondack Mountains as a direct link to emancipation (that is, he did not go there to aid people to freedom via the Underground Railroad). Instead, the Adirondacks related to elevating black people to a fuller freedom. The land experiment in the mountains held the promise of destroying the inferiority myth, a major basis for prejudice and slavery.

Brown also saw North Elba as a potential recruiting grounds for black soldiers in his Allegheny plan. According to Douglass, Brown had been "looking for colored men to whom he could safely reveal his secret" for thirty years and had almost given up. But upon meeting Douglass and others in 1847, Brown felt encouraged, "for he saw heads rising up in all directions, to whom he thought he could with safety impart his plan."[6]

With these various objectives in mind, John Brown and his family set out in hopes of finding a promised land in the Adirondacks. When they finally arrived in Westport, Essex County, New York, on May 22, 1849, the family was delayed for a day or two, waiting for a second wagon. When it arrived, John hired a black grantee named Thomas Jefferson to drive his team of horses and wagon, while John tended to the wagon carrying Mary and daughters Ruth, Annie, and Sarah. Sons Owen, Watson, Salmon, and Oliver drove a small herd of Devon cattle that had been purchased in Connecticut. Together, the large troop trudged westward to Elizabethtown and Keene, then along Old Mountain Road through a pass north of Pitchoff Mountain.[7]

Ruth Brown later recalled the adventure of that first trip into North Elba and how the family never tired of the grand mountain scenery. They stopped occasionally to get a cup of water from the sparkling streams that were "so clear we could see the bottom covered with clean sand and beautiful white pebbles." Her father also made them notice "how fragrant the air was, filled with the perfume of the spruce, hemlock, and balsams." He found something romantic in the Adirondack scenery, especially the mountains. There was a sort of thrill in his voice as if the mountain scenery was a demonstration of God's supreme power. "Everything reminds one of Omnipotence," he said.[8]

> [John Brown] was a lover of certain pastoral things,
> He had the shepherd's gift.
> When he walked at peace, when he drank from the watersprings,
> His eyes would lift

To see God, robed in a glory, but sometimes, too,
Merely the sky,
Untroubled by wrath or angels, vacant and blue,
Vacant and high. (Benet, *John Brown's Body*)

Old Military Road—the only road from the east through the mountains into North Elba—leveled out as it passed the first house, owned by Robert Scott. The second dwelling was located on Lot 110 on the north side of the road and belonged to Chapin and Caroline Flanders. The couple built the house and barn in the late 1820s. After moving to the nearby Town of Jay, they began renting the place, first to Robert Scott while he built his house nearby, and then to others. In similar fashion, John Brown rented the Flanders farm in 1849 until he had time to purchase his own lot, clear farmland, and build a house.

The Flanders place had cleared fields, a barn, and a one-story house with four rooms—a pantry, two bedrooms, and a large room that served as kitchen, dining room and parlor. In addition, the attic chamber could hold as many as four beds. The house seemed very small for a family of nine. "It is small," said John, "but the main thing is, all keep good-natured."[9]

Because Mary was ill, he hired a housekeeper (Mrs. Wait at first, then Mrs. Reed, both black women). He hired black men to assist with surveying, cutting timber, and carrying out other tasks. His generosity showed, especially when he paid several men to cut cordwood and then gave them the wood free-of-charge.[10] Yet, even before this rhythm of daily work got underway, unexpected things happened.

On the Browns' first morning at the Flanders farm, a young man named Cyrus Thomas arrived and asked if John Brown lived there. "Here is where he stays," said John. After escaping from slavery, Cyrus had looked for John in Springfield, Massachusetts, and hearing he was in the Adirondacks, came to find him. John immediately hired the young man to help at the farm and invited him to become the tenth occupant of the small house. The others did not complain since "Cyrus did not take more than his share of the room and was always good-natured."[11]

Dana's Visit and Mistaken Memories

A few weeks later, two white tourists and their guide showed up at the front door and asked for breakfast. It was common in those days for travelers on a tour of the Adirondacks to stop for a meal at a nearby farmhouse. On the morning of June 23, 1849, these men met Mr. Brown, "a thin, sinewy, hard-favored, clear-headed, honest minded man." Journal notes written by one of the travelers said Brown kept a good farm, owned "the best cattle and best farming utensils" in the region, and had "an unlimited family of children." He was "well-informed on most subjects, especially in the natural sciences, and he had books and had evidently made a diligent use of them."[12]

These were astute observations, not the vernacular of a common scribbler. This was the pen of Richard Henry Dana Jr., a Harvard graduate, lawyer, abolitionist, and author, famous for writing *Two Years Before the Mast: A Personal Narrative of Life at Sea* (1840). Dana had no idea that these jottings in his journal would become historically significant as an on-site record of the Browns' life at the Flanders farm. At the time, he regarded the family as unremarkable, perhaps even pitiable. "How on earth all these lived in that cabin was beyond our apprehension and almost beyond belief." Yet his guide said he had often lodged there—in the garret, with three others.

The Browns provided the men with a breakfast of "corn cakes, poor tea, good butter and eggs and unlimited supply of the best of milk." After the meal, Dana's party headed south through the woods to the McIntyre Iron Works where they explored the enterprise and the countryside, including a climb up New York's highest peak, Mount Marcy. On their return to North Elba, the group became lost in Indian Pass and spent a long, dreary night in the woods. The next morning, they hobbled out of the forest near the Flanders farm.

"Three more ragged, dirty and hungry men seldom called at a house for a breakfast," wrote Dana. "The Browns were very attentive, and Ruth immediately got us a large pitcher of the best of milk, with sweet bread and butter." Ruth refilled the milk pitcher and bread plate several times, until she became afraid the men would hurt themselves. She urged them to go upstairs and sleep until she could prepare a proper meal of venison and speckled brook trout. A few hours later, the men woke, ate supper, and climbed into a wagon that had come to take them to the nearby Osgood's Inn. Ruth recalled the men leaving with their boots in their hands—"for their feet were too much swollen to put them on." Undeterred by the misadventure, Dana spent the next day climbing Whiteface Mountain. The other two men were too lame to climb; they went fishing instead.[13]

After another night at the inn, the travelers started for home, stopping along the way to thank the Brown family for their kindness. "We found them at breakfast in the patriarchal mode," wrote Dana. "Mr. and Mrs.

Brown and their large family of children, with the hired men and women, including three Negroes, all at the table together." Besides the usual staples of meat, milk, bread, and butter, the breakfast included Indian meal cakes and maple molasses. That concluded Dana's journal entries of his three meetings with the Brown family. There was nothing extraordinary or especially thrilling about the visits, and Dana turned the page in his journal to begin describing his adventures at Ausable Chasm.

Years passed as life led Dana to other subjects and another continent, without a thought of Mr. Brown. The Civil War ended before Dana realized the man whom he had met in the Adirondacks was John Brown of Harpers Ferry fame. Realizing he had a scoop, Dana reworked his 1849 journal notes into an article, "How We Met John Brown," published in 1871 in the prestigious *Atlantic Monthly*. Although Dana tried to guard against the influence of intervening events, he faltered. He did not stick to his journal; he modified timelines, altered details, and added information. Did the new material come from Dana's retrieved memories or were they fabricated embellishments?

Dana believed he had visited the John Brown Farm (on Lot 95) written about in several accounts from the late 1850s and 1860s. He did not realize he had met the Browns while they lived at a rented place, the Flanders farm on Lot 110—five years before the famous house was built. Dana's article has caused (and still causes) major confusion about the two Brown residences in North Elba.[14] The article also created myths and misperceptions about Brown and his family.

Suddenly, in Dana's 1871 narrative, John Brown possessed a "marked countenance and a natural dignity of manner—that dignity which is unconscious, and comes from a superior habit of mind." He supposedly arrived at the farm leading a buckboard wagon that carried a black man and woman "with bundles," signifying some secret activity. Brown became a "strong abolitionist," and the neighborhood became "one of the termini of the Underground Railroad," according to Dana's guide, Mr. Aikens of Westport. "Negro families, mostly fugitive slaves," who had settled on Gerrit Smith's lands considered Brown "a kind of king among them."

Dana claimed, "I am not beating up memory for impressions." But memory can be a capricious creature and relying on other people's words can be just as problematic. Even Dana realized the dubious nature of the new "memories" and tried to explain why these noteworthy details were absent from his journal. He sensed that during his visits with the Browns, he had gone through "a fearful passage . . . with careless steps and unheeding eyes."

In fact, there was nothing to see or fear in 1849. More likely, Dana wanted to create a dramatic, publishable story in 1871, and fabricated tension and danger by his supposed witnessing of secret Underground Railroad activities, which transformed his meeting of Brown into some prophetic scene of heroism. It was years later, after reading other accounts and requesting information for his article from Aikens, that Dana heard the prevailing anecdotal stories and tall tales about fugitive slaves and an Underground Railroad in North Elba. The popular myth was difficult to quash and Dana's article was partly responsible for its continued existence.

For example, in *The Underground Railroad from Slavery to Freedom* (1898), Wilbur H. Siebert relied on the Dana story to conclude that it seemed probable that a "branch of the secret thoroughfare followed the valley of the Hudson River from Troy to the farm of John Brown, near North Elba." While the route looked feasible on a map, topography made it highly impractical, particularly in the Adirondack region. In 1933, when State Historian Alexander C. Flick printed a map of Underground Railroad routes in New York State, he showed a more reasonable route from Troy heading to Lake Champlain and northward. He also marked a "known route" from Westport to North Elba, but provided no justification for it other than that his map was based on Siebert's map. *The Underground Railroad in the Adirondack Region* (2004) included Flick's map, relabeled "Traditional View of Underground Railroad Routes in New York State." Thus, Dana's erroneous 1871 account had created a mythical route that transmuted into "traditional" reality.[15]

To the contrary, the established route of the Underground Railroad through Essex County ran close to Lake Champlain, with stations in Westport, Elizabethtown, Keeseville, and other towns. Routes also ran along the Vermont shore and via boats on Lake Champlain. There was no need to go inland to North Elba and mountain geography argued against it.[16] Of course, a runaway slave may have occasionally shown up in or passed through North Elba, but assisting fugitives was not the goal of Smith's experiment in the Adirondacks, nor was Brown there to run some secret smuggling operation. No reliable evidence supports the claim that Flanders farm, John Brown Farm, Timbucto, or the general area was an established route of the Underground Railroad. Nor is there evidence to support Dana's claim that the "Negro families" (settled in the neighborhood near John Brown) were "mostly fugitive slaves." The only known fugitive to live with or near the Browns was Cyrus Thomas, and his arrival was an off-the-cuff event (he was not a grantee nor was he fleeing to Canada).[17]

Despite its adverse impacts, Dana's 1871 account conveyed valuable insight into the extraordinary egalitarianism of the Brown family among the disparate abolitionist mindsets at the time. Dana found it strange that the subject of slavery never came up between him and the Browns since they were all antislavery activists. He suggested, "Perhaps the presence of the negroes may have restrained us, as we did not see the master of the house alone." How odd that Dana—an avowed abolitionist, member of the Boston Vigilance Committee, and lawyer who represented fugitive Anthony Burns—felt uncomfortable talking about slavery with black people.

A similar attitude popped up regarding the black friends at the supper table (which had been the breakfast table in the journal). Dana was surprised when Brown called them by their surnames, with prefixes of Mr. and Mrs. "It was plain," wrote Dana in 1871, "that they had never been so treated or spoken to often before, perhaps never until that day, for they had all the awkwardness of field hands on a plantation." Another odd observation, since Dana's journal referred to those at the table as "hired men and women" and made no mention of fugitives or clumsy behavior.

Most likely, it was Dana himself who was shocked by their presence and the gracious treatment shown by the Browns. The act of a white family eating at the table with black people was commonly viewed by white people as a troublesome signal of social equality. Even worse was the notion that only a man good enough to court and marry a daughter or sister should be seated at the same table with her, thus the presence of a black man suggested amalgamation. Dana's narrative demonstrated the attitude, even among some Northern abolitionists, that whites and blacks were not social equals.

White antislavery advocates and abolitionists, such as Dana, who shunned social interaction with black men and women (except perhaps the highly refined, wealthy, and educated), seemed two-faced, yet they were not uncommon. Antislavery societies led by white men often debated whether to allow black men (and women, black and white) to become members. Prejudice within the movement, along with the many Northern laws relegating free black people to an inferior position and lower social status worked against the arguments for emancipation. Proslavery advocates used it as proof of the hypocrisy of antislavery arguments and the supposed benevolence of slavery.

Sarah M. Grimke had addressed the issue at the 1838 Anti-Slavery Convention of American Women: "Prejudice against color is the very spirit of slavery, [and] sinful in those who indulge it . . . it is, therefore, the duty of abolitionists to identify themselves with these oppressed Americans, by sitting with them in places of worship, by appearing with them in our streets, by giving them our countenance in steamboats and stages, by visiting them at their homes and encouraging them to visit us, receiving them as we do our white fellow citizens."[18] John Brown and his family belonged to this *extraordinary* variety of white abolitionists. They not only preached and worked against slavery, but they also practiced brotherhood and sisterhood with black people. The Browns did not send Cyrus away to Canada or to live with a local black family, they brought him into their home (knowing the danger and social derision it entailed). No hint of colorphobia existed in their family. The Browns were kindred friends, allies, and schoolmates of the black families in North Elba.

Willis Hodges of Blacksville considered John Brown "a good and noble-hearted Christian gentleman who has always been a friend to the poor and oppressed, and particularly the friend of the poor slave." Hodges knew Brown would be "a welcome and useful neighbor" in the Adirondacks and praised him for sending "much aid and good words of cheer" even before he moved to the region. "I am not capable to express in words the goodness and greatness of this noble man." Like Brown, Hodges believed that words alone would not destroy slavery and racial repression. "Blood is the only thing that can wash the stain of slavery from this land," he wrote in 1849.[19]

This was another unusual aspect of John Brown's abolitionism; his views were more in line with black men such as Hodges than with white abolitionists. He favored practice and action over what he considered rhetoric and hypocrisy. For instance, he preferred to live among black friends and aid them directly. Not only did Brown survey his neighbors' lots in North Elba, but he also helped them sort out deeds and even tried to purchase a lot with them. James Henderson and Samuel and Thomas Jefferson were granted undesirable lots on mountainous land, so they settled their families on Lot 93 instead. They bought the old contract for the lot from a neighbor, but it had not been registered with Gerrit Smith. To settle the matter, Brown decided to join them in purchasing the lot and dividing it among them. He sent a payment of $225 for the deed and asked Smith to list the new owners of Lot 93 as Samuel Jefferson, Thomas Jefferson, James H. Henderson, John Brown, and Jason Brown.[20] For some reason, the deal fell through.

When land agent James McCune Smith visited Essex and Franklin Counties in September 1849, he found the black settlers a bit too reliant on the Brown family. McCune Smith felt the settlers had not done as well as they could for lack of start-up money, "backwardness of the season," and "partly from having waited too long for Mr. Browns team [of oxen]." He also feared they were "a little too dependent upon Mr. Brown's meal bin," rather than establishing their own self-sufficiency. Yet, the settlers were "making the woods ring with the music of their axe strokes" and made "a fine talk . . . about their feeling of independence." They had built log houses, cleared land for farming, and held antislavery church meetings at Iddo Osgood's house.[21]

McCune Smith met about sixty black people of all ages, men, and women,—many of them "hardy and industrious"—yet having varied experiences. Mr. Landrine had too much water on one lot and no water on another, so he gave up; Mr. Drummond (with wife and children) was "miserably idling his time here, if not criminally." Henderson appeared to be doing a good business. The thing that struck McCune Smith the most was "the evident impulse the *old* settlers had received," clearing more land in a single year than in the past three years combined. Maybe this northern countryside could still become a "land of promise." McCune Smith remained optimistic and predicted: "Could we get about 200 settlers in North Elba and then cut off all communication with the city, . . . things could be made to prosper."

These on-the-spot observations indicated that the enterprise remained small but somewhat cheerful. They also signaled latent troubles. McCune Smith's comment about cutting off news from the outside suggested that settlers were easily lured back to cities by family and friends or enticed by phony opportunities and folly. The remote location meant rough roads and difficult travel. The occupation of farmer did not appeal to everyone, but the black population was insufficient to support most other vocations.

The number of black settlers in North Elba never reached two hundred, or even one hundred. The total population of black people (men, women, and children, including nongrantees) was about 50 to 60 in 1850, 40 in 1855, and 22 in 1860.[22] And James McCune Smith was not among them.

Upon arrival at the lot deeded to him, McCune Smith wholeheartedly wanted to exchange the "bustling anxious life" of the city for the "majestic country." He felt like a "lord indeed" beneath the spruce and maple and birch, beside the brook. Despite his romantic exuberance, McCune Smith had no interest in making farming his occupation and the population was insufficient to support him as a physician. Perhaps, he was also dissuaded by the "superbly rough stump and corduroy road," which broke his wagon and left his party wandering lost in search of help.

A Theater of Social and Political Experiments

From the start of Gerrit Smith's land experiment, questions arose about his motive. A Vermont paper claimed the object of Smith's so-called charity was to increase the price on his remaining landholdings. Others believed he wanted to make voters of the black men so they would become supporters of the Liberty (Abolition) Party, a minor political party led by Smith. A North Carolina paper depicted Smith as "dreaming fondly that his black brethren would settle upon the estates [he gave them], thrive and raise up little darkies to worship Smith and vote the straight abolition ticket." Instead, they devoured his food, sold the land, and spent the money in "brass rings, red waistcoats, onions and whiskey." The article concluded that some black men became voters, thanks to Smith, but they refused "en masse" to vote for him.[23]

In New York State, adult slaves were emancipated in 1827, but legislation passed in 1821 prevented black men from voting unless they owned $250 in property. In early 1846, New York State considered eliminating the property requirement. Among the delegates to the State Constitutional Convention who favored the "Negro suffrage" measure were members of the Liberty Party, but also some Whigs and Democrats. Gerrit Smith refused to have the Liberty Party join hands with the nonabolitionists. He opposed the Negro suffrage measure because adhering to abolition principles was of "infinitely greater importance."[24]

Smith said he was less concerned with the unenfranchised than with how voters cast their ballots. "The great political evil of the world," he declared, "is not, that so few vote—but that they, who do vote, vote so ignorantly, so selfishly, so tyrannically." He admonished those who did not cast their vote "in the right spirit and the right ends," that is, for the Liberty Party, the only party that stood against slavery and disavowed slave owners.

Conversely, many black friends argued that suffrage was *the* principal issue and Smith should reevaluate the Liberty Party's position. The debate proved moot—New Yorkers voted to keep the $250 property requirement for black residents—but Smith had alienated many black abolitionists. Even before the final vote on Negro suffrage occurred in the fall, he tried to make amends—ostensibly by offering black men a pathway to the ballot through his land giveaway.

Initially, James McCune Smith despised Gerrit Smith's land program and accused him of "simplemindedly kowtowing to an economic system designed to cultivate inequality." McCune Smith saw no use in getting the vote by succumbing to the unjust land ownership requirement. "The negro *Man* is merged into the negro Landowner [leaving racism intact]. . . . What horrible mockery!" wrote McCune Smith. What good was land and a ballot if it cost his manhood?[25] Instead of working to remove the unjust property requirement, Gerrit Smith accepted its prejudice and made black men landowners. In essence, he and the land agents adopted the Jeffersonian notion of the yeoman farmer.

Smith wanted the black men to *earn* the vote through their own hard labor. He made them landowners of $40 in property; it would take years of hard toil for them to bring their property value to $250. This contradicted Smith's claims that voting was a "*natural* and indispensably protective right" and he would turn black men into voters, "Cost what it will."

Figure 2.2. Gerrit Smith, 1855. *Source:* Library of Congress. Public domain.

Inconsistent words and actions went beyond voting rights. Before Smith had even made out all the land deeds to black grantees, he became a candidate for US president in 1848. His political supporters came from the Liberty Party and Free Soil Party (which opposed expansion of slavery into the western territories but did not support immediate abolition). In his campaign pitch, Smith said: "Land Monopoly *I would disfavor*, whether on the part of Government or individuals. . . . Abolitionist though I am, I regard Land Monopoly—take the world together—as a far more abundant source of suffering and debasement, than is Slavery: and I add that whilst to abolish Chattel Slavery, is not to abolish Land Monopoly, to abolish Land Monopoly is to abolish Chattel Slavery."[26] How ironic that a rich, powerful white land baron claimed to be opposed to individuals holding a land monopoly. Smith deserved praise for generously donating some of his land to poor people, but he still owned vast tracts of land and served as landlord on many others. And he wanted to hold onto his lands—every man's homestead "SHOULD BE INALIENABLE"—while asking for "the public lands" be thrown open to settlers, "free of cost." Furthermore, Smith advised the black men: "Have no fellowship, political or ecclesiastical, with those, who hate or despise you. Turn your backs upon American Christianity and American politics, as upon the Devil himself—for he is their author." Smith wanted people to conform to *his* beliefs about land reform, to support *his* abolition schemes, and to back *his* church (Reform Church) and *his* political party (Liberty Party). He railed against James McCune Smith for having voted against his own interests by not voting for the Liberty Party. He claimed Frederick Douglass had voted for and advised his brothers to vote for "despisers of his race." Though Douglass might have been prudent (such as not wasting his vote on a Liberty candidate who had no chance of winning), Smith accused him of doing so "at the expense of self-respect."[27]

According to Smith, Negro suffrage was less important than *how* men voted. As he said in 1846, the "great political evil" was not that so few men could vote but that those who cast ballots did it "so ignorantly." Smith's words and political motives suggested his land gifts to blacks, supposedly supporting suffrage "justice," were not purely benevolent.

John Brown shunned this ranting and raving, this pontificating and castigating. He avoided membership in antislavery societies, churches, and political parties. The voting aspect of Smith's experiment never seemed a main concern to him. In January of 1849, before Brown moved to North Elba, he advised Willis Hodges, "Do not go to any expense about voting next spring, until we can get ready to take hold of that matter right." Yet one grantee in Blacksville voted in 1849, and four (including Hodges) voted in 1850, but none of them voted after 1850. A few Timbucto settlers probably voted in the mid-1850s.[28] However, talk about the subject attracted enough attention to suggest the possibility of a black man becoming supervisor of Keene in 1848.

A few years later, Essex County historian Winslow Watson stated that the "anomalous spectacle" had seemed probable, and at one time, it looked as if "the colored freeholders would obtain the political preponderance in the town [North Elba]." Though Watson indicated the political effort had been quelched, he claimed "an ulterior effort, connected with educational purposes" would still be made "to promote the occupation of North Elba by an African population."[29]

Many abolitionists viewed education "as even more important than political enfranchisement" in elevating the status of free black people. At a convention of black people assembled in Troy, New York, in 1841, it was stated: "Without education, the right of suffrage is a useless appendage. We might be made tools of the party, or imposed upon by false friends and designing demagogues." In a sermon preached to Smith grantees departing from Troy for their northern lands, Henry Highland Garnet said, "Train up your children in the way they should go, and be the patrons of education."[30]

John Brown had long dreamed of founding a black school and North Elba seemed to be a favorable location for the same reasons he chose New Richmond, Pennsylvania, back in 1834. It was sparsely populated and had no wicked people, thus there would be no opposition, or at least none that could not be influenced. He also realized that rallying teachers and supporters to become part of the community was important. In the spring of 1848, Brown had urged his son John Jr. and nephew George Delamater to go to the Smith lands, probably hoping the young men would serve as teachers.[31] Although Brown's plan fizzled, another group had already undertaken efforts to build a black school in the region.

At a General Conference of the African Methodist Episcopal Zion (AMEZ) Church held in 1844 in New York City, a committee was appointed to draft a constitution for an institute of learning. Four years later, the completed plan called for the establishment of a "Connectional Manual Labor School," whose purpose was to "elevate our whole people" by educating young black men, in general, and to prepare candidates for the ministry. The proposed location for the school: Essex County, New York. It would be named "Rush Academy," after Bishop S. Christopher Rush of New York City, who donated land he had purchased from Gerrit Smith. The 160-acre site was Lot 64 in Old Military Township 12 (near Averyville Road). It looked like North Elba was about to have a black educational institute.[32]

Undoubtedly, John Brown and his family were thrilled, but what did other townspeople think? In the span of only a few years, substantial changes occurred in this fledgling town and the prospect of even bigger change was on the horizon. About a dozen black families arrived in 1847 to 1849, and hundreds of more families were likely on their way, along with the prospect of a black school. Historian Winslow Watson described the sentiments of the people of the region as "deeply and vehemently opposed to being made the theatre of these social and political experiments."[33]

Chapter 3

Cultivators of Soil and Social Justice

> [Frederick Douglass] is doing more to instruct our young people and to indoctrinate them in the true republican principle, than any man has done since the revolution. *I therefore rejoice, and will rejoice,* and let none of my colored friends "faint and grow weary in well-doing, *for in due time we shall* reap if we faint not." "The *Lord our God* shall raise up for us a deliverer" in the very best possible time; and who shall pretend to prove that he is not *even now born*. . . . No! let no man's heart fail him; "but let us resolutely trust in God, and keep our *powder dry*."[1]
>
> —John Brown, *Frederick Douglass' Paper*, December 25, 1851

After aiding the grantees and getting his family settled at the farm, John Brown returned to Springfield, Massachusetts, to attend to his wool business. He took the best wool and left for England, gambling on a better price there. It was not to be. Brown's certitude failed him. He found "a great deal of stupid obstinate prejudice [against American wools] to contend with." Forced to sell the wool at greatly reduced prices, he was left with a financial disaster and numerous lawsuits.[2]

Mary Brown also left North Elba in August of 1849. Feeble health had plagued her for months and now death seemed to be looming. Believing the water cure was her only salvation, she headed to a facility in Northampton, Massachusetts—without asking John or writing to tell him. She knew he would not approve. John had little faith in the "cold-water practice" or

Figure 3.1. David Ruggles (1810–1849), abolitionist, member of New York Committee of Vigilance, and proprietor of Water-Cure in Northampton, Massachusetts. He believed in integration and dismissed the idea of separate institutions or organizations; he encouraged black men and women to become part of the general community by going to churches and schools that were open to all races. *Source:* Library of Congress. Public domain.

man-made medicines; he believed God provided one of the best medicines: "regular out-of-door labor."³

Mary had faith in the water cure, particularly the one operated by black abolitionist David Ruggles. In New York City, Ruggles had actively worked to aid an estimated six-hundred self-emancipated slaves, including Frederick

Douglass. After being attacked and forced to flee New York City, Ruggles moved to the interracial, utopian community of Northampton, Massachusetts, and healed his injuries through hydropathy. Although he had no medical degree or license and had gone blind, he began to assist others with their ailments. Ruggles examined his patients using touch and detected disease through electrical discharge in the body. His patients included both blacks and whites, including notable abolitionists William Lloyd Garrison and Sojourner Truth.[4]

Ruggles claimed he could cure everything from liver complaints to inflammation of the bowels, lame limbs, fever, and general debility. After examining Mary, he said she had "Neuralgia" (a disease of the nerves) and "a Scrofulous humour was seated on the glands" (suggesting tuberculosis). The doctor believed he could help her if she started a regiment of rest, a special diet, consumption of large amounts of water, and frequent baths. Mary agreed to stay in Northampton and take the cure.[5]

With both Mary and John absent from North Elba, Owen Brown ran the farm with the help of Cyrus Thomas, while Ruth Brown and Mrs. Reed took charge of the house and children. "I think we get along first rate here," Ruth wrote to Mary in early September of 1849, "much better than I expected." Her five charges were Watson (age thirteen), Salmon (twelve), Oliver (ten), Annie (five), and Sarah (two). The young girls had overcome their temptation to eat "green fruit" (which made them sick) and had stopped crying about going to bed. Nevertheless, Annie missed her mother "dreadful bad," and Sarah asked for her to come home. Ruth assured Mary there was no reason to rush home. "If the doctor can cure you . . . it is an opportunity you may not get again."[6] (Ruth's kind words proved prophetic; Ruggles died a month after Mary's visit.)

At the Flanders farm, Ruth sewed calico aprons for the girls, while Mrs. Reed made soap, hoping to fill an entire barrel since a pig died from overeating and there was plenty of soap grease. The women were also making butter and laying it over as fast as they could before the calves were taken away from the cows. They had gathered a mass of blackberries and half a washtub of huckleberries. Unfortunately, heavy frost killed the cucumbers, but the hops, peppers, and sage were saved.

While Mary stayed at the water cure, Ruth kept her up to date on their black neighbors. "The folks are all very well down to Timbucto," she reported, excepting Mr. Rice and Mr. Epps, who cut their feet while working on their new houses. Owen helped Mr. Hall build his house, "a very large one." Two of the Drummond children died within a day of each other. Mrs. Carasaw was making dresses for Sarah and Annie. Mrs. Cummin's son-in-law was "the most foolish colored man that I ever saw."

Figure 3.2. Mary Brown with Annie (left) and Sarah (right), 1851. *Source:* Library of Congress. Public domain.

Mrs. John Brown & two of her children, from daguerreotype –

The Browns had frequent interaction with the black settlers. In early October, John Brown Jr. and his wife Wealthy made a trip from Springfield and "visited most of the *important* places, such as Timbuctoo &c." Quite likely, he went to see the new houses of the Epps and Dickson families. Although it rained a lot during his visit, John Jr. appreciated the pure air and water in North Elba and joked about its remoteness giving "a total exemption from trouble by neighbor's geese."[8]

In November, Mary arrived home from the water cure with her physical and mental health improved, having heard much about abolition and women's rights from Ruggles and lecturer Lucy Stone. John also returned to the farm, happy to be home, but unlike Mary, his burdens had been multiplied by the wool business fiasco. Despite his financial loss, he immediately made plans to purchase land in North Elba. John had eyed 244 acres of land set on a high plateau—Lot 95—as a particularly good prospect. On

November 8, 1849, he requested Gerrit Smith to apply the $225 payment from the Lot 93 contract (which was never executed) toward the purchase of Lot 95. The next day, John, Jason, and Owen Brown signed the deed of purchase for $244.[9] (This property would later become the John Brown Farm Historic Site, but that was still years away.)

After completing the purchase of Lot 95, John was off to Springfield again. He traveled quite frequently as he worked to resolve debts of the wool business. While away in Springfield, Boston, Albany, and other cities, John often slept in soft, warm beds and ate fine foods, but they held "few charms," he said. "It does not make home. I feel lonely and restless." A supper of porridge and johnnycake with his family in a rustic cabin outshined a place such as the Massasoit Hotel in Springfield.[10]

During one stretch at home, John spent days "tracing out old lost boundaries." Every day, he started early and toiled late, returning from the work greatly refreshed and invigorated in "body and mind." According to one tale, not even the atrocious gnats and black flies bothered him. The black men who assisted him in the surveying work supposedly made a great fuss, "dancing and slapping themselves and complaining," while John stayed silent and ignored the pests. Then, when the surveying instrument had been set in place, he would calmly "pass his hand over his face, neck and exposed parts, quickly brushing all the troublesome flies away, and go on with his work."[11]

Everything about the North Elba area, including its "healthfulness," seemed to please John. "I have no question at all," he said. "I do not know where we could go to do better." The fine plank road from Westport to Elizabethtown was completed. The "colored brethren" had chopped trees on part of Lot 95 and Henry Thompson was clearing up the grounds. John deemed the land excellent for "stock growing and dairy business" and potatoes. "I have no where seen such Potatoes."[12]

During their first year at the Flanders farm, the Browns harvested thirty bushels of Irish potatoes, twenty bushels of oats, and eight tons of hay, and made sixty pounds of maple sugar and one hundred pounds of butter. They owned five milk cows, four working oxen, four other cattle, and two pigs. Value of livestock: $350. Value of animals slaughtered: $40. Family meals consisted of hearty farmer food: bread, butter, milk, cornmeal mush, pork, chicken, potatoes, turnips, carrots, and other items of their own raising. The nearby woods and waters provided venison and trout, but the most often mentioned wild edible was berries. "They grow in enormous quantities here, not in valleys but on high land," wrote Ruth. By early August of 1850, the family had already gathered fifteen bushels of berries, but they planned another excursion, which included camping out overnight. "We are all going to have a regular time of it, Mother and all."[13]

John supplemented the family's larder with barrels of salt, flour, mackerel, and other goods, often sending them from Orson Day's store in Whitehall or other places he was visiting. Other times John sent cash to buy cattle feed, a loom, or whatever the family needed. In addition to cash and goods, he sent letters expressing his regret at being away from the family. "I shall escape like a bird out of a cage the first moment I can get clear."[14]

His letters also doled out detailed suggestions and instructions. "Owen and Mr. Jefferson should use the horse team [to get hay from a neighbor] if the roads are in order." Then John added, "Great care should be taken in placing blinders [on the horses]." In the springtime, he wanted his sons to put up fences in two pastures and, if possible, to work the teams at least part of a day getting out manure and plowing. Another time, John cautioned not to "feed out the potatoes too freely" and suggested the milk cows be fed small potatoes until they depleted the supply, then cleaned oats could be used as feed. He instructed the boys to be "very careful to have no hay, or straw, wasted," putting down just enough bedding to keep the cattle from lying in the mire. In one of his explicit directives, John told his sons to grind a shovel to a sharp point and then use it to chop rutabaga so fine that it could be fed to the old cow.[15]

John Brown tried to be home to attend special events, such as the combined Essex and Clinton County Fair held in Elizabethtown on September 25, 1850. The local press bragged about the display of superb stock, beautiful home crafts, and various home industries that demonstrated "the naysayers" were wrong about northern New York. This "Rural Festival" established that the "hyperborean region" had "a high claim to pre-eminence in its agricultural character."[16]

The greatest sensation at the 1850 fair was the exhibition of a beautiful herd of Devon cattle. Everyone wondered, "Whose are these cattle, and from whence do they come?" The answer: John Brown of North Elba.

Brown's bull calves and cow calves won prizes at the fair, as did his adult cows and working oxen. In all, his cattle took nine prizes and won $11 in prize money. Townspeople were impressed and judged John Brown to be a welcome addition to the community. *The Essex County Republican* stated, "Essex County is deeply indebted to Mr. Brown," in part, because his livestock gave Essex County an advantage in its friendly competition with Clinton County. "We trust his public spirit and enterprise will be appreciated and adequately rewarded. We hope and believe that others will imitate his example and engage more efficiently in the introduction of improved stock into this county and region."

> He knew not only doom but the shape of the land,
> Reaping and sowing.
> He could take a lump of any earth in his hand
> And feel the growing.
> He was a farmer, he didn't think much of towns,
> The wheels, the vastness.
> He liked the wide fields, the yellows, the browns,
> The black ewe's fastness. (Benet, *John Brown's Body*)

As John was preparing for the fair, his daughter Ruth busied herself with preparations for her upcoming marriage to Henry Thompson. This included

Figure 3.3. Ruth Brown Thompson, eldest daughter of John Brown. *Source:* Ella Thompson Towne Scrapbook, the Huntington Library, San Marino, California. Used with permission.

Cultivators of Soil and Social Justice | 49

a trip to Whitehall to buy her wedding dress. She also began to assemble her wedding chattel: a good feather bed, five new pillows, six pairs of pillowcases, six pairs of sheets, and two new bed ticks (mattresses). Mary was getting some nice linen tablecloths that were made for her. As for furniture, Ruth possessed a nice table, a washstand, a large looking glass, and a set of cane chairs. Henry used his carpenter skills to make some other items, too.[17]

On September 26, 1850, Ruth and Henry said their wedding vows at his parents' house. Roswell and Jane Thompson were early settlers in North Elba, and some accounts credit them with having twenty-two or twenty-three children, but they were not that productive. The Thompsons had ten children: nine boys and one girl. After the wedding, Henry moved in with the Brown family. "I think [she] has done well," said John Brown. He approved of the way Henry got Ruth out of bed in the morning, "so as to have breakfast before light."[18]

Figure 3.4. Henry Thompson, husband of Ruth Brown, son of Roswell and Jane Thompson of North Elba, NY. *Source:* Ella Thompson Towne Scrapbook, the Huntington Library, San Marino, California. Used with permission.

Times of Trouble, Times of Vigilance

In addition to Ruth's marriage and the county fair, a major national event occurred on September 18, 1850. President Millard Fillmore signed the so-called Bloodhound Law. The revised Fugitive Slave Act (part of the Compromise of 1850) superseded the 1793 Fugitive Slave Act. Although the old law authorized states to seize and return escaped slaves to their owners and imposed penalties on anyone who aided in their flight, it was ineffectual due to varying state regulations and enforcements. The new, harsher 1850 law put power into the hands of the federal government and enacted stiffer fines and longer imprisonment for abettors of runaways. It also required (under threat of punishment) *citizens* to aid in capturing slaves. Some northern whites had never seen the brutality of slavery, but now they witnessed the capture and torture of black men, women, and children. White people also encountered threats on their doorsteps as their towns and homes were searched by marshals and slave hunters.

John Brown believed the horrific personal experiences brought by the 1850 fugitive slave law were "making more abolitionists than all the lectures that we have had for years."[19] That was evident in Essex County.

Citizens had organized their first antislavery convention on July 11, 1837, in Westport. The meeting announcement said they believed slavery to be "a heinous sin in the sight of God" and "a foul blot on our own national character." It was also a "great and grievous wrong to the slave" and required "immediate emancipation." Attendees of the convention formed the Essex County Anti-Slavery Society and adopted resolutions, but further actions were not forthcoming. In the early 1840s, Wendell Lansing of Keeseville, Essex County, found it harrowing to be "the friend of the slave" or "a conductor on the Underground Railroad, or to keep a station on that road." Abolitionists were called "n——lovers," and became the targets of "tar and feathers, or ancient eggs."[20] But after the Fugitive Slave Law was enacted in 1850, Lansing and other citizens were able to gather and discuss antislavery measures, sans tarring or egg throwing.

On October 16, 1850, Essex County men from the Towns of Jay, Keene, St. Armand, Wilmington, and North Elba met at the Jay Baptist Church and stated their verdict on slavery and the new law. The framers of the Constitution did not intend for that document to justify the extension and perpetuity of slavery; the framers spoke of slavery as "the greatest curse that could be inflicted on our country." The new fugitive slave law was unauthorized by the Constitution and should be repealed. The alleged fugitive should be able to use "any degree of resistance necessary" to prevent his capture.[21]

These Essex County citizens opposed slavery because they regarded it as "a sin against God and an outrage on the rights of men." They felt compelled "by duty to God and love to humanity" to use "all means" to eradicate it. They resolved the following:

> We the people of Jay, Wilmington, Keene, North Elba, and St. Armand are not unmindful of the fact that "eternal vigilance" is the price of liberty and we hold ourselves in readiness, at all times and under all circumstances, to unite in an honest effort to reform abuse and correct error, and in the discharge of such duty we will never swerve or falter; that "Principles not men" is our motto, and that if need be, party lines may be obliterated, if the character of our country abroad, and its honor at home, demand it.

Their statements asserted vigilance and unlawful resistance to the 1850 Fugitive Slave Law, yet these Essex County men did not attempt to hide their views. They voted to have their proceedings and resolutions printed in the *Essex County Republican, Ausable River Gazette, Albany Evening Journal,* and *Albany Atlas*. The full list of attendees was not given, but two of the most respected citizens of North Elba, Roswell Thompson and Iddo Osgood, were noted as members of the Resolutions Committee.

Although John Brown was not at the meeting, he supported his neighbors' statements, as did his family. The Browns pledged to disobey the law and to resist attempts to take any fugitives. "Our faithful boy Cyrus was one of that class," wrote Ruth, "and our feelings were so roused that we would all have defended him." Even if the women had to resort to throwing "hot water" on the slave catchers.[22] The women encountered no slave hunters or threats in North Elba, and Cyrus peacefully tended his crops of wheat, oats, turnips, and potatoes.

Concern for his many black friends drew John Brown back to Springfield, Massachusetts. He advised them to "trust in God and keep their powder dry" and helped form the League of Gileadites to protect themselves and fugitive slaves from slave catchers.[23] In addition to contesting the 1850 Fugitive Slave Law, John was busy battling business lawsuits, dealing with financial problems, and making living arrangements for his family. The lease on the Flanders farm would end soon and a house had not been built yet on Lot 95.

John's wealthy business partner, Simon Perkins, asked him to return to Akron, Ohio, to tend his sheep business. John accepted the offer and the family immediately prepared to move. They left North Elba in March of 1851, intending to return after a short-term stint in Ohio. Daughter Ruth stayed in North Elba with her husband Henry Thompson, and John kept in close communication with the couple. Before he even made it out of Essex County, John wrote to ask Henry to "open an account of debt and credit" since he would have a "good many errands" for him. In addition to selling John's "stuff" for him, Henry was informed that a neighbor was owed $7.09 payable in board, horse-feed, or oats; Henry's father was owed $2; and Alva Holt was to be given two thousand shingles. However, if the tax collector asked for $3, Henry should not pay him. Instead, John would proceed with a lawsuit.[24]

Having been involved in many business lawsuits regarding large sums of money (as much as $40,000), why would John contest a measly $3 tax bill? He was a man of principle, even in the smallest of actions. He believed he had been unjustly conned into paying school tax on land that he did not own or lease (he merely paid a small fee for letting his cattle roam there). Brown had already contacted the Elizabethtown law firm of Robert Safford Hale and Orlando Kellogg about filing a lawsuit to recoup his tax. Hale suggested that three dollars was a small sum and for every dollar Brown gained he would have to pay ten dollars in legal expenses. Hale told Brown it would be cheaper "to smother his indignation and let the affair drop."[25]

John Brown straightened himself, and with a most deliberate look said to Hale: "I am not aware, sir, that any opinion was asked of you upon that point, but upon a very different matter."

In recalling the incident, Hale said, "I never had a more complete snub."

After John moved to Ohio, he missed Ruth and Henry, "a part of my family in whose present and future interests I have an inexpressible concern." On one occasion, while conducting business in Troy, New York, he heard that smallpox was in a town near North Elba. He feared that Henry had not been vaccinated, so he made the 150-mile journey to assist them. Although Ruth and Henry were both well, Ruth appreciated her father's undertaking. "Was there ever such love and care as his!"[26]

In early January 1852, sadness fell on Ruth when her newborn baby died. Three months later, in Ohio, Mary birthed a large and strong baby boy, but whooping cough spread through the household and her baby died in mid-May. "Divine Providence has been cutting me loose, one cord after another . . ." wrote John. "I have so much to remind me that all ties must soon be severed, [yet] I am still clinging, like those who have hardly taken a single lesson."[27]

Times of trouble also fell on the black settlers. The 1850 Fugitive Slave Law threw a curveball at Timbucto. The location held less appeal for those grantees considering settling there; fleeing to Canada or staying put in a city looked more secure. Besides stunting population growth in Timbucto, the new law also diverted the attention of abolitionists toward intensified Underground Railroad activity. The Browns's temporary move to Ohio saddened the community, too, but Ruth and Henry Thompson remained in North Elba (and had Mrs. Dickson living with them for a while). John also stayed involved with the grantees, making occasional visits and relaying messages to them through letters to Henry.

When John visited North Elba in 1852, he found the black settlers "very comfortable" and in good spirits. "They have constant preaching on the Sabbath; and intelligence, morality, and religion appear to be all on the advance." James Henderson, whom John considered a "good man" and "very industrious," exemplified the promise of Timbucto. He was an Inspector of Elections for North Elba and seemed on his way to playing a leading role in the community—until he became lost in the winter woods and froze to death.[28] Unfortunately, history ignored his achievements and remembered him as the black man from Seneca Ray Stoddard's tale. "Well, he went out huntin' one day in winter and got lost in the woods. He had a compass with him, but when they found him they found where he had sat down on a log and picked his compass to pieces, and then sot there till he froze to death."[29] Henderson's demise emboldened critics to spout the notion that blacks were "ill adapted" for a northern climate and lacked the "experience and competency" to manage their affairs. It was an unjust characterization. The first death among the early white settlers was a man who perished "by cold in the woods." Brown himself nearly froze on the roadside in a winter storm. Like others, Henderson simply had bad luck.[30]

The death of James Henderson was the third setback in as many years, after the Fugitive Slave Law in 1850 and the Brown family's move to Ohio in 1851. Enthusiasm was souring and the black population diminished slightly from 1850 to 1855. Many things contributed to the slow decline of Timbucto: Smith's poor planning; the northern climate; some land unfit for agriculture; lack of cash and farming skills; white people who thwarted the efforts of the black settlers; the Browns' absence in Ohio extending to four years; and hard luck. All these factors played a part in Timbucto not attracting new pioneers and not holding on to the established settlers.

Three of the long-term black families in North Elba were those of Lyman Epps, Josiah Hasbrook, and William Appo. Lyman Erastus Epps was born a free man in Connecticut around 1815, the son of "a full-blooded Indian" father and a black mother. After the death of his first wife, Lyman moved to New York City, where he met and married his second wife, Amelia Ann (or Anna) Miller, who was born free in New York in 1817. Ann gave birth to a daughter, Evelene, in 1845, after which the Epps moved to Troy, New York, where they had a son, Lyman Jr., in 1847. The family, including Lyman's mother (who may have been a former slave), moved to North Elba around June of 1849, and more children (Albertine, Albert, Amelia Ann, and Kate) were born there.

Figure 3.5. Lyman Epps (circa 1815–1897), North Elba grantee. *Source:* Author's collection.

As a Smith grantee, Lyman Epps received a forty-acre lot, the southwest quarter of Lot 84, on the southern end of Bear Cub Road. He built a log cabin; raised sheep, milk cows, and cattle; grew a variety of crops (even corn); and guided tourists in the woods. He served as an inspector of elections and overseer of roads, and helped found a library, Sunday school, and church in the area. In 1863, Lyman and Ann bought Ruth and Henry Thompson's farm and moved to the south half of Lot 88 (abutting the John Brown Farm).[31]

Grantee Josiah Hasbrook was born in Ulster County, New York, and arrived at North Elba in 1849 with his wife, Susan, and five children. They settled on the thirty-five acres that Smith had granted them in the southeast quarter of Lot 9. The Hasbrook children were schoolmates and friends with the Brown children. When Josiah Sr. left the area in the late 1850s, three of his children stayed: Josiah Jr., Harriet, and Simeon. Simeon lived with Ruth and Henry Thompson in 1860. Josiah Jr. worked at the John Brown Farm and intended to go west with the Browns in 1863. Instead, he joined a war regiment and returned to the area after the war.

Not all the black men who owned land in North Elba were grantees. William Appo was too well-off to receive a grant; he purchased Lot 87 (148.6 acres) from Gerrit Smith. Appo was born free in Philadelphia, Pennsylvania, around 1808, and became a leading black musician, vocalist, and composer, touring in Philadelphia, New York, and Europe. With his wife and children, he lived in various places in the Northeast, including Troy, New York. Perhaps this is where he became friends with some Smith grantees and decided to buy land at Timbucto in July of 1848.

Evidence suggests that Appo only stayed at North Elba in the summer months, but he became good friends with the Browns and Eppses. Not long after Appo's wife died in 1863, he retired from teaching and moved to North Elba full-time. He married Albertine Epps, who was forty years his junior, and they had a daughter, Maud, born in 1872. William Appo died in 1880 and was buried in the Epps's plot in the North Elba Cemetery.[32]

Figure 3.6. Major Points of Interest and Residences in North Elba circa 1849–1860: (1) Robert Scott, Lot 117 and 118; (2) Chapin Flanders, Lot 110, rented by John Brown 1849–1851; (3) Little Red Schoolhouse; (4) John Brown, Lot 95, Browns lived there 1855–1863, present-day John Brown Farm State Historic Site; (5) Ruth Brown and Henry Thompson, southern half of Lot 88, and Mary Brown, northern half of Lot 88; (6) William Appo, Lot 87; (7) Sawmill and Starch Factory, along Ausable River; (8) T. S. Nash, Lot 101; (9) Archibald, Samuel, and John Thompson, Lot 106, 107, 108, became known as Intervales Farm; (10) Roswell Thompson, Lot 299; (11) Jackson Brewster (father of Byron R., Martha, and others); Lot 279; (12) James Henderson, Thomas Jefferson, and Samuel Jefferson lived on Lot 93; (13) North Elba Cemetery; (14) Iddo Osgood, Lots 85 and 86; (15) proposed site of Rush Academy, Lot 64; (16) Silas Frazier, part of Lot 51; (17) Horatio Hinckley, Lot 81 (and Lots 80, 73, 74), present-day Heaven Hill Farm; (18) Abbie Hinckley and Salmon Brown, western half of Lot 74, lived there 1860–1863; (19) Henry Dickson, southeastern quarter of Lot 83; and (20) Lyman Epps, southwestern quarter of Lot 84. *Source:* Map by David Hodges. Used with permission.

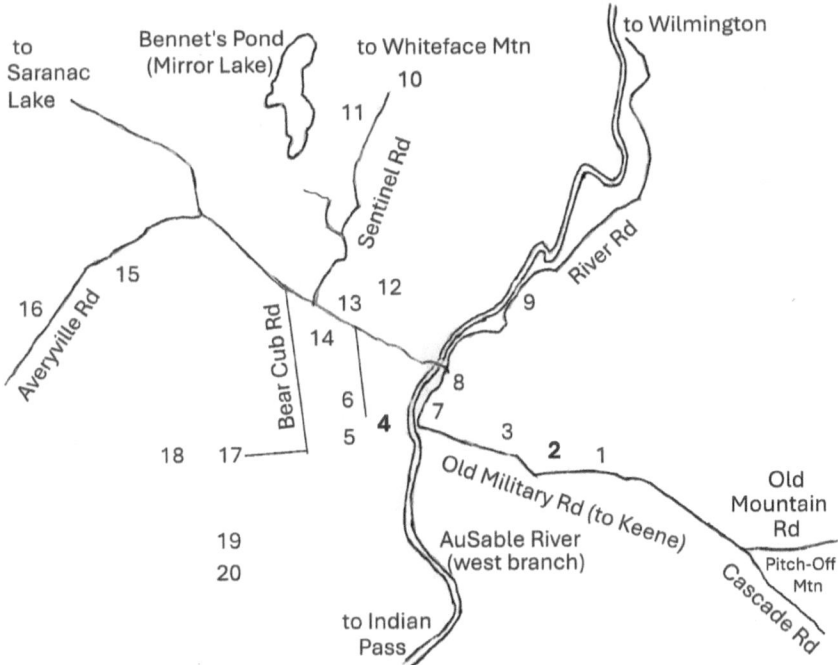

Chapter 4

The Genesis of the John Brown Farm and the Demise of Timbucto

> No place (of which I know) offers so many inducements to me, or any of my family, as that section; and I would wish when you make a move that you go in that direction. . . . [Henry and Ruth] appear satisfied that North Elba is about the place after all.
>
> —John Brown to his son John Jr., June 1854[1]

In Akron, Ohio, the John Brown family enjoyed the comfort of a fine house and the sureness of paid labor, yet John longed to return to the Adirondacks. When he visited North Elba in December of 1852, he found a few of his black friends had left and a few new ones had arrived; they maintained a small population of around forty. The black families hoped the Browns would come back to North Elba, which John seemed eager to do. He felt satisfied "to regard this as my home" and urged his son John Jr. to move to "Essex" (the term John frequently used to refer to the North Elba area). "The more I reflect on all the consequences likely to follow, the more I am disposed to encourage you to come here; and I take into the account as well as I can the present and future welfare of yourself and family, and prospects of usefulness."[2]

According to John, his son John Jr. had "Essex fever" and was not likely to recover. Ruth was happy to hear the news. She wanted John Jr. and Wealthy, her favorite brother and "sister," to move to North Elba. "Don't let your Essex fever cool off," she told them. She hoped they would decide to take some of the "all healing balm" of Essex County. Although it was cold and frosty in the winter, Ruth considered it a place to make a good living (for those willing to work) and the neighbors were good, kind people.[3]

In the spring of 1853, John Sr. started making plans for his return to North Elba, consulting with his daughter Ruth and son-in-law Henry Thompson about possible businesses and housing arrangements. As usual, John sent oodles of ideas. Even though a good sawmill was already operating nearby, would Henry be interested in running a sawmill business? Could Lot 95 be divided to accommodate the two families? Perhaps there were springs on the part lying east of the Ausable River that would be a good spot for a house. "Will it be any damage to you if you defer building your house . . . at least for another year?"[4]

John suggested Henry might want to get some logs peeled and start building John's house right away, since peeling bark was easiest in the spring. He said, "I expect to be quite satisfied with a log house for the rest of my days."[5]

> Go, cut down trees in the forest,
> And trim the straightest boughs;
> Cut down trees in the forest,
> And build me a wooden house. (Ralph Waldo Emerson,
>   "Boston Hymn," first read on Emancipation Day,
>   January 1, 1863).

The logs should be "hewed inside" and "peeled," explained John, and rather than laying the logs flat on top of each other, he wanted them saddled and notched at the corners. He also asked for a cellar under the house and a strong tight roof on top—"run a tie across from plate to plate so as to keep the roof from sagging." As for size, he suggested the building be two feet longer than the Flanders house, "done off below on the same plan," but with larger bedrooms. Last, John requested it be located "so as to avoid having to carry water uphill." Sometimes a house could be placed level with, or even below, the water source and yet have dry ground for a cellar, yard, and garden. "I would be at a good deal of pains to avoid lugging water up a steep place," he emphasized again.

After specifying all these details, John said these were only his "general ideas of a log house." He was not certain he would ever relocate to North Elba and live in the house. "Should I never get back," he wrote, "it may not in the end be a loss for you to build, and live, in such a House."

Henry Thompson wanted to please his father-in-law but, as a skilled carpenter, he preferred not to build with logs. When he asked the reason for logs, John said it was only for economy's sake and encouraged Henry to use his own good judgment. And, if possible, have the house ready by spring. The spring of 1854 came and went without Henry completing the house, but it did not matter since John delayed his move.

After visiting in June, John remained enamored with North Elba and was still trying to persuade John Jr. to move there. However, Jason warned his brother, "If you go to Essex, John, you will soon realize your dependance and the truth of Scripture where it says, 'who can stand before his cold?'" Going to North Elba meant living "7 months on the gain of 5 months." Owen also thought John Jr.'s plan had "a cold chilly wet look about it." He recalled that when he first went to the "romantic region" in the late spring, a man talked about hard frosts occurring in every month in the year. "I thought he was joking," said Owen, "but it was all true while I lived there. . . . on the 6th of June we could not clear away the manure from the Barn because it was half Ice yet."[6]

Despite his brothers' pessimism, John Jr. did not change his mind and he tried to convince Jason and Owen to leave Ohio and move to North Elba, too. Perhaps some of the Brown sons could have been persuaded to enlarge the family footprint in the Adirondacks. Instead, a firestorm ignited in Kansas and upended that possibility.

The Missouri Compromise of 1820, which prohibited slavery in states north of 36 degrees and 30 minutes, was repealed by the May 30, 1854, passage of the Kansas-Nebraska Act, which promoted popular sovereignty. This allowed settlers in *all* new states to decide whether the state would be free or slave. Although supporters of slavery promoted the act as a compromise, antislavery groups viewed it as an outright expansion of slavery. The Kansas Territory would be up for grabs. It fostered a lawless competition, an irrepressible conflict, which might even create a state of war in Kansas.

Some citizens from slave states came to settle in the territory, but many came from Missouri with the intent of casting proslavery votes in Kansas and then returning home. Armed with knives and guns, these proslavery "Border Ruffians" also intended to bully abolitionists and keep them from voting. Emigrant Aid Societies formed in free states and raised funds to assist families to take up homesteads in the Kansas Territory and vote for an antislavery government.

The Kansas situation irked John Brown, but he was already "committed to operate in another part of the field," to return to North Elba. However, if any of his sons felt inclined "to help defeat Satan and his legions" in Kansas, he had no objection. "If I were not so committed," he said, "I would be on my way this fall."[7]

Five of Brown's sons (John Jr., Jason, Owen, Frederick, and Salmon) decided to head to Kansas and establish homes among the free-state settlers near their aunt and uncle, Samuel and Florilla Adair. On October 1, the American Missionary Association commissioned Samuel, an antislavery advocate and minister, to settle near Osawatomie, Kansas. He and Florilla (a half-sister of John Brown) left Ohio in mid-October and, after a delay along the way, arrived in Osawatomie in late March 1855. They made a land claim, built a log cabin, held Sunday school, and preached to settlers. Being active in the cause of freedom, Adair was quickly labeled an abolitionist and subjected to threats by ruffians.

Meanwhile, John Brown agonized over his earlier decision. Rather than returning to the Adirondacks to help a few, could he benefit black people "on the whole" more by going to Kansas and helping to make it a free state? Since John had volunteered to aid the black settlers, he believed they had "a right to vote" as to the course he took. Presumably, they wanted John to return to North Elba, as they had expressed in 1852. So did Gerrit Smith. So did Ruth; she said her father was needed as much in North Elba as he was in Kansas.[8]

Then and there, in the fall of 1854, John abandoned the idea of going west. He did not pick up his rifle and run off to Kansas; he prepared to move back among the black settlers. And, coming with him and Mary would be Watson, Oliver, Annie, Sarah, and a new baby girl named Ellen, born on September 25, 1854—the thirteenth (and last) child of Mary and John. However, after getting encouraging news from the Adairs, John indicated that he would make a visit to Kansas, explore the territory, and consider settling there. But first he needed to move his family to North Elba.

Although Henry completed their house in early 1855, the family's move from Ohio to North Elba was postponed again. John's delay was utterly predictable, this time due to difficulty in getting funds to pay for the move. By May of 1855, he realized he would arrive too late to plant crops on Lot 95 and suggested that Ruth and Henry "plant or sow what you can" so something could be sprouting by the time the family arrived.[9]

In June, John Brown and his family finally made it to New York State and headed to Elizabethtown, then west to Keene, through Pitchoff Mountain pass, and into North Elba, past their old rental house. After crossing a branch of the Ausable River, they turned off the main road onto a byroad that started opposite the North Elba Cemetery. This lane (now Old John Brown Road) continued through a mixture of woods and open fields for about three-fourths of a mile before ending at a clearing on Lot 95. There stood the genesis of the present-day National Historic Landmark and New York State Historic Site—the John Brown Farm.

The house, built by Henry Thompson, was a plain dwelling with two rooms on the first floor: a northern room serving as sitting room and bedroom, a southern room serving as kitchen and a second bedroom. A central set of stairs led to a second-story, unfinished, open loft used for additional sleeping quarters. The structure consisted of a fieldstone foundation, earthen-floored cellar, timber frame, walls of milled lumber, and two brick chimneys. It was not a log cabin, but visitors described it as one and established the myth.

Many accounts also depicted the house as unfinished, half-finished, or worse. One called it "a leaky, drafty, cheerless shelter" that was "very primitive and crudely built" and "uninhabitable." Yet it was inhabited by the Brown family in June of 1855. It may have been drafty—the rooms were not plastered, the exterior unpainted, and the windows shutterless—but the house was not cheerless or incomplete. It was equal to or better than others in the region. Of the fifty-three houses in North Elba, only six were valued higher than the Browns' $500 dwelling (about $19,000 in today's value). The majority were log cabins worth an average of $50.[10]

In selecting the site of the house, Henry placed it near a spring to make it easy to fetch water. And he somewhat adhered to another of John's requests—for the house "to stand square with the world, longest East and West with doors opening through it North and South."[11] This was quintessential John Brown.

> Square with the world, as Square as earth to sun
> In the little things as in arduous duties done. (L. B. Mitchell,
>   "Square with the World," 1920)

Temples of faith throughout the world have stood with their walls built "four square with the walls of heaven." As the foundations of heaven and earth were stable, any building "four square" with them would be immovable. In Egypt, it was expressed: "such as a heaven in all its quarters" and "firm as the heavens." In the American Mid-West, it was believed that the world was divided into the competent who have "everything squared away" and the idiots "running in circles." Respectable people lived in houses that

Figure 4.1. John Brown's House (on Lot 95), North Elba, 1867. Earliest known photo of house, during ownership of Alexis Hinckley. After John's funeral in 1859, Mary used some of the donated funds to add two rooms to the house: one in 1860 for Salmon and Abbie; another in 1861 for Sarah. The addition (on right) was removed not long after 1867. Note the board fencing, big rock (far right), and cleared hill behind house. *Source:* Courtesy of the Adirondack Experience. Used with permission.

faced exactly east and west, or north and south. To do otherwise indicated a lack of dependability and trustworthiness, that is, such people may not be "fair and square" in their dealings.[12]

Contrary to John's wishes, the farmhouse doors opened east-west and the orientation of the house aligned with Whiteface Mountain, slightly east of due north. *Almost* square with the world.

Perhaps John's request extended beyond the physical house, to his spiritual house. Quite likely, he recalled the Bible passage, 2 Corinthians 5:19–20: "God put the world square with himself through the Messiah, giving the world a fresh start by offering forgiveness of sins." Maybe John wanted *himself* to stand square with the world. On Lot 95, he made a fresh start. He removed himself from business concerns, established a farm, aided his black neighbors, and began to hone his Allegheny Mountains plan. He

Figure 4.2. John Brown's House (on Lot 95), North Elba, circa 1870–1880. *Source:* New York Public Library. Public domain.

went into the wilderness and put himself square with God, offering his life to be used in whatever way necessary to eradicate the great sin of slavery and enact racial equality. The *way* was at the North Elba farm—or so it seemed.

In June of 1855, Ruth and Henry eagerly welcomed the arrival of John, Mary, and their five young children. After the happy homecoming, John read the pile of mail that included letters from his sons in Kansas. John Jr. wrote that the territory exceeded his expectations and held great prospect "for health, wealth, and usefulness." Salmon admired the "lovely prairies and wooded streams," which made Kansas seem like "a haven of rest." However, dreams of prosperity, "of fields of corn, orchards, and vineyards," were followed by outrage over the actions of proslavery men. "I feel more like fight now than I ever did before," wrote Salmon.[13]

John Jr. described how lawless bands of well-armed proslavery "Miscreants" roamed about intimidating and terrorizing free-state settlers, trying "to fasten Slavery upon this glorious land, by means no matter how foul."

Since the Browns' intention in Kansas was settlement, they brought only hunting weapons, not battle weapons. In total, the five brothers had one revolver, one good and one poor rifle, one small pistol, one Bowie knife, and two "slung shot" (a small metal ball or rock attached by a strap to the wrist and swung to strike a target). The Browns were quite ready and willing to fight the enemy, as were other antislavery men, if they could "thoroughly arm and organize themselves in military companies." John Jr. asked his father to send Colt revolvers, Minnie rifles, Bowie knives, and other arms. "We need them more than we do bread."[14]

John Sr. did not have guns or money to offer his sons, but he would get them—and bring them to Kansas himself and stand alongside his sons in defense against the proslavery forces. He immediately set out to make an appeal at an abolitionist convention in Syracuse. During the first day of meetings, Gerrit Smith read letters from the Brown brothers depicting the grim conditions in Kansas. The slavers and their allies had completely overpowered the Friends of Freedom, burning their houses and barns, destroying their crops, and maiming their cattle. "It was no longer a question of Negro Slavery," wrote the Browns, "but a question of Personal Liberty with the settlers from the Free States."[15]

Tears flowed as attendees listened to the letters. Then, John Brown stepped forward and delivered a fiery speech. As father of the five men, he declared that he was going to Kansas to aid in fighting the proslavery forces and encouraged others to join him or give funds for arms and supplies. Not everyone at the convention supported the use of violence. The age-old debate among abolitionists persisted—should actions be restricted to moral suasion and peaceful nonresistance measures, or should militant actions be employed? Convention officials declined to support or fund John Brown; they left it up to individuals to offer aid.

The Fugitive Slave Law and Kansas-Nebraska Act brought more abolitionists to conclude that slaveholders would never willingly end slavery—emancipation required militant force. Brown collected $60 from abolitionists who were willing to pay if others would do the work. In this sentiment, John Brown heard the call of God, so he buckled on his armor and answered: "Here am I." Ever since making a pledge to destroy slavery in 1837, he had kept his affairs "in such condition that in two weeks I could wind them up and be ready to obey that call; permitting nothing to stand in the way of duty—neither wife, children, nor worldly goods."[16]

Brown returned to North Elba to put things in order before leaving for Kansas. He prepared to leave his new farm, his wife and young children, and his black neighbors. He postponed his plans for an Allegheny campaign. Something unforeseen had shifted the topography from the mountains to the prairies. After twice resisting the call of Kansas, Brown succumbed to his duty to protect his family and other antislavery settlers. The *way* to eradicate slavery seemed to go through bloody Kansas. If there was "any other way to answer the end of my being," wrote Brown, "I would be quite content to be at North Elba."[17]

Unrealized Expectations and Unfair Judgments

According to the 1855 New York State census, twelve black men resided in North Elba (including Thomas Brown, who was listed as white). Eleven of them were denoted as "owners of land" and qualified as "voters" in the census: William Carasaw, Josiah Hasbrook, Lyman Epps, Leonard Worts, Lewis Pierce, Silas Frazier (nongrantee), Isaac Craig, Henry Dickson, Thomas Jefferson, Samuel Jefferson, and Thomas Brown. Six of them owned farms valued close to or exceeding the $250 property qualification for voting. Though they were poor, they lived in better circumstances than several of their white neighbors. Most of the grantees owned farm animals and implements. Many had a pig or two (Dickson had nine), a pair of oxen, a couple of horses, and a few milk cows and beef cattle. Pierce and Epps accomplished the most plowing with fourteen and six acres, respectively. The settlers had adjusted well to their new lives, but problems of some sort seemed to keep surfacing.

Lyman Epps heard rumors of black abolitionists planning to hold a celebration at North Elba "in honor of Gerrit Smith's benevolence" in donating land. It upset Epps that they would spend time and money on a party instead of using the resources to enable grantees "to settle on those lands, or otherwise make them available in securing a homestead for ourselves and for our children after us." Epps urged those who might emigrate to show gratitude to the donor, "in deeds and services, rather than in vain show and empty declamation."[18]

Epps refused to give up on his fellow grantees. "These lands are very valuable, and still increasing in value," and grantees should "redeem them," he wrote in *Frederick Douglass' Paper*. Some lands (near the Saranac River) had "beautiful pine lumber" and were increasing in lumber value. Although some grantees' lots had been sold for taxes, Epps knew they had two years to pay the back taxes and retain their land. Time was running out; the grantees needed to act. Otherwise, the lands would be turned over to the buyers who would make a fortune on what they derisively termed "N——Lands."

After reading Epps's letter, land agents Charles B. Ray and James McCune Smith tried to emphasize the potential timber value of the lands, but many grantees neglected back taxes and lost rights to their lands. Epps embraced an Adirondack life and knew the value of timber, yet it seemed that lumberjacking did not appeal to grantees in the city any more than farming. "Agricultural pursuits are not, as I think, suited to our condition," said Frederick Douglass at the 1853 Colored National Convention in Rochester, New York. Farming was a "noble profession," he said, but "it is almost impossible to get colored men to go on the land." They did not want to leave the city and their network of family and friends. Douglass explained one reason for this: "Slavery, more than all things else, robs its victims of self-reliance." He admitted the statement might have sounded strange coming from a black man, but he emphasized that he was dealing with facts. "There are exceptions," said Douglass, individuals whose agricultural pursuits provided the means of supporting and improving their families. He did not blame the others for lack of perseverance and zeal; he placed it in the context of slavery.[19]

Agricultural pursuits suited some people, but most turned their noses up at it (especially in the backwoods). Even the black farmers in North Elba often moved on to other places after a few years. They left the wilderness conditions of the Adirondack interior for places such as the Champlain Valley of New York and Vermont, which had a milder climate, cleared lands, access to transportation, and villages with stores, churches, mills, and so on. Though this out-migration was not unusual, visitors and writers often remarked on the black settlers' departures in racist terms. "Be it through the natural laziness of the African, or from the incapacity of the situation or soil," wrote Thomas Addison Richards in 1855, "none of the [Smith] settlers have long held their possessions." The black man was "by nature so indolent, so wanting in enterprise, and even in desire, that it is a question whether he would be able to raise a mullein in Paradise."[20]

Richards was wrong about the settlers. Although Smith and the land agents had given up on them, a few black settlers remained in North Elba and the Brown family had rejoined them. Together, the Browns and the black families farmed, labored, prayed, hiked, and attended school. As for Richards's bigotry, it likely stemmed from his affection for the South, which he depicted in his landscape paintings of slave plantations. Worse still, a similar racial insult came from the pen of Gerrit Smith.

In 1857, Gerrit Smith admitted that his expectations had not been "fully realized." Of the three thousand black men who received land grants, half of them had either "sold their land, or been so careless as to allow it to be sold for taxes." Fewer than fifty grantees continued to hold physical possession of their land, and most of those were in the central part of the state. Many of the unoccupied parcels were in Essex and Franklin Counties, where "the winters are long, the snows deep, and the soil thin." White men managed there "only by very hard work and very frugal habits," said Smith. "Why, then, considering the character of the colored people, should we expect them to do much in such a country?"[21]

Those were stunning words, nevertheless, Smith went on to say "the character of the colored people" was improving, "but the mass are ignorant and thriftless." They should quit making excuses for their continued degradation and "swear that they will be Pariahs and lepers no longer."

That was quite an indictment from the initiator of the "scheme of justice." His judgmental words gave powerful ammunition to his foes. The press delivered the epitaph for Smith's land scheme—it was an "utter failure." A few years later, a Virginian described the grantees as "lazy, filthy and thievish" men who "would neither work, learn, or pray." He proposed "the failure of the North Elba scheme" might be due to "the unfitness of the negro for a state of freedom." This was the *curse* that Frederick Douglass warned about back in 1848 and 1849.[22]

Long before the roofs of the Timbucto cabins turned to rot, facts were sidestepped and the blame game was in full stride. Gerrit Smith never admitted his role in its failure, nor did his biographer Octavius Brooks Frothingham. In 1878, Frothingham said the grantees had "none of the qualities that make the farmer." Smith's "heroic hope" that the land grants would "rouse the blacks to manhood" proved to be illusive. The fault for the demise lay, "not so much in the land or its donor, as in the inefficiency of the people who desired a Capua, and rebelled when they found a New England."[23]

It was Smith who *promised* them an Eden paradise and what they found was not "a New England"; Smith gave them an isolated northern wilderness. It was Smith who loudly and widely pitched his empty, undesirable land in terms of divine self-regeneration and Romanticism. And, while Smith gloried in the praise for his benevolence and took credit for his altruistic gift to poor blacks, he took none of the blame. As a perfectionist, he did not acknowledge his failure to anticipate the practical needs of the black settlers, thus about 98 percent of them rebuked his offer to move to the Adirondack land.

When he gave land to poor white men in 1849 to 1850, he gave them each ten dollars and offered them forty dollars if they didn't want the land. He also gave fifty dollars to poor white women so they could buy land. No such help was offered to black men and women. Smith made out the deeds and that was it. He never offered guidance, sent supplies or cash, or visited them. Smith "took no interest in their welfare."[24]

Instead, as initiator and spokesperson for the land experiment, he established the myth that the project proved the inferiority of black people. He set a precedent for future judgments, not only of the land experiment, but also of the black settlers and Timbucto.

Like Frothingham, most historians and writers considered the experiment a failure and finding a culprit was easy work. Ignore Smith's faults. Ignore facts and fairness. Blame the black grantees, who were often erroneously described as escaped slaves or Southern fugitives. No one did it with as much audacity and repugnance as Alfred Donaldson in his John Brown chapter in *A History of the Adirondacks* (1921). Parts of Donaldson's text were wholeheartedly racist.

> As a matter of fact, of course, the attempt to combine an escaped slave with a so-called Adirondack farm was about as promising of agricultural results as would be the placing of an Italian lizard on a Norwegian iceberg.
>
> The farms allotted to the negroes consisted of forty acres each, but the natural gregariousness of the race tended to defeat the purpose of these individual holdings. The darkies began to build their shanties in one place, instead of on their separate grants. Before long about ten families had huddled their houses together down by the brook. . . . The shanties were square, crudely built of logs, with flat roofs, out of which little stovepipes protruded at varying angles. The last touch of pure negroism was a large but dilapidated red flag that floated above the settlement, bearing the half-humorous, half-pathetic legend "Timbuctoo"—a name that was applied to the whole vicinity for several years.[25]

Although this account was labeled *History*, it lacked historical accuracy and integrity. Donaldson took the memories of old-timers, without fact checking their narratives, and whipped them up into a fictional and racist narrative. The settlers were not escaped slaves, there were never ten families huddled together, and there was no evidence of a red flag bearing the legend

"Timbuctoo" or of the name applying to the entire area for several years. To the contrary, Timbucto was only used in 1848 and 1849 to refer to the black community in North Elba.

It was not only Donaldson who spread confusion about Timbucto and the black settlers. Some accounts were not racist, they were just wrong. In one account, Lyman Epps Jr. claimed "slaves" came to Lake Placid by means of the 'underground railway' and many of them settled in the vicinity of Averyville and Freeman's home. "Practically all died," he said, "owing to the extreme cold weather and scarcity of food." Another well-known local, O. Byron Brewster, claimed "Timbuctoo" had been the "Indian name" for the town (North Elba) and suggested that it had been given that name by "smug Keene and Jay people." According to Brewster, Timbucto had nothing to do with the "pitiful settlement of colored people" known by the name of "Freeman's Home," which was changed to Cascadeville a few years later.[26]

Though myths and misinterpretations about the black farmers in North Elba existed before and after Donaldson's account, his text propelled it to a new level. Donaldson resurrected the name Timbucto, changed its spelling, and mocked it as laughable and sad. Because subsequent writers, including scholars and historians, repeated his sensational, racist prose as fact, Donaldson's account was largely responsible for annihilating the cultural heritage and factual history of the black settlers.

His text also unfairly judged John Brown's relationship with the settlers. Donaldson claimed that Brown dismissed the idea of a black colony in North Elba as "pure chimera" and gave up on it "in 1851" when he moved to Ohio. Pure fiction.[27]

Contemporaries of Brown such as Wendell Phillips, Willis Hodges, and Gerrit Smith did not blame the demise of Timbucto on him. Phillips praised Brown for moving among the black settlers in North Elba so that "he might be by to hold them up with his strong right arm, and a heart that never failed; and whenever you probe that life you find nothing but disinterestedness." Willis Hodges recalled how Brown worked to help black settlers establish homes in Essex County. "Brown supplied goods to the starving people from his own means, labored on their behalf, and preached to them." Gerrit Smith praised Brown as "friend and father" to the settlers. "His kindnesses to the little colored colony in gifts of barrels of flour and other necessaries, and, above all, in advice and guidance, were numberless," wrote Smith. "His care for it was incessant."[28]

Yet some recent accounts continue to fault Brown. He was not "a kind of father" to the grantees, nor did his family help them enough. Brown "sacrificed" dozens of people still living on Adirondack lands when he left for Kansas. If not for Brown's arrival "on a red warhorse," the Timbucto colony would "rescue the U.S. from white supremacy."[29] Among the astounding statements is one from the *Dreaming of Timbuctoo* exhibit (2001), asserting that the settlement of "Timbuctoo" failed for many reasons, one of them being "the late arrival of their mentor, John Brown." None of the reasons involved Gerrit Smith.

Like many other incidents and experiments in American history, memories fade, facts get twisted, and pieces are forgotten. Each generation looks to the past, often through rose-colored glasses or in search of evidence supporting a contemporary agenda. Smith's land giveaway was a worthy and noble cause, and it is admirable that Timbucto has attracted attention and recognition in the 2000s. However, hindsight can obscure the context and relevance of the past and presentism can fabricate a misleading or fabled portrayal of history.

Smith's scheme did not elevate the black race, destroy prejudice and inferiority, or lead to the destruction of slavery. There were not eight or twelve "black settlements" in the Adirondacks. These so-called settlements consisted of a group of people spread across a geographic area and several consisted of fewer than five families. They were integrated communities, not independent black settlements, and only Timbucto and Blacksville were large enough to be considered communities. Neither should they be called "black suffrage settlements." Smith's land giveaway was not a scheme solely "to gain access to the vote." Voting was not the only goal or even the major objective of the black settlers. The project did not enable three thousand men or "numberless black New Yorkers" to vote—the number was close to twenty.[30]

Timbucto was not lost or deferred or othered. People wrote about it in hundreds of articles and books about John Brown and in accounts of Adirondack history. The reality was that the goals of Timbucto were unrealized and many factors contributed to its demise—some preventable, some out of anyone's control, and few having to do with the character of the black settlers or John Brown. But there is no intrinsic dishonor in failure. Other settlements in the Adirondacks did not prosper; the first white community in North Elba went bust in 1817. Plenty of utopian communes, such as Brook Farm, flourished and vanished within a few years. Many black farming communities popped up in the 1840s and 1850s in the Northwest Territories and most fell apart due to poor planning, disagreements, or other forces. Yet, there are unexpected positive outcomes and exceptions. In Cass County,

Michigan, Quaker settlers welcomed black farmers and created a thriving community. Among the communes, Northampton was more interracial than most, had 120 members in 1844, and resulted in David Ruggles's Water Cure and Mary Brown's healing.

Among the few settlers who took a risk in moving to the Adirondacks, several became admirable and honorable citizens. The Epps, Carasaw, Hasbrook, Appo, and other families remained for years in North Elba. "Some of the best farms which I have seen in that region are still in the hands of colored men," wrote Thomas Higginson in 1859 and James Redpath repeated it in 1860.[31] Later, several prominent black writers such as Benjamin Quarles and Archibald and Francis Grimke also described positive aspects of Smith's project. The best-known account was written by author, sociologist, and National Association for the Advancement of Colored People (NAACP) leader W. E. B. Du Bois. His 1909 biography of John Brown acknowledged the shortcomings of the climate, the settlers' farming skills, and Gerrit Smith ("it was not a well thought-out scheme"), yet Du Bois said the project "turned out some good Negro farmers" and "gave some of its best Negro citizens of today to northern New York." Smith's experiment was "not wholly a failure," but Du Bois felt it might have done more if planned better, and "much if not all of its success was due to John Brown."[32]

Chapter 5

Middling Tuff Times

[The proslavery border ruffians] hate him as they would a snake, but their hatred is composed nine tenths of fear . . . [John Brown] is a strange, resolute, repulsive, iron-willed, inexorable old man. He stands like a solitary rock in a more mobile society, a fiery nature, and a cold temper, and a cool head—a volcano beneath a covering of snow.

—Abolitionist William A. Phillips,
Kansas lawyer and journalist, 1856[1]

When John Brown and son-in-law Henry Thompson headed to Kansas in August of 1855, their families in North Elba held to the solace: "If it is so dreadful for us to part, with the hope of meeting again, how dreadful must be the separation for life of hundreds of poor slaves." Oliver Brown soon joined his father on the journey to Kansas while Watson remained in North Elba to help his mother. When Mary and Watson wrote about being lonesome at the farm, Salmon Brown reminded them that they had volunteered to go to "that cold and miserable land" and would have to "wind it through for a while."[2]

The conditions Salmon faced in Kansas were tough, too. The thunderstorms were some of the heaviest he ever experienced "since Noah's flood" and it looked as though the whole of Kansas would drown. The spirit of the antislavery people seemed to be drenched already and they were willing to negotiate with the "hellish pro-slavery" people. Salmon predicted "the great ulcer of this boasted republic" would soon break and, within the year,

Figure 5.1. Watson Brown, son of John and Mary. *Source:* Library of Congress. Public domain.

Kansas would be in open insurrection. John Jr.'s wife, Wealthy Brown, presented another possibility. "Perhaps, we shall all get shot for disobeying their beautiful laws." She reasoned they might as well die for a noble cause in Kansas "as freeze to death" in North Elba.[3]

John Brown sent a plethora of ideas on how to winterize the farmhouse. After haying season ended, he wanted Watson to get some good clapboards from the mill and haul them into the barn. He also asked for Henry Thompson's brother John or someone to be hired to nail down the shingles and clapboard, and "finish off the outside of the House good."

Plaster made of lime and sand could be used to cover the interior walls. Also, John wanted the cellar dug out and walled up. All of this was to be done before the freezing cold of winter arrived.[4]

Work on the house required money; therefore, in early September John directed the sale of his cattle being kept in Connecticut. The funds would be sent to Watson, and John explained how he should sign his name on the draft, "across the back . . . about two inches from the top end." John also said to be frugal with the money because he expected "to be very poor."

Poor, indeed.

When John, Henry, and Oliver set out from Chicago on the long overland journey through Iowa and Missouri, they traveled with a heavily loaded wagon and one horse, slept in a tent, and survived on crackers, herring, boiled eggs, tea, and a little milk. For fresh meat, they shot prairie chickens, having three for breakfast one morning. They also had "plenty of quinine and bark etc." to cure Henry's case of ague. However, when the trio finally reached the Kansas territory on October 5, 1855, John had only sixty cents and was forced to write and ask his father for a $50 loan.[5]

Most of the family in Brownsville, Kansas, were near starvation and engulfed in sickness and bitter cold. However, when John wrote to Mary, he understated the terrible situation in Kansas sympathizing with her seemingly "widowed state" in the "miserable Frosty region" of New York. "May God abundantly reward all your sacrifices for the cause of humanity," he wrote, "and a thousand-fold more than compensate your lack of worldly connections!"[6]

To improve conditions at North Elba, Ruth (who was two months pregnant) and her young son Johnny moved into the farmhouse with Mary and her children. John approved of the arrangement and advised them: "Try to be cheerful," "hope in God," and "encourage each other." As freezing weather approached in November, the work of winterizing the farmhouse had not been done, so John suggested another way to keep out the cold, by covering the outside with "cheap straight-edged boards." He advised Watson to run the boards from the ground to the eaves "barn fashion" and to hammer the nails only partway so the boards could be removed later and reused.

Regarding Mary, John complained that he had not gotten a "scratch" from her. "It seems that my Wife has *worn out* her *Pen* entirely." He told her to buy another cow if they needed more milk and to get other things they needed. "Do not any of you go without what you need." John hoped the money from the sale of his cattle had arrived, but week after week went by as Mary and Watson waited for the funds. When they were down to their last loaf of bread, they asked John's father for a $50 loan.[7]

The family members in North Elba were more isolated than ever. Almost the entire family was in Kansas, along with the Adairs, and now Mary's brother, Orson Day, decided to make a new start there after foreclosure of his store in Whitehall, New York. Henry Thompson, with the help of John, Salmon and Oliver, built a house for the Day family in Kansas. By then the situation had cooled down, in part, due to freezing weather. In early February of 1856, temperatures dropped to 28 degrees below zero. Oliver had two frozen toes, Owen a frozen foot, and Henry a frozen nose.

John admitted they were having "middling tuff times," but they had enough to eat and reason for "unfeigned gratitude." When the snow melted, it would cause high water and the Missourians would find it difficult to invade Kansas. "God by his Elements may protect Kansas for some time." John told those at North Elba not to worry about anyone in Kansas. "Trust us to the care of Him who feeds the young ravens when they cry." However, John was soon grieved to hear that Mary had suffered through dire circumstances and borrowed money from his father. Instead of expressing sympathy, he scolded her for not telling him of her needs sooner.[8]

The arrival of spring in the Adirondacks did not chase away Mary's blues. In mid-May, snow still covered the mountains and even some of the fields; nary a bud appeared on the beech and maple trees. Yet, Mary picked up her pen and assured her husband that things were "middling well," despite Ellen suffering a little "with worms." They had made three gallons of molasses, a little vinegar, and sixty-four pounds of maple sugar. Watson had already sowed four acres and was getting ready to plant carrots, turnips, and potatoes. The grass had grown enough for the cattle to feed on it. Old Spott, the cow, was giving "a nice mess of milk" and Watson's two little pigs were fat. With funds sent by John, the family paid off their debts and bought leather to make new shoes for Mary and the girls.[9]

Without Henry by her side, Ruth had been dreadfully sad during her nine months of pregnancy. Separation was difficult for Henry, too, but he felt he had "a sacrifice to make, a duty to perform" in Kansas. He could not have "a conscience void of offence" if he left the work unfinished. He needed to put his "hand to the plough" and labor "until School is out."[10]

Despite Ruth's fear that her baby "would not be right," she birthed a healthy girl on May 9, 1856 (the birthday of John Brown). The baby weighed eight pounds five ounces and had dark blue eyes, reddish hair, and "a well-proportioned head (I think)." Ruth wrote to Henry, "I never look at her without thinking of you, my dear husband; I want to see you more than ever and I hope the lord will spare your life to return to me again." In the meantime, she assured him that she had the best of care from Grandmothers Thompson and Brown and the old neighbor Mrs. Peacock. As she ended her letter, Ruth asked Henry what he wanted to name the baby. They agreed on Ella Jane Thompson.[11]

The Kansas War

For months, things were "middling tuff" in Kansas as proslavery men threatened to make a second attack on the town of Lawrence, the stronghold of the free-state people. Then, on May 21, David R. Atchison, a former senator of Missouri, made a speech to about 750 proslavery ruffians near Lawrence. "We have entered that damned town, and taught the damned Abolitionists a Southern lesson," he said. Now they were about to attack it again to show that Kansas belonged to them. "Come on, boys! Now do your duty," he yelled. If a woman dressed as a soldier and carried a rifle, "trample her under your feet as you would a snake!" If anyone should stand in the way, "blow them to hell with a chunk of cold lead."[12]

The citizens of Lawrence put up little resistance, even handing over their only cannon. Yet the proslavery ruffians raided, burned, and pillaged Lawrence, which included the destruction of the antislavery headquarters and two newspaper presses.

> America the land of Liberty?
> I tell you what!—I'll put a chunk of lead
> Inside your brain if you say that to me;
> I'll raise your skull-top for you off your head.
> America's the land of Slavery now—
> To Slavery's cause the North I mean to win;
> And if what I assert you won't allow,
> I'll rip you open uppards to the chin. ("Song of the Border Ruffian")[13]

The proslavery victors celebrated, unaware of the reign of terror they had set in motion. "A bloody collision in Kansas seems all but inevitable," declared the *New-York Tribune*, "a collision which can hardly fail to shake the Union to its center."[14]

John Brown and his men had buckled on their armor and gone to Lawrence, but they did not arrive in time to stop the attack. When they returned home to the Pottawatomie Creek area, a posted Notice told all free-state men to leave within thirty days, otherwise their throats would be cut. The Browns and their neighbors had every reason to believe these threats. One friend put it bluntly: "We expect to be butchered, every Free State settler in our region."[15]

The next day, Brown heard that abolitionist Senator Charles Sumner was on the floor of the US Senate speaking about crimes in Kansas when he was physically struck and severely beaten by a cane-wielding Southerner. The news infuriated Brown; he was tired of hearing the word *caution*. Drastic action was necessary to prevent the slaughter of his family and neighbors, to foil future attacks on Lawrence and other towns, and to deter the triumph of slavery. "We must show by actual work that there are two sides to this thing," said Brown, "and that they cannot go on with impunity."[16]

May 24, 1856. One year had passed since John Brown Jr. wrote to his father about the need for guns and swords in Kansas. After those weapons arrived, they remained clean of blood and battle for three seasons—until this day. Soon afterward, Mary Brown received a letter from John saying, "We were . . . accused of murdering five men at Pottawatomie, and great efforts have since been made by the Missourians and their ruffian allies to capture us."[17]

Of course, John was not going to give any particulars in a letter that authorities might intercept. Only later would Mary learn the gory details. Around midnight on May 24, John had organized a raid along Pottawatomie Creek, seizing five proslavery men from their houses and killing them with broadswords. Later, Salmon admitted his part in committing the slayings but said, "It was all that saved the Territory from being overrun with drunken land-pirates from the Southern States . . . It was done to save life, and to strike terror through their wicked ranks." John claimed he did not personally kill any of the men, but admitted he ordered the acts. He said, "God is my judge."[18]

Newspapers publicized the incident, and ever since, it has been disected, debated, and squeezed through the wringer. In the Kansas territory, many horrifying atrocities, threats, and acts of war were occuring on both sides. The press had labelled it "the Kansas War" months before John Brown even arrived in the territory.[19] Why did the Pottawatomie killings attract so much attention? Because they struck terror into the hearts of *proslavery* men?

The proslavery forces had been operating almost unrestricted since early 1855. Benjamin F. Stringfellow, a General in the Missouri Militia, told his men that their "rights and property" were in danger, thus, they were justified in "violating laws, state or national." He told them to go into "every election district in Kansas . . . and vote at the point of the bowie-knife and the revolver." If the ruffians found any "scoundrel" who was associated in any way with "free-soilism" or abolition, they should keep him from voting, that is, "exterminate him."[20]

The horrors of ruffianism continued through 1855 and 1856. Near Lawrence, a man reported that his brother-in-law was "shot through the head . . . and his scalp exhibited in fiendish exultation by his murderer." The assassin declared: "I went out for the scalp of a d—d abolitionist, and I have got one." In another incident, ruffians assaulted a woman because she resided with a family suspected of speaking to free-state men. When the woman stepped out of the house during the night, four men seized her and took her away into a ravine where she was "stripped of all her clothing, her hands and feet fastened, her *tongue* drawn out, a string *tied* about it and secured around her neck." Somehow, she crawled back to the house and aroused help.[21]

In contrast to those events, the Pottawatomie killings drew immediate reaction and retribution. A proslavery posse captured Jason and John Jr. (who was not at Pottawatomie), placed them in irons, and forced them to endure horrendous conditions before turning them over to authorities who held them in jail for months. Meanwhile, Brown's men defeated proslavery forces at the Battle of Black Jack. It was the first clear victory for the free-state forces in Kansas, though it came with consequences. Henry Thompson had a bullet lodged in his body, Salmon Brown accidentally wounded himself a few days later, and authorities were actively hunting for Brown's men. As soon as Henry and Salmon recovered, Oliver and William Thompson (who had come to help his brother) traveled with them back to North Elba.[22]

John Brown's notoriety grew even greater after the Battle of Osawatomie on August 30. Missouri ruffians attacked Brown's forces, who were outnumbered (perhaps as much as 10 to 1), but Brown's men fought and killed many of the enemy before retreating. John Brown walked away with the monikers "Captain Brown" and "Osawatomie Brown." However, the battle had dire consequences. John wrote to Mary, "Dear Fredk was shot dead without warning." Frederick had not even taken part in the fighting, and was unarmed, when Martin White, a proslavery man, killed him.[23]

When Watson and Salmon heard the news of Frederick's murder, they stopped digging potatoes in the North Elba fields and immediately set out for Kansas to kill Martin White. The young men reached Iowa before their father sent word to forsake revenge and to remember they do what they do for a principle. Watson returned to his wife (Isabelle Thompson, Henry's sister, whom he had married in September 1856) in North Elba, while Salmon planned to go to Cleveland and learn the carpentry trade.

In Kansas, the Browns lost their cabins, crops, books, papers, and dear Frederick. They were left almost destitute, and the cause of freedom for which they had sacrificed so much seemed almost lost, too. However, when John returned to New York State, he received support rather than rebuke from abolition friends. The Kansas war changed some minds about the use of violence. For example, although Gerrit Smith was a politician and supporter of the peace movement, he said: "Political action is just now our greatest evil—our greatest danger. We are looking after ballots, when our eyes should be fixed on bayonets. We are counting votes, when we should be mustering armed men. We are looking after the interests of civil rulers, when we should be seeking after military rulers. . . . Missouri will be the battlefield in her turn and then slavery will be driven to the wall!"[24]

After visiting Smith and Frederick Douglass, John returned to North Elba, having been absent for a year and a half. The farm was still John Brown's *home*—symbolically, more than physically. It was where he sent money and provisions, where his wife and young children lived and farmed, and where he longed to lay his head at night. That head looked strange to little Ellen who had been a baby when her father left for Kansas. Ellen was so afraid of John that Annie had to sit on his knee beside her as he sang "Blow Ye the Trumpet, Blow."[25]

John kept his stay short. He did not want it known his home was in North Elba; he wanted his family to be safe there. He returned to his work with unflinching resolve. "God sees it," said John. "I have only a short time to live—only one death to die, and I will die fighting for this cause. There will be no peace in this land until slavery is done for. I will give them something else to do than to extend slave territory. I will carry the war into Africa."[26]

Carrying the war into Africa meant taking it into the domain of the slave power. It meant striking offensively at the heart of the enterprise. But his Allegheny plan could not be talked up yet; the Kansas conflict had to be concluded first. For that, John Brown needed money and he hoped the abolitionists of New England would supply it.

In mid-January of 1857, Brown arrived in Boston and met with the young schoolteacher Franklin Sanborn, who was Secretary of the Massachusetts Kansas Committee. After hearing Brown's account of Kansas, Sanborn introduced him to other notable men, most importantly, four staunch abolitionists: Thomas Wentworth Higginson, a minister and journalist; George Luther Stearns, a wealthy businessman and president of the Massachusetts Kansas Committee; Rev. Theodore Parker, a Unitarian minister; and Dr. Samuel Gridley Howe, physician and educator of the blind. These four men, along with Sanborn and Gerrit Smith, became known as the Secret Six—the white men John Brown turned to for counsel, encouragement, and financial aid.

Though John Brown found encouragement in New England, he did not find adequate funding, so he made a public appeal via the newspapers. He explained that he had limited means when he first engaged "in the struggle for Liberty in Kansas" and now found himself "more destitute." Yet he still wanted to continue his efforts and believed the "friends of Freedom" would answer his call. "I ask all honest lovers of Liberty and Human Rights, both male and female, to hold up my hands by contributing pecuniary aid. . . . I will endeavor to make a judicious and faithful application of all such means as I may be supplied with." The *Brooklyn Evening Star* printed Brown's entire letter, after they mocked him ("Poor fellow! . . . J. B., 'sly J. B.'") and called his appeal a "most delicious piece of political mendicancy." The headline asked, "When Will It Stop?"[27]

Instead of stopping, Brown expanded his plea. In April, he merged his appeal letter with extracts of his speeches and transformed it into an essay known as "Old John Brown's Farewell." He described what happened in Kansas—how he, his family, and his brave men "suffered hunger, cold, nakedness, and some of them sickness, wounds, imprisonment in irons, with extreme cruel treatment, and others death." They had been "lying on the ground for months in most sickly, unwholesome and uncomfortable places, some of the time with sick and wounded destitute of any shelter, and hunted like wolves, sustained in part by Indians." Brown said they had done this "in order to sustain a cause which every citizen of this 'glorious Republic' is under moral obligation to do, . . . a cause in which every man, woman and child of the entire human family has a deep and awful interest." He never asked for or expected wages. Yet, "amid all the wealth, luxury, and extravagance of this 'heaven-exalted' people," he could not even secure "the necessary supplies of the common soldier."[28]

Brown concluded, "How are the mighty fallen!"

Soon thereafter, funds and weapons began to flow and Brown believed he could raise the necessary resources to return to Kansas. Meanwhile, thoughts of mortality arose in his mind. While traveling throughout New England, Brown visited his relatives in Canton, Connecticut, and discovered his grandfather's old memorial stone near the cemetery. After receiving his relatives' permission to take the unused stone, he shipped it to Westport, New York, and arranged to have an inscription in memory of his son Frederick carved on the back of it: "murdered . . . for adherence to the cause of freedom." Then he wrote to Mary that he wanted the old stone to mark *his* grave at the farm.[29] With a price on John Brown's head and Uncle Sam's hounds on his heels, there was a real possibility that he would not return from Kansas alive.

Though he had never asked for help in providing for his family, in mid-March of 1857, Brown made a private appeal for $1,000 to Amos A. Lawrence of Boston. Brown proposed the purchase of "an improved piece of land" that would enable his wife and five younger children to "procure a Subsistence" if he never returned from Kansas. Though Mary was "a good economist and a real old fashioned business woman," Brown described her sacrifice in going through two winters "in our open cold house, unfinished outside and not plastered."[30]

Lawrence replied that he was short of cash, having donated large amounts to the Kansas effort. He told Brown not to worry about his family; they would be cared for if anything happened to him while he was working for the cause. "The family of 'Captain John Brown of Osawatomie' will not be turned out to starve in this country," wrote Lawrence, "until Liberty herself is driven out."

Assuming he had secured a commitment for the $1,000, John made an agreement with Franklin and Samuel Thompson to buy Lot 88 (which they had bought on land contract from Gerrit Smith). Lot 88 bordered the west side of the Brown farm (Lot 95) and half of the 160 acres would be given to Mary and half to Ruth (who already lived on the south half of the lot). On May 15, John met Samuel Thompson at Smith's land office in Peterboro and paid Thompson $150 toward the sale. Then Smith transferred the contract to Brown.[31]

However, complications slowed the collection of the $1,000 funding. Lawrence and other supporters believed they had never made personal commitments to the aid. Brown firmly insisted he had been given a guarantee. In explaining the situation to Sanborn, Brown said his wife willingly endured self-sacrifice and was "not above getting her bread over the washtub," though she never spoke of her trials or troubles. Why should his wife and family suffer while he performed a service that was "equally the duty of millions?" Those millions did not miss a single hearty meal in their efforts. Brown believed "the cheapest and most proper way" to provide for his family was to secure a piece of land for Mary and Ruth in North Elba. The women would find it "far less humiliating" to accept land rather than cash.[32]

As Sanborn worked out a way to get the funds, Brown traveled to Iowa, feeling "exceedingly mortified" over his unfulfilled promise to Franklin and Samuel Thompson. When Brown heard the funds had been secured in early August, he thanked Sanborn for the aid to his family. "The parting with my wife and young uneducated children," wrote Brown, "without income, supplies of clothing, provisions, or even a comfortable house to live in, or money to provide such things, with at least a fair chance that it was to be a last and final separation, had lain heavy on me." John's description was rather dramatic, with a pinch of hyperbole, though he also admitted the situation "was about as much a matter of self-sacrifice and self-devotion on the part of my wife as on my own, and about as much her act as my own."[33]

In mid-August of 1857, Franklin Sanborn went to Peterboro with the $1,000 draft in hand. Since the Thompsons still had outstanding payments to Gerrit Smith for the original contract, Sanborn assigned the draft to Smith, who kept $288.89. Then Smith signed the deeds and Sanborn traveled to North Elba to distribute the remaining funds and land deeds.

When he arrived at the Brown farm, two sons were working to extend the clearing. They had cut some trees and were getting the logs together before burning off the land. The women were busy gathering and drying wild red raspberries, so they might enjoy sauce and pies during the winter. Sanborn noted that the house was "not much more than a frame, boarded and clapboarded, and much of it lathed, but with only two or three plastered rooms." Ruth and Henry lived in a smaller house across the pasture on Lot 88. When Sanborn visited them, Ruth entertained him with anecdotes of her father while Henry told of his own adventures in Kansas, including the fight at Black Jack, where he was wounded and still carried the rifle ball in his body.[34]

During his two-day stay, Sanborn paid $571.13 to the Thompson brothers to complete the land purchase and then transferred the deeds, with Mary given the north half of Lot 88 and Ruth the south half. The remaining sum of $25.45 was given to Mary and "could not have been better bestowed," observed Sanborn. The family raised much of what they needed but had little cash "for the purchase of necessaries not raised by them." However, Sanborn recognized the "striking" contrast between the standard of living in "thriving towns of Massachusetts" and the Brown family's "rude and primitive" existence with no elegance and very few comforts. The outside world would consider them impoverished, but different standards prevailed in North Elba. In the entire town, "there was scarcely a house worth a thousand dollars, or one which was finished throughout."[35]

Almost everybody there was poor, recalled neighbor Byron Brewster, and "the Browns certainly were." Byron knew because, as a boy, he had worked for board and lodging at the Brown farm. Another neighbor boy, John G. Fay, remembered how his family lived back then. "Dad used to kill two bucks every fall, take them with horse and sleigh to Plattsburgh, sell them and bring home yarn, calico, [baking] soda and spices, etc., for the winter. Three hundred pounds of maple sugar, four hundred pounds of pork, and our own cows, were a living, fit for a king, those days."[36]

Even allowing for some inflation (or deflation) in memory, Brewster and Fay established a sense of ordinary life among North Elbans. Circumstances certainly held no elegance, but they were not dire, either. The Browns had a frame house; good farmland, pastures, and sugar maple trees; sheep, cattle, milk cows, and pigs; and deer in the woods, trout in the streams, and berries in the meadows. Salmon Brown recalled, "Frugality was observed from a moral standpoint but, one and all, we were a well-fed well-clad lot." John also sent letters and cash and supplies such as flour, sugar, rice, and salt fish. He was "never stingy in his family," said Ruth, "but always provided liberally for us, whenever he was able to do so."[37]

Though the Browns lacked possessions, the comforts of home were familial and spiritual. They persevered as a simple, God-fearing family destined to never become rich, to never be able to help the poor and oppressed from an abundance of wealth and property. Instead, the Browns' contributions came through sacrifice and what Sanborn called "the narrow path of poverty."[38]

Some historians and biographers have linked John Brown's long absences from home to the poor living conditions and claimed he deserted his family. Mary Brown felt differently; she said John always left home full of sorrow. "Many and many a time he has bid me good-bye hardly able to speak for his tears, saying he might never see me again." When away in Kansas, he thought of Mary in her "widowed state" and yearned to be with her. "I sometimes allow myself to dream a little of enjoying the comforts of home," he wrote, "but I do not dare to dream much."[39]

John's frequent absences also suggested he had complete faith in Mary "to be both mother and guardian of his flock." A friend described Mary and

Ruth as "fully sensible of the greatness of the struggle" against slavery and willingly bearing their part in the cause. "The women must stint" in North Elba because it cost money for John and the men to do their antislavery work in Kansas. John relied on Mary and Ruth as devoted and hardworking women; they were not just doing so-called women's work, it was vital work.[40]

Sanborn felt rewarded in being the guest of the Browns, a family in which "a manly and womanly resolution and generosity prevailed." They all seemed "cheerful in the midst of poverty and anxieties."[41]

A few weeks after Sanborn's 1857 visit, on the cold and stormy fifteenth day of October, Salmon Brown married Abbie Hinckley. An eighty-year-old neighbor lamented that the couple had married "on such a tempestuous day." She feared their married life might prove unhappy, "but upon learning that none of the wedding cake was burned," the superstitious woman concluded

Figure 5.2 Salmon Brown, son of John and Mary. *Source:* West Virginia State Archives. Used with permission.

Middling Tuff Times | 87

their marriage might possibly be harmonious. And it was. Years later, Abbie recalled her life as a newlywed in North Elba.

> [Salmon] Brown, who was a man of great determination and energy, went into the forest and cleared several acres of land and built a house of hewed logs, and also a barn. We had a cow, a yoke of oxen, some sheep and poultry. We also made several hundred pounds of maple sugar a year, the most of which we sold for eight cents a pound. It was a lonesome old hole in the woods, but I was happy with my husband and children and did not know enough to realize that we were shut off from most everything that is supposed to contribute to comfort and happiness. We surely lived the simple life.[42]

Figure 5.3 Abbie Hinckley Brown, wife of Salmon, sister of Alexis Hinckley. *Source:* West Virginia State Archives. Used with permission.

Chapter 6

High Peaks and Higher Law

What is wanted is men, not of policy, but of probity—who recognize a higher law than the Constitution, or the decision of the majority.

—Henry David Thoreau, "Slavery in Massachusetts"

Henry David Thoreau, Ralph Waldo Emerson, and their Concord friends were ridiculed as "monks sitting cross-legged on the floor" for choosing to "abstain entirely" from the antislavery movement. Yet John Brown found them to be kindred souls, not monkish men, when he met them in early 1857.[1] For a decade, Emerson and Thoreau had been speaking and writing about the connection of nature to the evils of slavery and the conflict of human laws with a higher law.

"Nothing is more absurd than . . . to complain of a party of men united in opposition to Slavery," said Emerson. "As well complain of gravity, or the ebb of the tide. Who makes the Abolitionist? The Slaveholder." Emerson asserted that slavery was a violation of nature's laws and would eventually be punished. "Whatever is false cannot be enacted. This law of nature is universal: gravity is only one of its languages; justice is another. Any attempt to violate it is punished, and recoils on the man. . . . The sky has not lost its azure because our eyes are sick. . . . Nature is not so helpless but it can rid itself of every crime."[2] Thoreau felt less optimistic about nature's law enacting justice. In 1854, slavery in the South and the capturing of black men in the North made him feel as if he had "lost his country." Even at Walden Pond, he found walks in nature spoiled by thoughts of wicked men. Then, one day he saw a waterlily in a swamp—a fine, white flower growing out of the "slime and muck of earth." To Thoreau, the lily represented the possibility of men of "purity and courage" rising up despite the "sloth and vice of man." Just as "Nature had not been a partner to the Missouri Compromise," men of virtue should stand up and refuse to compromise, wrote Thoreau. Slavery and servility should be buried or perhaps used "for manure."[3]

Thoreau and Emerson were not the only ones saying that the laws of the state needed to conform to a higher law. In 1850, Senator William H. Seward (New York) said, "We hold no arbitrary authority over anything, whether acquired lawfully or seized by usurpation. The Constitution regulates our stewardship; the Constitution devotes the domain to union, to justice, to defense, to welfare, and to liberty. But there is a higher law than the Constitution." At their 1850 meeting, Essex County abolitionists approved of Seward's words and declared the fugitive slave law to be "utterly unauthorized by the Constitution as well as by the teachings of reason and Religion."[4]

Thoreau took the teachings further. "In fact," he said, "I will quietly after my fashion, declare war with the State." He went to jail for refusing to pay tax to a government that sanctioned human slavery. Since the government unjustly imprisoned men, "the true place for a just man is also a prison." Thoreau's imprisonment lasted only one night (friends paid his taxes and authorities released him), but he reasoned, "It matters not how small the beginning may seem to be, what is once well done is done forever." He continued to believe that "one honest man" of the North willing to withdraw from the "copartnership" of our government with slavery, and locked up in the county jail, would lead to the abolition of slavery in America.[5]

Where would that man come from? Thoreau suggested: "A township where one primitive forest waves above while another primitive forest rots below—such a town is fitted to raise not only corn and potatoes, but poets and philosophers for the coming ages. In such a soil grew Homer and Confucius and the rest, and out of such a wilderness comes the Reformer eating locusts and wild honey." This man was John Brown who came from the wilds of northern New York, raising potatoes and eating black flies and maple sugar.

When Thoreau and Emerson first met Brown in early 1857, they dined and conversed with him and attended his speech to a crowd of more than a hundred people at the Concord Town Hall. Thoreau described Brown as a man "of great common-sense," like those who once stood at Concord Bridge, on Lexington Common, and on Bunker Hill, only Brown was "firmer and higher-principled." The heroes of American Independence bravely faced their country's foes, but Brown "had the courage to face his country herself when she was in the wrong."[6]

Emerson said everyone who heard Brown speak was impressed by his "simple, artless goodness and his sublime courage." For example, Brown believed in two instruments, the Golden Rule and the Declaration of Independence, and declared that it was "better that a whole generation of men, women and children should pass away by a violent death than that a word of either should be violated."[7]

After the talk, Emerson donated $25, Thoreau "a trifle," and others according to their means. More importantly, these two transcendental tree-huggers, or "Frogpondians" as Edgar Allan Poe sardonically called them, were enthralled by the rough, rugged abolitionist named John Brown. Emerson and Thoreau were not scared by Brown's talk of Kansas atrocities and violence. "In wildness is the preservation of the world," said Thoreau. By wildness, he meant the freedom to follow one's true nature, including the wild streak. "Whether or not we acknowledge it, there is a savage in all of us, even the most civilized, and that primal nature will show itself in impassioned or inspired moments."[8]

In wildness and wilderness, there is a bit of heaven and hell. Alfred Lord Tennyson called it "Nature, red in tooth and claw." Modern versions of the Bible use the word *wilderness* nearly three hundred times, referring to a variety of physical geographies and psychological states. Generally, wilderness is both an evil place in need of subjugation and a divine refuge where God makes himself known—some combination of revelation or rebirth with a side dish of danger and depravation. It is often an isolated and inhospitable place where a person is utterly vulnerable; they have cut themselves off from their past and their supports and entered the wilderness in an attempt to make a fresh start, to undergo self-discovery and find wisdom.

As Americans began to abandon negative, fearful notions of wilderness by the 1840s, some sought out the Western frontier. Others explored the wild frontier still existing in New York—in the Adirondacks. City dwellers sought an escape from dirty, crowded conditions. Invalids longed to be free of illness and looked for a cure. For example, Rev. Joel Headley suffered "an attack on the brain" and took to the woods seeking "mental repose and physical strength." He found that the Adirondacks provided a perfect antidote to "the haunts of men" and "overcivilized" urban life.[9]

Wilderness mountains reached toward heaven, bringing one "closer to God" and divine inspiration. Headley climbed more than a mile into

Figure 6.1. "Off Tahawus—East, July 19, 1859." Ink wash sketch (2015.57.1i) of two men sitting near the summit of Tahawus (Mount Marcy) looking east. From Alfred Pancoast Boller sketchbook. *Source:* Courtesy of the Adirondack Experience. Used with permission.

the sky, to the summit of the highest peak, Mount Marcy, and beheld a scene of "vagueness, terror, sublimity, strength, and beauty." It made him feel that God had designed and wrought the Adirondacks "as a symbol of His omnipotence." Headley's conclusion: "God is great!" and "Man is nothing here."

Artists in search of America's sublime scenery were particularly fond of Indian Pass, the abyss between Mount McIntyre (Algonquin Peak) and Wallface Mountain filled with a jungle of house-sized rocks and dark caverns. Author and poet Charles Fenno Hoffman admired it as "one of the most savage and stupendous among the many wild and imposing scenes at the sources of the Hudson."[10] Landscape painter Jervis McEntee said, "It is one of those wild scenes so full of majesty and sublimity which the Creator has formed for us to look upon that we may the better comprehend his boundless power."[11]

The Brown family appreciated the romantic aspect of nature; Indian Pass was just outside their window. However, unlike the artists, health seekers, and other visitors, the Browns experienced the reality of living there. When John Brown said everything reminded him of Omnipotence, he added a caveat—"and where if you do get your crops cut off once in a while, you will feel your dependence."[12]

When frost or hail or insects brought devastation, it reminded farmers of their human frailty and insignificance. When Ruth and Henry's crops needed rain, and the skies finally poured, John wrote to them: "It is a great mercy to us that we frequently are made to understand most thoroughly our absolute dependence on a power quite above ourselves."[13] In a deeper sense, Brown's words harken to Bible passages about going into the wilderness and casting off "earthly props." When people are uprooted and endure hardship, they experience a feeling of weakness and desperation, inducing them to renew their faith in God and live a higher life.

John Brown certainly understood the practical side of nature. On one of his trips home, he could not find anyone to take him from Keene to North Elba. Being anxious to get home, he started walking in the deep snow. After going a few miles, he got so tired and lame that he plopped down in the road to rest. He got up after a while, walked as far as he could, and sat down again. He proceeded in that way until he was overcome by fatigue and lay down in the deep snow, convinced he would die. A man passed John but did not notice him lying there. Though in great pain, John finally started walking again and somehow reached Robert Scott's house. Scott hitched up his wagon and took the frozen man home.[14]

The Browns did not shy away from blunt reality. As farmers and breeders, they experienced the miracle of birth and the finality of death, the sprouting of seeds and the process of decay, the glory of sun and rain and the violence of wind and ice. The Browns dared to look God and Nature in the face. At least most of them did. Jason thought North Elba was a good place "for a colony of Norwegians" who had never heard of a "temperate climate." He cheekily referred to North Elba as "Father's New Palestine." Owen also felt North Elba was too cold to be a promised land, but unlike Jason, he climbed a few mountains and felt the potency of the landscape. From the summit of Mount McIntyre (Algonquin Peak), the second highest mountain in the state, Owen said he could see "all the kingdom of the earth." He stayed there all night with no company except his dog.[15]

Watson, Salmon, and Annie Brown, along with nine friends, climbed Whiteface Mountain, but not by tramping up the popular route from the east with its gradual ascent. On July 3, 1857, the group rode a barge boat up Lake Placid to the head of the lake. From there, they walked through the woods to the base of the mountain and then climbed up the bare rock slide to the summit. The clear day gave them views of the St. Lawrence River, the Green Mountains of Vermont, and Lake Champlain. Annie even spotted a steamboat and eight or nine sailboats on Lake Champlain. She

Figure 6.2. "Whiteface (Mountain), from Lake Placid," by Harry Fenn. From "The Adirondack Region," in William Cullen Bryant, ed., *Picturesque America*, vol. II (D. Appleton, 1874), 420. *Source:* Author's collection.

also bragged that they camped overnight—in a terrible rainstorm—and she stood on top of Whiteface Mountain on the Fourth of July.[16]

Annie and her two female friends were among the first women to climb Whiteface up the slides from the west and to camp overnight on the summit. Her friend Simeon Hasbrook was likely one of the first black youths to stand atop Whiteface. The trip may have also initiated some romance; two of the climbers, Salmon Brown and Abbie Hinckley, married in the fall.

The Browns and their friends appreciated mountain life, and the extra income from serving as mountain guides. On two occasions in 1858, Henry Thompson guided gentlemen from Middlebury College up Mount Marcy and "made $13.00 in that way." His younger brother Dauphin guided author

Alfred Billings Street up the slides to the summit of Whiteface Mountain. Lyman Epps cleared a trail and guided tourists through Indian Pass.[17]

Visitors came to the Adirondacks not only to explore the mountains—some wanted to cleanse their minds and renew their spiritual and creative powers. "In the woods, the mask that society compels one to wear is cast aside," wrote Headley, "and the restraints which the thousand eyes and reckless tongue about him fasten on the heart are thrown off, and the soul rejoices in its liberty."[18] This kind of experience lured Ralph Waldo Emerson to the lake region of the Adirondacks. Emerson, poet James Russell Lowell, scientist Louis Agassiz, and seven other friends left Boston to commune with nature at what became known as the Philosophers' Camp in 1858.

At Follensby Pond (east of Tupper Lake), their idea of *roughing it* included ten guides—one per man—and some "rather Cockneyish" activities. After emptying dozens of bottles of ale, the men tested their mark by shooting bullets into them. Later, Emerson used his new double-barreled gun to shoot what was probably the first game he ever bagged, "a peetweet" (sandpiper).[19] These Romantics spent two weeks experiencing a rather watered-down version of wilderness life. "We flee away from cities," wrote Emerson, "but we bring the best of cities with us. We praise the forest life, but will

Figure 6.3. Philosophers' Camp, from *Frank Leslie's Illustrated Newspaper*, 1858. *Source:* "Sporting Tour in August 1858 of F. S. Stallknecht and Charles S. Whitehead," *Frank Leslie's Illustrated Newspaper*, 1858. Public domain.

we sacrifice our dear-bought lore of books and arts and trained experiment, or count the Sioux a match for Agassiz? O no, not we!"[20]

Wilderness as an ideal was appealing to these refined, gentlemen—the Adirondacks cured their ills, filled them with inspiration, and perhaps opened a pathway to the Muse—but a few weeks of sleeping in a bark hut on beds of evergreen branches was enough for them. "Civilized" life took place in cities and that was where these Romantics wanted to live.

However, Emerson realized that in the Adirondack woods the worth of a man was not based on formal education or fine threads.

> Look to yourselves, ye polished gentlemen!
> No city airs or arts pass current here.
> Your rank is all reversed; let men of cloth
> Bow to the stalwart churls in overalls:
> They are the doctors of the wilderness,
> And we the low-prized laymen.
> In sooth, red flannel is a saucy test
> Which few can put on with impunity. (Ralph Waldo Emerson,
>   "The Adirondacs," 1858)

If Henry David Thoreau had gone to Follensby Pond, he would have idolized the guides, too, for he believed Man needed "wild and dusky knowledge more than lettered learning." Staying in the house produced a softness, "not to say thinness of skin," said Thoreau, whereas living outdoors produced a roughness of character. Something in the sun, wind, and mountain air fed the spirit and caused man to grow "to greater perfection intellectually as well as physically." In such an environment, thoughts were clearer and fresher; understanding more comprehensive and as broad as the plains; and intellect on a grander scale, like thunder booming among the mighty mountains. Thoreau claimed that not even Adam in paradise was "more favorably situated on the whole than the backwoodsman in this country."[21]

The Browns praised the beauty and healthfulness of the region and liked being "doctors of the wilderness" in red flannel and overalls (though, it is claimed John Brown himself always wore linen and a brown frock coat, never donning a flannel shirt). Nevertheless, they did not come to North Elba seeking mountain views or pursuing freedom from illness or city life; they were freedom seekers of a different sort. The Browns came to assist the black settlers with finding freedom from oppression and prejudice.

> Say, where hath Freedom made her home,
> In what retired dell?
> To her seclusion I would come,
> In quietude to dwell.
> Away among *the mountains* high,
> Tis said that she did flee,
> Then let me to those *mountains* fly,
> For there I shall be free.
> There I shall feel *the* flowing wind,
> Dear nature's breath divine,
> Beneath a shelt'ring rock reclin'd,
> Beside *the* waving pine,
> There watch *the* bright clouds sailing high,
> Through heaven's concave flee;
> Oh! let me to *the mountains* fly,
> For there I shall be free. (George Cooper, "Mountain Liberty,"
>   1842)

While Gerrit Smith and his land agents romanticized the wilderness and its capacity for equality, few of the black settlers recorded their feelings. One of the few comments about the wilderness came from Willis Hodges of Franklin County. He wrote that they lived *"under our own vine and fig tree*, with none to molest us or make us afraid." He also ended his autobiography with these thoughts: "I hope that those of my colored friends, both bond and free, who read or hear about this little book will be inspired to press forward in their fight for freedom and equal rights . . . We may not live to view the promised land of freedom and justice; we may die in the wilderness of slavery and injustice . . . but our children or children's children will possess the land, if God is God, and a just God."[22]

Hodges's text personified the duality of wilderness. Many Bible passages and spirituals implored Christians to "go into the wilderness" and find God, yet others described the wilderness as a place of danger, and possibly death. The spiritual "O, ain't I glad I've got out the wilderness" signaled that wilderness was not suitable for the people of God. Writers and speakers often used the Biblical phrase "wilderness of slavery" to refer to the ironic and sad reality in America, "that no slave breathes its pure air or treads its free soil."[23]

John Brown believed in nature-given rights for all: "That Nature hath freely given to all Men, a full Supply of Air, Water, and Land; for their sustenance, and mutual happiness, That No Man has any right to deprive his fellow Man, of these Inherent rights." He wrote those words in his 1858 "Declaration of Liberty," as one of the reasons for a revolt against the institution of slavery. He also expanded the "unalienable rights" to include "equal rights, privileges, and justice to all, irrespective of Sex, or Nation." His Declaration also advocated "Fraternal Kindness" and the duty of Man "to promote the Happiness, Mental, Moral, and Physical elevation of his fellow Man." Those who violated these principles would bring upon themselves "certain and fearful retribution, which is the Natural, and Necessary penalty of evil Doing."[24]

Like Thoreau and Emerson, Brown connected human rights with nature. "I expect nothing but to 'endure hardness,'" said John, "but I expect to effect mighty conquest, even though it be like the last victory of Samson."[25]

Decades later, a visitor to the North Elba farm imagined John Brown standing there, "brooding over the horrors of slavery" and "foreseeing the impending struggle for liberty." He thought of Brown looking at the "titanic mountains" and hearing the rush of strong rivers and "songs of resounding tempests." Perhaps this setting inspired the radical abolitionist to do his duty and act, "to descend like a mountain torrent, and sweep the black curse from out the land."[26]

Another writer took the theory further. In a city, a man might not reach extremes; a man would see opportunities for adjustment and find ways of getting along with dissenting views. But mountains do not compromise. The visitor suggested the following:

> Let a man sit in this farmhouse, or lie in the shadow of this rock day after day while the sun strides across the sky, or the wind, rain, hail, and snow beat up and down the valley; let him brood upon the wrongs of an oppressed race; let him read his Old Testament—yes, or his New; let him consider the inwardness of Clay compromises and Buchanan diplomacy; let him meditate upon politicians, editors, clergymen, and men of property; . . . let him think these thoughts year after year; let him test the resulting theories in a debated land with Sharp's rifles and the bowie knife—he will become a dangerous man, a fanatic, and perhaps a saint.[27]

John Brown was a rugged frontiersman of uncompromising principle who believed in a higher law. Did that make him dangerous? Red in tooth and claw? Or, as Thoreau posited, did "callous palms" make a man "conversant with finer tissues of self-respect and heroism?"[28]

Chapter 7

Carrying the War into Africa

> [John] had been waiting twenty years for some opportunity to free the slaves; we had all been waiting with him, the proper time when he should put his resolve into action, and when at last the enterprise of Harpers Ferry was planned, we all thought that the time had now come . . . we all looked to it as fulfilling the hopes of many years!
>
> —Mary Brown to reporter, November 1859[1]

In the final days of 1857, John Brown was in Iowa trying to sell his teams and wagon and "move in a different direction." His son Owen and nine others accompanied him and "all of them are pledged to stand by the work." By late January 1858, John had traveled to Frederick Douglass's house in Rochester, New York. "I am (praised be God!) once more in York State," John wrote to his family, but since there was a $1,000 reward on his head, he needed to conceal his whereabouts. He warned his family, "Do not noise it about that I am in these parts." John commanded everyone—including himself—to have "courage, courage, courage!" With the "unseen Hand" of God guiding him, he might accomplish "the great work" of his life. Then he would be permitted to return home and "rest at evening."[2]

The great work in the Alleghenies had been planned for years and now the time to act was "very near at hand." At the home of Douglass, Brown was busy writing his "Provisional Constitution" and "Declaration of Liberty." He greatly valued Douglass's friendship because he appreciated Brown's "theories" and "labors." In general, Brown found "a much more

Figure 7.1. John Brown, circa 1859, from drawing by W. E. Bowman. Although John is often remembered with a long beard, he did not grow it until late 1857 or early 1858, as a disguise against those seeking to arrest him. *Source:* Library of Congress. Public domain.

earnest feeling among the colored people than ever before." He heard "the language of Providence" tell him to "Try on."[3]

Unjust actions, such as the Dred Scott court decision of 1857, also pushed Brown to intensify his efforts. The Supreme Court ruled against Dred Scott (a slave), stating that he had no right to sue in federal court because, under the US Constitution, slaves and descendants of slaves were not citizens. The ruling, written by Chief Justice Roger Taney, accepted the doctrine that black people had "no rights which the White Man is bound to respect." Taney defined whites as the superior race and blacks as subordinate, and alleged the ranking was in accord with natural relations, and universally accepted, thus indisputable and fixed forever.

Slaveholders applauded the Dred Scott decision; abolitionists reacted with shock and horror. John Brown described the situation as slaves enduring "perpetual imprisonment and hopeless servitude" or else "absolute extermination." Stopping the slave power was paramount and urgent. Suasion seemed futile. As Brown had said in Kansas, "All talk and no cider—great cry and little wool." It was time to act, time to carry the war into Africa—to take the Underground Railroad above ground and into the heart of the slave power. When Brown told his general plan to the Secret Six who had gathered at Gerrit Smith's mansion in Peterboro, they voiced many objections but eventually decided to support and fund Brown's course of action.[4]

Not knowing who might read his mail, John adopted the alias "Nelson Hawkins" and used code words for the enterprise. In one letter, he recruited "scholars" (soldiers) for his "school" (army). In other letters, John referred to the enterprise as a surveying operation, mining business, or farming venture. In urging Franklin Sanborn to join the cause, John referred to "the ample field I labor in" and the "rich harvest," which the present and future generations could "reap from its successful cultivation." He even revealed that the prospect of becoming a "reaper" in the great harvest had made him overcome a desire to die and instead become "rather anxious to live for a few years more."[5]

After visiting friends in Brooklyn, Boston, Philadelphia, and New Haven, John arrived in North Elba on March 23. He discussed details of the Allegheny plan with family and close friends. Some men would head to Pennsylvania in May, while others would arrive later, with the raid on Virginia scheduled to begin on July 4, 1858, to commemorate the signing of the Declaration of Independence.

John hoped to enlist his sons Salmon, Oliver, and Watson, and his son-in-law, Henry Thompson. However, after they had returned from the Kansas fighting, "the boys" made a resolution to "learn and practice war no more." Upon hearing this in March of 1857, John wrote that he had not solicited them to engage in war and that he felt "no more love of the business than they do." However, he thought "there may be possibly in their day what is more to be dreaded, if such things do not now exist." Those words proved prophetic, and in 1858, some of "the boys" pledged themselves to engage in battle again. Some did not.[6]

John was especially eager to have Henry join him. "I would rather now have him 'for another term' than to have a hundred average scholars." Although John implored him to "go to school," Henry made up his mind to stay with his family. "If I thought the success of the enterprise depended on my going, I should go at once," he wrote. "Nothing but three little helpless children keeps me at home."[7]

Ruth felt selfish when she thought of the women slaves who were deprived of both husband and children, but she could not bear the thought of Henry leaving again and the likelihood of him never returning. Although Ruth anticipated fatal consequences, she tried to be optimistic about her father's fate. "God has been with you thus far," she wrote to him, "and will still be with you in your great and benevolent work." She ended the letter with a melancholy line from her son, Johnny: "Tell Grandfather that I hope he will live to come back here again."

Oliver Brown was "fully determined to go" if he could receive about $60 to help with his obligations. No doubt that included his wife, Martha Evelyn Brewster, whom he married on April 7, 1858. When John heard news of the wedding, he was dumbfounded that his nineteen-year-old son should marry so young. Yet Martha was only fifteen. Regardless of her age, the Browns found her to be cheerful, dignified and earnest, and she supported the fight against slavery even though some of her relatives opposed the Browns' abolitionist stance. The marriage meant Martha would have a home with Oliver's family when he left to join his father's army.[8]

As for other possible recruits, Timbucto grantee Lyman Epps had not decided while neighbor Alexis Hinckley was ready to go. John claimed to be satisfied with "who shall go out surveying," but then he suggested that Henry might manage the farms for both families and allow Watson to go. In anticipation of the answer, John enclosed $25 to help pay traveling expenses for Watson. A few days later, Brown wrote again, saying he left the choosing of recruits to the "united wisdom" of those in North Elba, though, as usual, he gave advice. John suggested that Salmon might assume responsibility for the families in North Elba and allow Lyman Epps, Watson, and Henry to join him (in addition to Oliver and Alexis Hinckley).[9]

John Brown soon headed to St. Catherines, Ontario, Canada, where he found "abundant material" of the "right quality," that is, recruits for his army. He also met Harriet Tubman, the legendary "Moses" of Underground Railroad fame, who had extensive knowledge of the Allegheny Mountains. Tubman "hooked on" and agreed to solicit her Canadian friends for money and recruits. She even volunteered to join Brown's forces.[10]

Figure 7.2. Oliver Brown and wife, Martha Brewster Brown, 1859. *Source:* Library of Congress. Public domain.

With the help of black abolitionist Dr. Martin R. Delany, Brown organized a convention for May 8 and 10 in Chatham, Ontario, a hub for black men and women who had left the United States. The meeting had two purposes: enlist soldiers and gain support for the "Provisional Constitution and Ordinance for the Proscribed and Oppressed People of the United States." The document was not full of hollow words; it made a clear statement of Brown's opposition to slavery and the Dred Scott ruling and his dedication to equality. Having black men back his plan and fight beside him was vital to John Brown.

At the Chatham convention, Brown explained his plan to invade the South and liberate slaves, then march farther south, using small-scale, surprise raids to weaken and destabilize the slave system until it eventually collapsed. His "Provisional Constitution" set forth a plan for an independent, slave-free nation that would exist until the United States exterminated slavery. "These articles are not for the overthrow of Government," stated Article 46. There was no plan for a coup or dissolution of the Union, only for a transfer of power "for the time being." According to Brown, the document would govern actions and prevent anarchy once the revolution began. The convention attendees, thirty-some black men and a few white men, approved the document. Brown also succeeded in signing up thirteen recruits in Canada.[11]

Meanwhile, in North Elba, the men made final choices about going or staying. Their decisions proved moot. Hugh Forbes, the military instructor for Brown's men, leaked information and threatened to expose the entire plan. Rather than taking hasty or rash steps, Brown held to his "invariable rule" of not doing anything "while I do not know what to do." He told the recruits in North Elba to "wait for further advice in the matter." He cautioned Mary to be prudent "in all that is said, written, or done." Upon the advice of the Secret Six, Brown postponed the plan.[12]

It was hard to know what effect the delay would have, but it seemed to temper enthusiasm and instill doubts in some recruits. It also halted John Jr.'s move to North Elba. He had become convinced it was a good place to make a living and to settle his family. Back in 1857, he tried to find a place with southeast exposure to the sun, a good supply of maple trees, a water source, and "a fine view of your glorious mountain scenery." The islands of Lake Placid seemed an intriguing possibility for pasture lands and perhaps a home (with a scow or skiff for access). But when he visited the region in late March of 1858, John Jr. looked at the islands and considered other options. He found "wild lands having excellent sugar orchards on them, of from two hundred to one thousand good maple-trees" that could be purchased for about one dollar per acre. Other lands were "excellent for rye, spring-wheat, oats, potatoes, carrots, turnips, etc., and in some places hardy apples can be raised to advantage."[13]

The beautiful scenery, especially along the new road through Cascade Pass, impressed John Jr. He also enjoyed hearing Dillon Osgood preach at the red schoolhouse and joining Lyman Epps and others in singing at Henry's house. For sure, he had "Essex fever," and in April, he bought eighty acres in North Elba. Yet despite his eagerness to move, John Jr. was forced to stay put because of the uncertainty of the Allegheny plan. His father knew of his great disappointment but advised him to stay in Ohio rather than start a new venture, which might require more funds.[14]

In early June, John Sr. made a short visit to North Elba. Upon leaving, he stopped in Westport to send the family a barrel each of pork, flour, and salt; 110 pounds of codfish; a small package of seed potatoes; cotton sheeting; and a pair of boots for Watson. When John reached Ohio, he wrote his customary sheaf of advice, instructing the boys to build a square pen, "leaving the pen open at the bottom so that the Pigs could run out and in; to be fed by themselves."[15] The family managed quite well through the summer. Oliver and Martha worked for the Hinckleys for three months and made $50. Ruth and Henry grew some of the best crops ever, having a good yield of wheat, potatoes, onions, cucumbers, turnips, carrots, and peas. Even young Johnny planted a garden and raised potatoes, corn, beans, peas, onions, and lettuce.

In September, the Brown family harvested crops and stacked wood in preparation for the onslaught of winter. John sent $50 to Mary so she could pay for a borrowed barrel of flour, settle other small debts, and buy items "to supply substantial comforts for the family." He also hoped to send funds for another yoke of oxen. In the meantime, the family would have to find a man to help get logs or hire an oxen team for a few days. "Do the best you can," he wrote, "and neither be hasty or get discouraged."[16]

John Brown spent most of the summer and fall of 1858 in Iowa and Kansas, ready to pounce if fighting broke out, but staying relatively quiet until mid-December. When a slave from Missouri said his family was about to be sold, John and a group of men went into Missouri and liberated eleven slaves from three plantations with only one casualty, a slave owner who attempted to draw a weapon. Afraid to put any details in a letter, he wrote to Mary: "You will I suppose get Kansas news through the *newspapers*."[17]

The group evaded marshals and proslavery men who pursued them for more than two months as they made the 1,500-mile journey to Canada. Along the way, a woman gave birth to a baby boy, whom she named John Brown, thus making twelve freed persons. When they arrived safely in Canada, John said: "Lord, permit Thy servant to die in peace; for mine eyes have seen Thy salvation! I could not brook the thought that any ill should befall you,—least of all, that you should be taken back to slavery. The arm of Jehovah protected us."[18]

John had successfully "carried the war into Africa," into the slave state of Missouri. Maybe John *could* accomplish his ambitious Allegheny plan with minimal bloodshed. Maybe he *was* an instrument of God. He was also a wanted man again; Missouri offered $3,000 for his capture. That did not keep him from leaving Canada and returning to the United States to rekindle his postponed plan. On the suggestion of Harriet Tubman, John scheduled the Harpers Ferry raid for Independence Day 1859, but it would be delayed until the fall.

In late March of 1859, John sent $150 to Mary for "a good, well broke, well matched, young yoke of oxen (not unruly)" and for debts or necessities. The next month, he went to North Elba for a short visit. When he left, he stopped in Westport and shipped the family 130 pounds of codfish, 40-some yards of calico, two pounds of tea, a pound of allspice, an ounce of nutmeg, and ten spools of thread. When he reached Troy, he sent more supplies: a barrel of clear pork, two barrels flour, some sole leather, a calf skin, and two bunches of cotton yarn.[19]

Even while recruiting soldiers and preparing for great action elsewhere, John seemed determined to keep the family well supplied and to attend to the smallest details at the farm. He wanted Cloverseed and Hungarian grass seed to be sowed on one-sixth of an acre *as an experiment*. He also asked the women to help the boys pick up stones and sticks on the meadows before the grass grew too high. The family picked rocks, planted seeds, and kept up with other farm chores.

With the addition of 80 acres on Lot 88, the Brown farm had 80 improved acres and 260 unimproved, worth $500. In 1859, they harvested ten bushels of hay, seventeen of wheat, twenty-five of buckwheat, one thousand of potatoes, and other crops. The Browns owned four milch (milk) cows, two oxen, and two cattle, along with twenty-two sheep and three pigs, which valued $254. They also produced one hundred pounds of butter and an astonishing one thousand pounds of maple sugar.[20]

Ruth and Henry Thompson's farm (on the south half of Lot 88) had twenty-five improved acres and fifty-five unimproved, worth $500. They harvested five bushels of hay, eighteen of wheat, forty-seven of buckwheat, sixty-one of rye, one hundred of oats, and three hundred of potatoes. They had three milch cows, two oxen, and three cattle, along with twenty-six sheep and four pigs, which valued $354. During the year, they produced one hundred pounds of butter and six hundred of maple sugar. Together, the Brown and Thompson families amassed a good stockpile.

Back in the spring of 1859, John had traveled to New England to meet with the Secret Six. He also stopped in Concord and lectured at the Town Hall again. "He impressed me as a person of surpassing sense, courage, and religious earnestness," recalled Amos Bronson Alcott. "A man of reserves, yet he inspired confidence in his integrity and good judgment," and he did not conceal his hatred of slavery. Brown seemed ready "to strike a blow for freedom at the fitting moment," said Alcott. "I thought him the manliest of men and the type and synonym of the just."[21]

After his lectures and meetings in Massachusetts, John returned to North Elba and preached a Sunday service at the red schoolhouse that doubled as a religious meetinghouse. Only twice had Mary Brown heard the slave mentioned by the regular preachers. But when a Sunday meeting was held "under the auspices of John Brown," the Lord heard plenty of thunder about slavery.[22]

On that first Sunday in June of 1859, John read scripture and then spoke about his antislavery actions in Kansas, saying they were in accordance with the laws laid down in the Bible. Next, he told of liberating slaves from Missouri plantations and taking them to freedom in Canada. John acknowledged that his group killed one of the slave owners who tried to protect his so-called property, but claimed his actions to be right, even to the taking of a life. Most of the listeners rebuked John's radical idea of buckling on armor and spilling a little blood in the hope of preventing much greater bloodshed. They wanted nothing to do with his future plans. "He has now gone back west," an attendee wrote, "to what part of the country, or for what purpose, no one knows."[23]

Almost no one. When Mary and the children said goodbye to John, they knew where he was headed—to Chambersburg, Pennsylvania, and then into Maryland, to rent a farm within a few miles of Harpers Ferry, Virginia. They knew his purpose, too. John Brown was again carrying the war into Africa. He planned to march into Harpers Ferry, take control of the Federal Armory and Arsenal, liberate slaves in the vicinity, and then retreat to the mountains.

Even though Ruth's daughter Ella was only three years old, she said she remembered the day her grandfather left for Harpers Ferry. Her mother had a music lesson with William Appo that day, and when Ella cut her finger and cried, Appo rocked her to sleep on a "Rockee" (a long rocking chair). Thomas Peacock also claimed to recall that day, when he would have been about six. He was planting potatoes with his father on John Brown's farm and saw a big meeting of neighbors at the house. A few days later, Brown said farewell, kissed everyone goodbye, and rode off. When Thomas's father heard news of the raid and Brown's hanging, he was greatly upset and did not eat or sleep for several weeks.[24]

Like Ella, Thomas shared his memories many decades later, so their tales may be whimsical or apocryphal. Other such claims included Brown stopping to visit abolitionist Phineas Norton in Keene and saying, "Watch the *Tribune* and you will see where I am going and what I intend to do." According to local legend, Brown then proceeded to Elizabethtown where he spent the Sabbath with Levi DeWitt Brown, attending services at the old Baptist Church.[25] Who knew about the Harpers Ferry plan and how much they knew is still debated. Evidence suggests that Brown family members, the Secret Six, and a few other supporters and friends were privy to the general scheme and some specific details.

The famous Adirondack guide Bill Nye knew the Brown family intimately and recalled how John often spoke about the topics of the day, always getting directly to the point. "He had a kind of convincing way of expressing his views, and, withal, a commanding way that would win," said Nye. John was so convincing that Nye considered going to Harpers Ferry with him on his last trip, even though Nye said, "I had no idea that he was going to do what he did."[26]

According to Lyman Epps, Brown was very careful about talking freely since many neighbors had proslavery sympathies. Epps believed Brown had weighed all the possible outcomes of his plan, even the "idea of sacrificing himself." He recalled Brown saying, "Who would not be willing to dance on nothing between heaven and earth to free the nation from this cursed slavery?"[27]

After the plan was put into motion, secrecy was imperative. Having previously used the names Nelson Hawkins and Shubel Morgan, John Brown now called himself "Isaac Smith," and associate John Kagi became "John Henrie." It was a method of concealment from enemies and also rooted in suspicion of the prying eyes of the postal service. In 1859, John instructed Mary to enclose letters in a small envelope, put a stamp on it, seal it, and address it to I. Smith and Sons, Harpers Ferry, Virginia. That small envelope needed to be put in a stamped envelope addressed to John Henrie, Chambersburg, Pennsylvania. "I need not say, do all your directing and sealing at home, and not at the post-office."[28]

The Browns had neighbors of both proslavery and antislavery persuasion, but even some of the latter believed the abolitionists were too radical. When *Uncle Tom's Cabin* came out in 1852, they refused to read it because it was "in a novel style." They claimed to feel deeply for the slave but thought the abolitionists did harm by coming out so strong and taking such high ground. "Their plan is to use moral suasion," said Henry Thompson, "and very mild means—a plan which I think will do about as much good as it would to pacify a raging Tiger with the promise of a good meal by and by."²⁹

Preparations for Harpers Ferry

Facing slavery on its own turf required fierce devotion, unflinching nerve, and selflessness. Not many people would even contemplate joining a foray into Harpers Ferry. That was not important to Brown; the quality of the men mattered much more than the number of recruits. "A few men in the right, and knowing they are right, can overturn a mighty king," said Brown. "Fifty men, twenty men, in the Alleghenies, could break slavery to pieces in two years."³⁰ For those who considered joining Brown, there were various factors and circumstances to mull over. There was no right or wrong answer. In the end, each individual conscience had to weigh the options.

Salmon Brown did not serve as a recruit for Harpers Ferry. "One of the boys had to stay at home," said his wife, Abbie. "That lot fell to Salmon." His decision to stay may also have been influenced by his not wanting to fight again or his not wanting to leave Abbie because she was pregnant. Abbie's brother, Alexis Hinckley, planned to join the recruits in 1858 and in 1859, but his wife became ill, so he did not go. Lyman Epps considered going, but said, "I had a wife and six children to provide for." Henry Thompson also stayed home, however, his brothers William and Dauphin volunteered to go and to pay their own expenses.³¹

The total number of men from North Elba: five (John and four recruits). But the only person who immediately headed south with John was his son Oliver. Oliver carried a lock of Martha's hair with him, but nevertheless, he missed her terribly and wished he had a photo of her. To compensate for his loneliness, Oliver sent Martha a copy of his photo and asked her to frame it because, "I may want some day to see how I looked when I was young."³² His fretting was unnecessary. He soon had an opportunity to hold Martha in his arms.

Isaac Smith (John Brown) posed as a cattle buyer from New York and rented the Kennedy farm as headquarters for the recruits who would be arriving. However, he neglected one critical detail—women. An army of men without any womenfolk could arouse the suspicions of neighbors, so Oliver returned home to bring two women down to the Kennedy farm in Maryland. He reunited with Martha in North Elba, while Mary considered John's request for her and Annie to come to the Kennedy farm for a few weeks. "You will have no more exposure here than at North Elba," wrote John. ". . . It will be *likely to prove* the most valuable service you can ever render to the world."[33]

If Mary went, then five-year-old Ellen would be left with Martha and Sarah; Sarah was only eleven and daughter-in-law Martha only sixteen. And Watson's wife, Belle, was nine months pregnant. Should Mary leave these young women to manage without her? What if "a few weeks" turned into months?

John's letter provided an alternative. "If you cannot come," he wrote, "I would be glad to have Martha and Annie come on." Since Martha wanted to be with Oliver, it was decided that the two girls would go to the Kennedy farm. On the morning they were to leave, Martha slipped on the stairs and sprained her ankle, then she fainted. Everyone assumed she would have to stay home and recover, but Martha insisted on going with Oliver to Maryland.

Because Martha went instead of Mary, historians often criticize Mary and accuse her of lacking family loyalty and showing ambivalence about the Harpers Ferry campaign. While John considered Mary's presence in Maryland "most valuable," he knew he had kept her "tumbling here and there, over a stormy and tempestuous sea" for many years. She had moved from house to house, from state to state; suffered the loss of many children, often while John was away; and worked and sacrificed for the cause. John believed he had no right to ask more of her. As he had done previously with the selection of recruits, he deferred to Mary since she knew best the circumstances at North Elba. She decided that her valuable service was needed to tend the children, manage the farm, and serve as midwife. Mary wrote to John that she hoped he would be "blessed with health and success in the great and good cause" in which he was engaged. She knew not to put any specific details in a letter.[34]

Since the "freight" (weapons) had not yet arrived in Maryland, Watson stayed in North Elba to finish haying. He had cut his foot and was glad to have time for it to heal. The delay also allowed him to be with his wife, Belle, when she gave birth to their son, "a fine little fellow and one of the best natured children I ever saw," according to Ruth. It pleased the Brown family that the couple named the baby Frederick (Freddy) after his uncle who was killed in Kansas. Freddy turned two weeks old just as it was time for Watson and Dauphin and William Thompson to head south. After bidding everyone goodbye, Watson rushed out of the house crying as though his heart would break. He seemed to realize he was leaving his wife and little boy forever.[35]

When William parted with his young wife, she clung to him and said, "Oh! William, don't go, I shall never see you again." He responded, "Mary, what is my life compared to the millions of poor slaves."

Oliver, Martha, and Annie arrived at the Kennedy farm on July 16, followed by Watson, William, and Dauphin on August 6. They joined the other occupants: John Brown, Owen Brown, and Jeremiah Anderson (who fought with free-state forces in Kansas and assisted Brown in freeing slaves in Missouri). Recruit John E. Cook, another member of John's forces in Kansas, lived in Harpers Ferry, getting to know the townspeople and the layout of the armory. John (Henrie) Kagi resided in Chambersburg, Pennsylvania, to assist recruits as they arrived one, two, or more at a time—Charles Plummer Tidd, Aaron Dwight Stevens, William Leeman, and Albert Hazlett, all veterans of the Kansas war.

Edwin and Barclay Coppoc, Quaker brothers from Springdale, Iowa, arrived within a few weeks. Stewart Taylor, a young man from Canada, came in August, as did Dangerfield Newby, a formerly enslaved mulatto whose wife and seven children were slaves in Virginia. According to Annie, none of the men joined the company to become heroes, they joined in order "to do to others, as they would have others do to them" and to "tell Pharaoh to let my people go."[36]

Annie and Martha knew the recruits quite well. While the two young women posed as housekeepers, their real work was to keep "the outside world" from discovering the men. John feared that people would become suspicious of the large group, particularly the presence of black men. Others could help with the housework, but John depended on Annie to be a lookout and let nothing interfere with her "constant watchfulness." An investigation of the house would be a disaster—not only the discovery of the men but crates full of rifles were used as chairs in the dining room while a box of pistols rested near Martha's bed.

The recruits had to stay inside and if a stranger approached, the girls warned the men and they climbed into the loft and stayed quiet. The routine became quite tiresome, so they passed the time by singing, playing checkers, and reading. Yet the men yearned for exercise, so whenever a thunderstorm rolled in, "they would jump about and play, making all kinds of noise" since no one could hear them. Of course, the girls stayed alert even during the storm parties.

Figure 7.3. Annie Brown, daughter of John and Mary, in her teens. *Source:* Library of Congress. Public domain.

A neighbor named Huffmaster was especially nosy. "No one can ever imagine the pestering torment that little barefooted woman and her four little children were to us," said Annie. Mrs. Huffmaster invented all kinds of excuses to visit the Kennedy farm. She often noticed the clothes hanging to dry and said, "Your men folks has a right smart lot of shirts."

Eventually Mrs. Huffmaster managed to see two of the black men and suspected the "Smiths" were helping slaves escape to the North. She promised to keep quiet about it, but Annie feared she was a spy. It was like "standing on a powder magazine, after a slow match had been lighted."[37]

The "Smiths" had another scare in mid-August when Martha became quite ill. Eventually, they determined her condition: Martha was pregnant.[38]

Besides the tense times, there were also poignant moments at the Kennedy farm. One day John sat near Annie as she was sewing. Suddenly two wrens banged into the door and then flew back to their nest under the porch roof. Several times the birds returned to the door and twittered as if in great distress. John and Annie went out to the porch and discovered a snake crawling near the top of a post, about to devour the baby birds in the nest. John killed the snake, which made the parent wrens sing a song of joy and thanks.[39]

John thought it odd the way the birds had asked for him to help and suggested it might be "an omen of success." Annie did not think her father was superstitious. She believed he always felt "God called him" and placed him in the position of crushing the tyrant.

Chapter 8

The Anguish of Harpers Ferry

> How very little we can possibly lose? Certainly the cause is enough to *live* for, if not to [die] for. I have only had *this one* opportunity in a life of nearly sixty years; and could I be continued ten times as long again, I might not again have another equal opportunity. God has honored but comparatively a very small part of mankind with any possible chance for such mighty and soul satisfying rewards.
>
> —John Brown to Franklin Sanborn, February 24, 1858

The days passed as John Brown waited for more recruits, more money, and the rest of the 950 pikes he had ordered. He desperately wanted to enlist Frederick Douglass as a member of his army and arranged a secret meeting in Chambersburg from August 19 to 21. "I want you for a special purpose," Brown told Douglass. "When I strike, the bees will begin to swarm, and I shall want you to help hive them." Douglass refused to join, warning Brown that he would never get out of Harpers Ferry alive—he was "going into a perfect steel-trap." However, Douglass's companion, former slave Shields Green, said, "I b'lieve I'll go wid de ole man."[1]

Such were the disparate views of Brown's plan. Some felt it was hopeless, doomed to fail, a suicide mission, while others thought it was necessary to strike a blow regardless of the consequences to personal life. It was not a completely new premise. As early as 1854, abolitionist James Redpath toured the Southern states (as a spy) and wrote articles about his findings under the pseudonym John Ball Jr. "North Carolina could be involuntarily made a member of the free states by a general stampede of the slaves," he wrote, "if the Abolitionists would send down a trusty Band of 'Liberators,' provided with compasses, pistols and a little money for the fugitives."[2]

In 1859, five months before the Harpers Ferry invasion, Redpath published his articles in book form and dedicated the volume to John Brown. "To you, old Hero," wrote Redpath, ". . . You are willing to recognize the negro as a brother," and believe those who take away or withhold his rights have committed a crime that should be punished. "Peacefully if we can, but forcibly and by bloodshed if we must!" Redpath affirmed, "You, Old Hero! Believe that the slave should be aided and urged to insurrection, and hence do I lay this tribute at your feet."[3]

Private and public hints of Brown's plan were materializing, some from recruits' letters to their mothers and darlings. "If every one must write some *girl*"; said John, "or some other extra friend telling, or showing our location; and telling (*as some have done*) all about our matters; we might as well get the whole published *at once*, in the New York Herald." John ordered all correspondences, except those "on business *of the Co.*," stopped for the present time.[4] His directive came too late.

After hearing of the plan, David J. Gue agreed with Brown's mission, but feared the men would meet "certain death." He tried to save them by telling federal government officials that "Old John Brown" was leading a "movement." On August 25, 1859, Gue's anonymous letter arrived at the office of the Secretary of War and informed him of a "secret association" that was planning "the liberation of the slaves at the South by a general insurrection." The writer explained that black men had been drilling in Canada and waiting to rendezvous in the mountains of Virginia, where John Brown planned to strike a blow at Harpers Ferry. The attack would happen in a few weeks so "whatever is done must be done at once."[5]

Anonymous letters arrived quite often at the secretary's office and received little attention. Free blacks from Canada marching into Virginia? A white man arming black men and leading an insurrection? It was unfathomable that anyone would devise such an absurd scheme; the secretary of War ignored the warning.

Another intimation appeared one month before the raid—a speech by Gerrit Smith published in the *Liberator*. "It is, perhaps, too late to bring slavery to an end by peaceable means . . . it must go out in blood," said Smith. He believed that no recourse was left to blacks but God and insurrection. "For insurrections, then, we may look any year, any month, any day. A terrible remedy for a terrible wrong." While Smith and Redpath used the term *insurrection*, John Brown did not. He repeatedly stated that his goal was to liberate slaves, not to incite violence against slave owners or citizens. He was going into a Southern state to free enslaved people and establish a base in the mountains that would serve as a Subterranean Pass Way for freedom seekers.[6]

A last hint of what was about to happen appeared in the *National Anti-Slavery Standard* on October 15, 1859, one day before the raid commenced. "Let us lay our fugitive track above ground," wrote Rev. A. L. Post, "and man it, if possible, with such men as 'Old John Brown,' of Kansas notoriety."[7]

Keep Up Good Courage

In early September, Oliver Brown wrote to his wife Martha: "Our work is going on very slowly, but we think satisfactorily. . . . I think there is no good reason why any of us should be discouraged; for if we have done but one good act, life is not a failure." Similarly, Watson wrote to his wife Belle, "I would gladly come home and stay with you always but for the cause which brought me here,—a desire to do something for others, and not live wholly for my own happiness." He told her, "I think of you all day, and dream of you at night."[8]

By mid-September, it was already snowing at North Elba and the mountains were covered in whiteness. It was so cold and windy that Belle had to sit as close to the stove as she could without burning her skirts. "This place is too frosty to live in," she wrote to Watson. The cucumbers vines were killed. The corn did not grow well; even after boiling it twice, "it was altogether green." Of course, the potatoes grew marvelously.[9]

"O! that I could be with you," wrote Belle, "but I will try to be contented as I am." The Brown family was very kind to her and helped take care of baby Freddy. Even five-year-old Ellen sat and rocked him in the rocking chair since he did not yet have a cradle. Belle told Watson not to worry, but to "keep up good courage . . . and come back as soon as possible. I think of you all night in my dreams."

At the Kennedy farmhouse, another recruit finally arrived, a young black man named Osborne Perry Anderson from Chatham, Ontario, Canada. The pikes arrived, too, and the time to execute the plan grew nearer. John decided the girls should leave the farm. On September 29, Oliver escorted Martha and Annie to Troy, New York.

The girls reached North Elba safely, and soon afterward a package of four blankets arrived. A letter from John directed that Martha should have the first choice because he thought her "fairly entitled *to particular* notice," presumably because of her pregnancy. As for Belle, Abbie, and Annie, he suggested they "*cast lots*" for a choice of the other blankets. John also sent his blessings and hoped to soon have $50 to help the family through the winter. In the meantime, he suggested, "Begin early to take good care of all your animals, and pinch them at the close of the winter, if you must at all."[10]

A week later, John found he had time to send one more letter. He told Mary to use any leftover money "to make all as comfortable as may be for the present." That included his daughters-in-law; he considered "the whole as one family" and welcomed all to have a home with Mary "until we return." John remained optimistic that the men would "return" to North Elba and reunite with family.[11]

Oliver sent a final letter to his pregnant wife at the North Elba farm telling her to "keep up good, cheerful spirits" and to get plenty of rest, sleep, "and out-door exercise." As for his outlook, the thought of her strengthened his will to do right. "It is when I look at your picture that I am wholly ashamed of my every meanness, weakness, and folly. . . . I am more and more determined every day to live a more unselfish life."[12]

The recruits were eager to begin their work, especially after another slave murder, the fifth to occur within a few miles of the Kennedy farm since the men arrived. Watson told his wife, Belle, "there is a better day a-coming." However, if he should never see her again, "Believe me yours wholly and forever in love." He signed the letter "Your affectionate husband" and dated it October 14, 1859.[13]

The next day, three recruits showed up at the Kennedy farm: John Copeland and his nephew Lewis Leary (black men from Oberlin, Ohio) and Francis Jackson Meriam (a white man from Boston). Brown was thrilled to have the stalwart black soldiers, and though Meriam was somewhat frail, he came ready to fight. More importantly, he brought $600 in gold. Brown interpreted this as a sign from God and scheduled the raid for the next evening, Sunday, October 16, 1859.

News Arrives at North Elba

The Browns in North Elba did not know the exact date on which the Harpers Ferry raid would begin. As they waited for news, farm life continued as routinely as possible. Salmon tended to the potato field that Oliver had cleared and planted on the hill behind the Brown farmhouse in the spring. When Oliver decided to go south with his father, he sold the potato patch to Salmon, and in the fall of 1859, Salmon and young Byron Brewster harvested 4,500 bushels of potatoes. That fourteen-year-old "dug and picked potatoes to beat any boy's work that I ever saw," said Salmon. Most of the potatoes were hauled in the "old ox-cart that was on mother's place" to the local starch factory.[14]

In late October, Martha Brewster Brown went to the North Elba post office and heard talk that John Brown and his men were under arrest. Such rumors circulated often, so the family had no reason to believe this one. They waited anxiously for further news. When Martha returned to the post office a few days later, a newspaper had arrived in the mail. She opened it and read a headline announcing the death of her husband, Oliver Brown. The paper also told of the death of his brother Watson and the capture of his father, John Brown.

When Martha arrived home, Annie Brown (being the fastest reader) was chosen to narrate. "So I read that long account from beginning to end, aloud, without faltering," said Annie. "I was stunned, and my senses so benumbed that I did not comprehend the meaning of the words I pronounced."[15]

John Brown's small group of soldiers had marched into Harpers Ferry on the night of October 16. A railroad station employee, Heyward Shepherd refused to obey directives and Brown's men shot the free black man, who died from his wound. After crossing the bridge, a few of the men took over the US Armory and Arsenal. Another group freed several slaves from nearby properties and took their owners as hostages. When the townspeople woke in the morning, they found the streets and bridge guarded by armed men, some white and some black. The town flew into a panic and reported an attack by fifty men. Soon, the raiders had become "a gang of Negroes" backed by 200 to 300 whites. Other reports said the "Great Insurrection at Harper's Ferry" involved 500 to 700 men. Later in the day, it was realized that the raiding party consisted of only about twenty men led by John Brown.[16]

A detachment of Charles Town (Virginia) Guards reached the town and killed some raiders near the bridge. Five others were chased out of the Armory, most of them shot and killed in the river. Random firing continued for an hour or more. Several citizens were killed and several insurgents were "biting the dust." The *New-York Tribune* reported, "Three of the rioters are lying dead in the streets, three are lying dead in the river. And several are said to be lying in the Armory enclosure."[17]

John Brown and many of the raiders were barricaded in the engine house with their hostages. Brown offered to release the hostages if he were allowed to march out of town with his men, but the proposal was refused.

Figure 8.1. Townspeople (left) and raiders in engine house (right) exchanging rifle fire at Harpers Ferry, Virginia, October 16–17, 1859. *Source:* Library of Congress. Public domain.

United States Marines under the command of Colonel Robert E. Lee were called to the scene. As the marines waited for daylight to make a move, rumors suggested that the rioters would be hanged as soon as they were captured. On the morning of October 18, the raiders were offered safe passage to the jail. Again, Brown refused; he preferred to meet his fate "with his rifle in his hands" rather than "dying for the amusement of a crowd."[18]

The marines stormed the engine house and the first one to enter was shot dead. In addition to the casualties of the Marine and Heyward Shepherd, the insurgents had killed G. W. Turner, Thomas Boerly, and Harpers Ferry Mayor Fontaine Beckham. About eight townspeople were wounded. Most of the raiders in the engine house were killed or wounded during the foray. The earliest reports stated that John Brown was "mortally wounded" and "dying," and Aaron Stevens was wounded badly and could not possibly recover. Soon thereafter, newspaper accounts stated the status of the men.[19]

John Brown, nine wounds but will recover

Aaron Stevens, wounded but will recover

Oliver and Watson Brown, sons of John, dead

William and Dauphin Thompson of North Elba, dead

Dangerfield Newby and Lewis Leary, black men of Ohio, raised in Virginia, dead

William Leeman, dead

John Kagi, Jeremiah Anderson, and Stewart Taylor, dead

Charles Tidd, dead (had escaped and lived)

Edwin Coppoc, unhurt but prisoner

John Copeland and Shields Green, both black men raised in the South, unhurt but prisoners

John E. Cook and Albert Hazlett, escaped (were later captured and imprisoned)

Osborne Anderson, a black man, escaped

Owen Brown, Barclay Coppoc, and Francis Meriam (men who had not gone into the village), escaped

"My father had often spoke of the possibility of failure . . . ," said Ruth, "and had endeavored to prepare our minds for it, but I did not think failure possible. . . . It was bitterly unjust that father should be brought low after all his sufferings and unselfish struggles, and that the wicked slave-power should triumph." Ruth could not sleep nor shed a tear; she felt "rebellious and hard." But when she went to the Brown farm, her heart softened and tears flowed upon seeing her mother "pallid as death" and the young widows sitting by the fireside "bowed by grief." The anguish of those three young widows was heartrending—Martha Brewster Brown, sixteen years old and pregnant; Belle Thompson Brown, a new mother, who also lost her two brothers; and Mary Brown Thompson, alone.[20]

There was also the terrible agony of Annie, who had known most of the raiders. Three of them were her brothers and she loved the others as

Figure 8.2. "Harpers Ferry Insurrection—Burying the Dead Insurgents." The dead raiders were thrown into a trench beside the Shenandoah River near Harpers Ferry. *Frank Leslie's Illustrated Newspaper,* November 5, 1859. *Source:* Library of Congress. Public domain.

brothers, having lived at the Kennedy farm for eleven weeks. "We were most of us struck dumb," said Annie, "horrorstricken with a grief too deep and hard to find expression in words or even tears. I do not think I have ever fully recovered from the mental shock I received then."[21]

Annie did not shed a tear, nor sleep or eat, for several days; she looked wild and inconsolable. In fear of Annie's "terrible state of mind," Ruth asked her music teacher, William Appo, to play for them. He played an instrumental piece or two and then sang "The Dying Warrior," which caused Annie's tears to fall.[22]

A Visit from Higginson

The weary hours dragged by, and all looked dark and gloomy in North Elba. The Brown family feared there was no sympathy for John, not even from his abolitionist friends. While some did abandon him, others were doing all they could to help. Since John Brown's trial would proceed first, Thomas Wentworth Higginson of the Secret Six, along with other Boston friends, gathered funds for Brown's defense and sent a lawyer to Charles Town, Virginia, where John and the other prisoners were being held in the county jail. Higginson then turned his efforts toward a rescue, but John refused any such attempt. Thinking that Mary could shake her husband's doggedness and ultimately help in his rescue, Higginson sought to convince her to see John in the Virginia jail. This mission motivated the Bostonian journalist to venture into "the enchanted land of the Adirondack," having no notion of the scene awaiting him at the Brown home or of the adventure of the journey. Or that his travelogue would become a classic piece of Adirondack literature.[23]

Higginson chose the "least frequented and most difficult" route to the Brown's upstate New York homestead, from Keeseville to Wilmington and then along the new road through the grand Wilmington Notch. "You soon find yourself facing a wall of mountain," he wrote, "with only glimpses of one wild gap through which you must penetrate." The Notch seemed "beyond the world" to him, yet North Elba was "beyond the Notch" and a wild mountain road was beyond that. "But the house we seek is not even on that road, but behind it and beyond it."

After another mile or two, Higginson followed a path through the forest until he came to a proper clearing. "There is a little frame house, unpainted, set in a girdle of black stumps, and with all heaven about it for a wider girdle, on a high hillside; forests on north and west; the glorious line of the Adirondacks on the east; and on the south one slender road leading off to Westport, a road so straight that you could sight a United States Marshall for five miles." The Brown family welcomed Higginson into their home. "I shall never forget the effect it had on us," wrote Ruth, "the clouds began to disappear, and a ray of sunshine revived our saddened hearts."[24]

In turn, the familial scene uplifted Higginson. He called them "heroic mountaineers" and a "most noble race of suffering saints." A father was under sentence of death, a brother fleeing for his life, two other brothers killed, and two brothers of their extended family killed. Yet these loved ones were not crushed by death and doom.[25]

"Now that word *killed*," wrote Higginson, "is a word which one hardly cares to mention in a mourning household circle," especially under the agonizing circumstance of "coffin-less graves in a hostile land." Yet every member of that family could pronounce that awful word "with perfect quietness; never, of course, lightly, but always quietly." To the Brown family, "killing means simply dying—nothing more; one gate into heaven, and that one a good deal frequented by their family: that is all."[26]

When photographs were brought out, someone said, "This is Oliver, one of those who were killed at Harpers Ferry." As the words drifted about the room, his seventeen-year-old widow, Martha, sat sewing "and her finger did not tremble as she drew the thread." In this household, "danger and death fit into the ordinary grooves of daily life," observed Higginson, ". . . breakfast and dinner are provided, children cared for, and all external existence has the same smoothness that one observes at Niagara, just above the American Falls."

When he told the family there was little hope of acquittal or rescue of John, they responded with only one question: "Does it seem as if freedom were to gain or lose by this?"

Like John Brown, they were "absolutely devoted to a principle." Their foremost concern was that the events might bring some benefit to the poor slaves. "My husband always believed," said Mary, "that he was to be an instrument in the hands of Providence, and I believe it too."

The next morning, as Higginson prepared to leave, he talked with Salmon about the sacrifices of the family. Salmon looked up in a quiet, manly way and said, "I sometimes think that is what we came into the world for—to make sacrifices."

The Brown family and their friends made a mountain of sacrifices. Now, Mary was leaving her loved ones to go on a journey to Virginia. Her daughters, sons, and grandchildren would not see her for more than a month.

The first words from John Brown to his family soon arrived in North Elba. "We were fighting for our lives at Harpers Ferry." He wrote about how Watson, Oliver, William, and Dauphin were "killed" and he received several saber cuts in his head and bayonet stabs in his body. Though thousands were thirsting for his blood, he felt "no consciousness of guilt in the matter" and no disgrace of being imprisoned. Instead, he was quite cheerful "in the assurance that God reigns and will overrule all for his glory and the best possible good." The afflictions and tribulations were only "for a moment," and "shall work out for us far more exceeding and eternal weight of glory." John advised his beloved family to be firm and humble believers, and "Never forget the poor, nor think anything you bestow on them to be lost to you, even though they may be black as Ebedmelech."[27]

Reactions to the Harpers Ferry Raid

The *Charleston* (SC) *Mercury* called the Harpers Ferry raid a "trifling affair" and a "silly invasion" perpetrated by "reckless fanatics." The paper considered it "absurd" that state and national military troops had to be called to suppress the raiders. Even Virginia's Governor Henry Wise noted the fright and cowardice among the people of Harpers Ferry. He summarized the affair as a handful of men holding a population of nearly two thousand at bay for about thirty-four hours. "Well, Governor," said someone in the crowd, "you must remember we were locked together like sheep."[28]

"Yes, I know that," said Governor Wise, "but I must say I think you acted like sheep also."

Virginians needed to restore their honor and chivalry. "We cannot stand such insults and outrages as those at Harpers Ferry," declared Governor Wise. It would bring us "suffering worse than the death of our citizens," it would be "the death of a State."[29]

John Brown's assault on Virginia shocked most people in the South. Despite promises of brotherhood from some Northerners, the raid proved that factions of Northern men intended hostility and insurrection. There were fearless, armed, white and black men willing to die to end slavery. "So perish all the enemies of our country!" exclaimed a North Carolina newspaper. The "fanatics" would see "death and disgrace await those who attempt to overturn the institutions of the South." Antislavery men of the North "cannot and will not justify" the vile acts of this "cut-throat gang."[30] Southerners fully expected *everyone* to condemn Brown and his men.

Some did. Abolitionist William Lloyd Garrison initially called the raid "a misguided, wild, and apparently insane" effort to emancipate the slaves through insurrection. Other Northerners declared John Brown to be a menace, murderer, and traitor. Slavery might be a sin, they reasoned, but states rights and the *Constitution* had to be upheld. Brown broke the law and should be punished. His violence and law-breaking not only gave fodder to his critics, but it also posed problems for his friends. Alleged conspirators and funders of the raid were hunted for questioning and prosecution as the South attempted to tie Brown's actions to the Republican Party, thus destroying their political opponents.[31]

Before fleeing the country, Frederick Douglass penned an editorial, "Capt. John Brown Not Insane," for his monthly paper. He considered Brown's conduct at Harpers Ferry "perfectly natural and simple on its face." Believing the Declaration of Independence to be true and the Bible to be a guide to human conduct, Brown "threw himself against the serried ranks of American oppression." According to Douglass, moral suasion was useless on slaveholders. "It is vain to reason with them. One might as well hunt bears with ethics and political economy for weapons, as to seek to 'pluck the spoiled out of the hand of the oppressor' by the mere force of moral law. Slavery is a system of brute force. It shields itself behind might, rather than right. It must be met with its own weapons. Capt. Brown has initiated a new mode of carrying on the crusade of freedom."[32]

Franklin Sanborn and Samuel Howe of the Secret Six also left the country for a short time. Peculiarly, Gerrit Smith became extremely paranoid that federal officials were coming to question him about his part in the Harpers Ferry affair. He turned into "a raving lunatic" and was taken to the New York State Lunatic Asylum at Utica. After spending several weeks at the Asylum (with doses of cannabis and morphine) and a few more weeks under the roof of his doctor's home, Smith returned to Peterboro, though he was still quite feeble. Months later, he wrote his first public statement since his breakdown. He claimed the "great shock" from the death of John Brown and his two sons hastened his already overworked body and brain into a crisis, and he soon "went down under a troop of hallucinations."[33]

Another worrisome event haunted Gerrit Smith, too. His nephew by marriage, Claggett Fitzhugh, who lived near the Pennsylvania-Maryland border, came upon a stranger exiting the woods on October 26. Fitzhugh escorted the man into town and then seized him and turned him over to authorities. The captured man was raider John Cook. Smith's nephew had foiled the escape of one of John Brown's men and sent him to the gallows.

However, the idea that most haunted and distressed Smith was "that my friends and relatives in the South believed that I had plotted their murder." Perhaps that concern was part of the reason Smith insisted he had no previous knowledge of Brown's plans at Harpers Ferry (despite evidence and witnesses to the contrary). According to historian John Stauffer, Smith lost his perspective on reality and "forfeited his close friendships with blacks . . . he could not overcome the deep recesses of his racism."[34]

Smith's reaction to the Harpers Ferry raid was extreme. Other antislavery voices simply paused and hesitated to make public statements of support, particularly Quakers whose pacifism clashed with the use of violence.

However, the South's expectation that all Northerners would out-and-out rebuke Brown fell flat, especially in Concord. As biographer David Reynolds points out, "when those truly intimate with Brown . . . were trying to cover up their connection with him, Thoreau was going out of his way to suggest that he was his friend and confidant."[35]

Thoreau scolded the "herd of newspapers and magazines" for their editorial comments about Brown's raid and rebuked those who "wash your skirts of him." In his public speech, "A Plea for Captain John Brown," in Concord on October 30, 1859, he said the following:

> We do not know the facts about it. It was evidently far from being a wild and desperate attempt. His enemy, Mr. Vallandigham, is compelled to say, that "it was among the best planned and executed conspiracies that ever failed."
>
> . . . I hear another ask, Yankee-like, "What will he gain by it?" as if he [John Brown] expected to fill his pockets by this enterprise. Such a one has no idea of gain but in this worldly sense. If it does not lead to a "surprise" party, if he does not get a new pair of boots, or a vote of thanks, it must be a failure. But he won't gain any thing by it.[36]

Thoreau said the time would come when people would see John Brown had enacted "a brave and humane deed" at Harpers Ferry. The major issue was not the use of violence and guns, "but the spirit in which you use it." According to Brown, a man had a perfect right to interfere by force with the slaveholder to rescue the slave, and Thoreau agreed with him.

> I do not wish to kill nor to be killed, but I can foresee circumstances in which both these things would be by me unavoidable. We preserve the so-called peace of our community by deeds of petty violence every day. Look at the policeman's billy and handcuffs! Look at the jail! Look at the gallows! Look at the chaplain of the regiment!
>
> We are hoping only to live safely on the outskirts of this provisional army. So we defend ourselves and our hen-roosts, and maintain slavery. I know that the mass of my countrymen think that the only righteous use that can be made of Sharpe's rifles and revolvers is to fight duels with them, when we are insulted by other nations, or to hunt Indians, or shoot fugitive

slaves with them, or the like. I think that for once the Sharpe's rifles and the revolvers were employed in a righteous cause. The tools were in the hands of one who could use them.

While denying any direct involvement with the raid, black abolitionist Charles H. Langston publicly expressed agreement with Brown's principles. "His actions were in perfect harmony with, and resulted from the teaching of the Bible, of our Revolutionary fathers and of every true and faithful anti-slavery man in this country and the world." Langston declared that the Bible commands us to remember those in bonds as being bound with them, and the fathers of our country's revolution taught us that resistance to tyrants is obedience to God. "The man who takes from his brothers his liberty, becomes a tyrant and thus forfeits his rights to *live*."[37]

When the government sided with injustice, it revealed itself to be a "brute force, or worse, a demoniacal force . . . ," said Thoreau. "Is it not possible that an individual may be right and a government wrong? Are laws to be enforced simply because they are made? Or declared by any number of men to be good, if they are *not* good?"[38]

The words of people like Langston and Thoreau gained sympathy and admiration for Brown and shifted public opinion in the North. Some people re-evaluated the use of violence and the morality of man's laws and the horrors of slavery. For example: Lydia Maria Child believed in peace principles and could not sympathize with the methods Brown chose. But she honored his intentions in the cause of freedom. "I admire your courage, moral and physical," she wrote to Brown. "I reverence you for the humanity which tempered your zeal. I sympathize with you in your cruel bereavement, your sufferings, and your wrongs. In brief, I love you and bless you."[39]

Ralph Waldo Emerson called John Brown "the new saint" and predicted he would "make the gallows glorious like the cross."[40] Frances Ellen Watkins (Harper) declared a similar fate in her touching, eloquent letter to Brown.

> In the name of the young girl sold from the warm clasp of a mother's arms to the clutches of a libertine or a profligate,—in the name of the slave mother, her heart rocked to and fro by the agony of her mournful separations,—I thank you, that you have been brave enough to reach out your hands to the crushed and blighted of my race. You have rocked the bloody Bastille; and I hope that from your sad fate great good may arise to the cause of freedom. . . .

> The Cross becomes a glorious ensign when Calvary's pale-browed sufferer yields up his life upon it. And, if Universal Freedom is ever to be the dominant power of the land, your bodies may be only her first stepping stones to dominion. . . . God writes national judgments upon national sins.
>
> . . . We may earnestly hope that your fate will not be a vain lesson, that it will intensify our hatred of Slavery and love of freedom, and that your martyr grave will be a sacred altar upon which men will record their vows of undying hatred to that system which tramples on man and bids defiance to God.[41]

Several news accounts also praised Brown. "If a man builds his house over a volcano," snapped the *Albany Evening Journal*, "it is not those who warn him of his danger that are to blame for its eruptions." "Blood will have blood," bellowed a Northerner, "and the crimes of Southern slaveholders will yet work out a fearful retribution on their own heads." A Philadelphia abolitionist predicted the death of slavery: "This is the beginning of the end."[42]

The trial of John Brown lasted only six days. An attempt was made to save his life by pleading insanity. Higginson believed it was done with good intention, but the result would "degrade one of the age's prime heroes into a mere monomaniac." John flatly refused to cooperate in the insanity plea. Mary did likewise. "I couldn't say . . . that my husband was insane—even to save his life; because he wasn't." Another time, Mary said that if John were insane, "he had been consistent in his insanity from the very first moment she knew him."[43]

Even John's nemesis Virginia Governor Henry Wise said: "Those who think Brown mad make a mistake. . . . He is a man of clear head, of courage, fortitude and simple ingenuousness. He is cool, collected and indomitable." Wise followed up those statements by calling Brown "a fanatic, vain and garrulous," but also "firm, truthful and intelligent."[44]

Bravery and honesty did not matter; the Virginia Court found him guilty of murder, treason, and conspiring with slaves to rebel. Prior to his sentencing on November 2, 1859, John Brown made a spontaneous appeal to the Court.

> In the first place, I deny everything but what I have all along admitted, of a design on my part to free slaves. . . . Had I so interfered in behalf of the rich, the powerful, the intelligent, the so-called great, or in behalf of any of their friends, . . . it

Figure 8.3. John Brown's Trial at Charlestown, Virginia, painting by David C. Lithgow, 1923. On display at the Essex County Courthouse, Elizabethtown, New York. *Source:* Wikimedia Commons. Public domain.

would have been all right, and every man in this court would have deemed it an act worthy of reward rather than punishment.

This Court acknowledges, too, as I suppose, the validity of the law of God . . . which teaches me that, "All things whatsoever I would that men should do to me, I should do even so to them." It teaches me further, to "Remember them that are in bonds as bound with them." I endeavored to act up to that instruction. . . .

> Now, if it is deemed necessary that I should forfeit my life for the furtherance of the ends of justice, and mingle my blood further with the blood of my children and with the blood of millions in this slave country whose rights are disregarded by wicked, cruel, and unjust enactments, I say let it be done. . . . I feel no consciousness of guilt.

When John finished speaking, the Judge sentenced him to be hanged on December 2. Mary read the decree in a newspaper, but she made no outburst. She just bowed her head for a few minutes and then said: "I have always prayed that my husband might be killed in fight rather than fall alive into the hands of the slaveholders; but I cannot regret it now, in view of the noble words of Freedom which it has been his privilege to utter."[45]

Mary saw that John was sending his message to the country through his letters and speeches. In a letter to her, he wrote: "I will here say that the sacrifices *you* and I, have been called to make in behalf of the *cause we love*, the *cause of God and of humanity*; do still not seem to me as at all too great. I have been *whipped* as the saying *is*; but am sure I can recover all the lost capital occasioned by that disaster; by only hanging a few moments by the neck."[46]

"I cannot even come and look at you," responded Mary. "O, it is hard! . . . When you were at home last June I did not think that I took your hand for the last time. But may *Thy* will, O Lord, be done." She praised his speech to the court, saying he could not have accomplished so much for the cause if he had preached in the pulpit for ten lives such as his. "You know that Moses was not allowed to go into the land of Canaan; so you are not allowed to see your desire carried out. Man deviseth his way, but the Lord directeth his steps."[47]

Ruth longed to see her father but knew that the Lord was with him and would never forsake him. She asked him to remember her "to *all those noble prisoners, colored* as well as white." Her son Johnny sent a message: "Tell Grandfather that I know he is in prison because he tried to do good." And Henry sent word that although John's life would be taken, his deeds and influence would "live to be remembered and do good."[48]

John Brown had no fear of hanging. On his last Sabbath day on Earth, he was shedding tears, but they were not tears of grief and sorrow. "I am weeping for joy; and gratitude that I can in no other way express," he wrote to his sisters. He explained that death would be "an Infinite gain" for him and "of *untold* benefit" to the cause.[49]

On November 28, John Jr. wrote a letter to his father, referring to it as "my last words to you on this side of Heaven." He tried to comfort and assure his father that though his sons and daughters might be poor in worldly goods, they felt rich in the legacy of their father's life and deeds. "O, how can we help mourning for you . . . our dear lost father. No, not lost; for, 'though you die, yet shall you rise again.' For a brief period, you must pass beyond our sight . . . but still you will live—live in the hearts of your children, and in the hearts of millions of poor Africa's sons and daughters, who will yet love to call you father."[50]

Chapter 9

Vying for John Brown's Body

> Make me a grave where'er you will,
> In a lowly plain, or a lofty hill;
> Make it among earth's humblest graves,
> But not in a land where men are slaves.
>
> —Frances E. Watkins (Harper), "Bury Me in a Free Land," 1858

John Brown made it clear that, after his execution, he wanted to be buried at the hardscrabble farm amid the wild mountain scenery. The request was not a spur-of-the-moment dying wish; he had given it serious thought for years. Upon finding his grandfather's memorial stone replaced by a new one in Connecticut, he sent the old stone to North Elba in 1857. When he returned to Kansas, he sensed he might not get out alive and expressed his wish to Mary to be buried at the farm with the stone as his grave marker. After being sentenced to hang in 1859, he repeated his request to be laid to rest at the farm beside the big rock where he liked to sit and read his Bible. Perhaps Brown recalled Psalm 18:2: "The Lord is my rock and my fortress and my deliverer; my God is my rock."

John Brown's body seemed destined to be amouldering in the grave in New York State at the place he called home. It is often stated in a matter-of-fact way, as natural as maple sap flowing in the Adirondack springtime. It is his grave that would transform the humble home into a shrine, a Mecca of national and international significance. However, getting Virginia to hand over Brown's body and then transporting it six-hundred miles by train, wagon, boat, sail ferry, and sleigh to North Elba were not easy tasks. The entire undertaking was full of physical hurdles and political hostilities. Virginian foes and abolitionist friends were both plotting ways to exploit John Brown's body—even before he was dead.

Proposals for the Body

In late November of 1859, James Miller McKim expressed his hope that Brown's body would be exhibited in Philadelphia and then sent to Boston for interment. Henry Wright tried to have John Brown persuaded to give his body to the Anti-Slavery Society so money could be raised for an illustrious burial and grandiose monument. Another abolitionist suggested enclosing Brown's body in a metal coffin, with the face exposed (and kept on ice). In this way, his body could be paraded through cities and be of "great propaganda value."[1]

Some Virginians thought the North would carve up Brown's body and "convert his bones into buttons and tooth-picks, and tooth powder" and turn his sinews into "hoops for women's skirts." Virginia Governor Henry Wise believed Northerners intended to dissever Brown's body—"the head buried in Massachusetts, the heart and the arms and the legs, and the dismembered body, each piece to go to separate States, and that each would erect a monument thereon."[2] Therefore, Governor Wise refused to let the North have the body; instead he considered proposals from Southerners.

The *Richmond Examiner* suggested Brown's body should be "chopped into small pieces, in the Chinese manner, and distributed *in terrorem* all over the land." A piece of his "traitorous flesh" would be skewered and put on display in every square mile of Virginia. Doctor M. E. Bickle wanted to use his special embalming process to make Brown's body look lifelike and then exhibit it throughout the South as a warning to the slaves. After that, Bickle would exhibit the body in the North and procure money from abolitionists. He proposed giving half of the profits to Virginia as compensation for expenses due to Brown's raid; the rest of the profits would be kept by Bickle.[3]

Governor Wise dismissed that ghoulish money-making scheme. He also dismissed the offer of showman P. T. Barnum who was willing to pay $100 for Brown's clothes and a pike, if accompanied by a certificate of authenticity. Wise favored the plan of Winchester Medical College to display the heads of Brown and the other hanged raiders in its museum collection. The college was also willing to take the entire bodies if the transfer would not cost more than $5 each. Wise liked this plan since it achieved his main objective: keeping those who were hanged from being buried in Virginia soil.[4]

Brown rebuked the proposals of Wise and foiled the plans of his abolitionist friends; he wanted a simple burial in New York. He asked Mary to come and gather his body after Virginia applied "the finishing stroke." If she could afford the trip and endure the troubles along the way. If the people of Virginia would allow her to come. Brown also wanted Mary to collect the remains of their sons Watson and Oliver, and neighbors William and Dauphin Thompson. He suggested a way to make it easy to carry the remains of the five men to North Elba—gather some wood, set a fire, and "burn the flesh, then collect our bones and put them in a large box."[5]

Practical—but morbid, and insufferable for Mary. In the end, John told her not to grieve if she was unable to obtain the bodies: "It can make little difference what is done with them." However, as James Redpath wrote a few weeks later: "With his sword and his voice John Brown had demonstrated the unutterable villainy of slavery. His corpse was destined to continue the lesson."[6]

Gazing Stock

In early November, Mary Brown had left North Elba with Thomas Higginson, ostensibly to go see John in jail. They barely made it out of town before their buggy broke and they had to walk to the village of Jay. They found another buggy and made it to Burlington, Vermont, that evening. The next day they took the train to Boston, the conductors giving Mary free passage when they learned her identity. Upon arriving in Boston, a crowd of twenty-five to thirty friends greeted her. A man named Fiske handed Mary $20 and a pair of gloves—"and came back twice to give good advice." Others gave her money and handkerchiefs and shoes and kisses. She received more than $100 by the time she began her trip southward, first by steamboat to New York City and then by train to Philadelphia. Abolitionist James Miller McKim met her there, and the next day he escorted her on the train to Baltimore.[7]

Family members in North Elba received word that Mary was safe and "everything will go well." But the broken buggy seemed to have been an omen that things would go awry.

When John heard that Mary was coming to visit him in jail, he sent word to her, "Do not, for God's sake, come here now."[8]

By the time she received the message, Mary was already at a friend's house in Baltimore. Somehow, she managed to get to the train depot and find McKim before he left. She returned with him to Philadelphia, where she learned the reasons for John's refusal to see her. He said,

> If my Wife were to come here just now, it would only tend to distract her mind ten-fold . . . [and] deepen my affliction a thousand-fold. I beg of her to be calm, and submissive; and not to go wild on my account. I lack for nothing. And was feeling quite cheerful before I learned she talked of coming on. I ask her to compose her mind and to remain quiet till the last of this Month; out of pity to me.[9]

When Mary heard this, her tears flowed freely and she responded: "Tell my husband, I can spare him for the sake of the cause! . . . I can resign him to God, sure that it is His hand that strikes the blow!"[10]

After three days in Philadelphia, Mary headed to Perth Amboy, NJ, to the home of Rebecca Spring, who had just returned from visiting John in jail. While at Spring's house, Mary received a letter from John saying he was somewhat recovered from his wounds. He also gave another reason for not wanting her to visit him: she might be made "a gazing stock" and have to endure gawks and threats from "all sorts of creatures." A second letter from John said he had a "strong desire" to see Mary again but thanked her for heeding his request to stay away. For this, he felt a renewed obligation to his "ever faithful and beloved wife."[11]

Upon returning to Philadelphia, Mary composed a carefully worded letter (with the help of minister William H. Furness) in hopes of convincing Governor Wise to give her the bodies of her husband and sons. The letter emphasized that she did not ask for John's life, she requested only that his mortal remains be delivered to her for decent and tender interment. "Little as it is that I ask," wrote Mary, "if you will grant my request, your humanity in this particular shall have the sincerest thanks of his wife and children."[12]

Governor Wise appreciated Mary's wisdom in understanding his "position of duty" and assured her that he did not take the slightest pleasure in the execution. "Sympathizing as I do with your affliction," he wrote, "you shall have the exertion of my authority and personal influence to assist you in gathering the bones of your sons and your husband." Wise instructed his Major General to guard Brown's body from mutilation after the hanging, then place it in a plain coffin and deliver it to Mary Brown in Harpers Ferry.[13]

As she read Wise's reply, Mary began to sob and no one could comfort her. Perhaps she had held onto a smidgeon of hope that the governor might show mercy and stay the execution. His letter annihilated every possibility of John avoiding the noose. In that moment, Mary did not feel up to making the toilsome journey to Virginia and wanted a friend to act as her agent. By morning, she decided to go, feeling certain John's body could be recovered but doubting "the bodies of Oliver and Watson will be found."[14]

Sarah and James McKim would accompany her, but they also wanted a personal male escort for Mary. The role involved risk of assault, arrest, or worse. A substantial number of infantry and cavalry regiments patrolled the Harpers Ferry and Charles Town area, and the local newspaper assailed abolitionists as "pusillanimous wretches"—long-faced, lily-livered, and self-righteous. "We confess to a supreme hatred for the whole of them, male and female." Despite the danger, lawyer Hector Tyndale volunteered to accompany the wife of John Brown into Virginia. He did not even know the Browns, but he felt sympathy for them and did what he would want a gentleman to do for his wife.[15]

Mary Brown and her three escorts arrived in Harpers Ferry on November 30, two days before John's execution. Although Governor Wise had consented to their visit, the authorities prevented their progress to the Charles Town jail. The party of two men and two women seemed "dangerously strong."[16]

That same day, Wise claimed he had no fear of strangers or attacks; the great presence of troops in the region was because he considered it a fine time "to put the state in military training." Boys could be taught "how to carry biscuit in their knap sacks and to arrange bullets in their cartridge boxes." When one of the boys fired a shot at a man who would not halt, the town flew into a panic for four hours until it was discovered that the soldier had killed a cow. *The New York Tribune* reasoned, "As a cow will frighten a private doing sentry duty, one live Northern woman and two Northern men might reasonably be expected to intimidate a Virginia army."[17]

The two Northern men must have frightened someone in Harpers Ferry. As Tyndale and McKim were on a walk, they heard "a sharp report and the whistling of a bullet close to them." Though they could not discover who fired the shot, "they felt that they were exposed to the dangers of assassination from an enemy."[18]

The next morning, December 1, the order came that only Mary could go to Charles Town, she could only see "prisoner Brown," and she must return the same day. Mary's desire to see John outweighed her angst of going to the jail without her friends. But she would not be alone. Captain

Philip Moore of Richmond rode in the carriage with her and "a file of dragoons" with rifles escorted them. During the eight-mile journey, Mary told Captain Moore that she had always felt a deep interest in the cause in which her husband was engaged. She resented the idea that John had done anything to deserve death or taint his name with dishonor. "She regarded him as a martyr in a righteous cause," recalled Captain Moore, "and was proud to be the wife of such a man. The gallows, she said, had no terrors for her or for him."[19]

Charles Town buzzed with the news that Mary Brown was on her way. Three brass cannons were placed aside the two already stationed in front of the jail. Eight hundred to a thousand men, with glittering bayonets, pistols, and swords, "formed a hollow square through which the carriage passed with Mrs. Brown." As Mary entered the jail, the jailor's wife thoroughly searched her. There was a notion that Mary might give John a weapon or some strychnine with which he could commit suicide. Thus, the military "might be deprived of the extreme pleasure of choking the man to death." Of course, nothing suspicious was found on Mary, yet officers kept a strict watch over the couple. The visit took place in the jail cell with John in chains, and Mary noted that to keep the chains from galling his ankles, John wore two pairs of woolen socks with pieces of paper stuffed into them.[20]

Figure 9.1. "Mrs. Brown Escorted from Harper's Ferry to the Jail at Charlestown to Have an Interview with her Husband, the Day Before he was Hanged." Mary Brown in carriage, escorted by armed soldiers on December 1. *Frank Leslie's Illustrated Newspaper*, December 17, 1859. *Source:* Author's collection; public domain.

The couple embraced and then spoke about the settlement of property. For the most part, John passed everything to Mary, having full confidence in her ability to manage it for the benefit of the children. He expressed to Mary that it would be pleasant to live longer, but "as it was the will of God he should close his career," he was content. If it was deemed best that he should be "legally murdered" for the good of the cause, he was prepared to submit to his fate without a murmur. Mary became disturbed at these remarks, and John told her to "cheer up," for his spirit would soon be with her again, reunited in heaven.[21]

Figure 9.2. "John Brown's Last Interview with his Wife in the Jail at Charlestown, VA." *Frank Leslie's Illustrated Newspaper*, December 17, 1859. *Source:* Author's collection; public domain.

JOHN BROWN'S LAST INTERVIEW WITH HIS WIFE IN THE JAIL AT CHARLESTOWN, VA.

Vying for John Brown's Body | 139

Mary and John ate supper with the jailer and his wife in their residence, which was attached to the jail. After supper, they returned to John's cell, and he endorsed several checks and gave Mary his letters and papers. Though John wanted Mary to remain with him all night, an officer denied the appeal and requested her to return to Harpers Ferry. The husband and wife parted, both seeming to be fully self-possessed and composed.

After Mary's departure, the wild excitement in Charles Town subsided. The streets were empty except for the armed patrols and the ether of anticipation. "Tomorrow, as the clock strikes twelve," reported the *National Era*, "the solemn tragedy commenced on the plains of Kansas in 1855 will end by the falling of the drop on the plains of Charlestown."

December 2, 1859

As the sun rose on the morning of December 2, soldiers with polished bayonets marched about Charles Town, keeping order in the crowds, preventing admission of unknown persons, and scouting the nearby woods for potential rescuers. A twelve-pound howitzer stood near a large field where stakes rose from the soil to mark positions for the military companies. A scaffold sprouted at the center of the field, a scaffold expressly for John Brown.

> The *Outer John Brown* they will torture and kill,
> And tumble it into a grave,
> But the *Inner John Brown* may trouble them still,
> By its whisperings round with the slave.
> Stand firm, John Brown!
> Death nears you, John Brown, Old Outer John Brown,
> And marks you as food for the worm;
> Nor death nor the worm can harm Inner John Brown,
> So Inner John Brown, stand firm!
> Stand firm, John Brown! (David Barker, "To John Brown,"
>   December 2, 1859)[22]

Soldiers paraded about the field with the "pomp and circumstance of war." Virginia seemed compelled to orchestrate every detail. For example, the Sheriff examined hanging ropes from three states. Missouri sent a hemp rope made by the slaves of Mrs. Doyle, wanting vengeance for the murder of her husband by Brown's men in Kansas in 1856. That rope was found

140 | John Brown in New York

unfit to sustain Brown's weight, as was a cotton rope from South Carolina. A third rope, a hemp one from Kentucky, proved strong enough to be trusted with John Brown's neck.[23]

At eleven o'clock, John Brown left the jailhouse dressed in "a black frock-coat, black pantaloons, black vest, black slouch hat, white socks, and slippers of predominating red." He refused to have any clergy pray with him or accompany him to the scaffold. Brown said he would rather be joined by "barefooted, barelegged, ragged slave children and their old gray-headed slave mother."[24] Authorities did not allow any black friends to accompany him, nor did he kiss a black child as he descended the jail steps. News reporters created the myth, and soon the imagined scene became enshrined in art and poetry. Brown's only act as he left the jail was to pass a note to a guard. The small scrap of paper carried his final, prophetic message—words that would be printed and repeated throughout the country. "I, John Brown, am now quite certain that the crimes of this guilty land will never be purged away; but with Blood. I had as I now think: vainly flattered myself that without very much bloodshed: it might be done."

Brown boarded an open wagon and took his seat on a pine box, which contained his coffin. Two files of riflemen flanked the wagon as it jostled through the field to the awaiting scaffold. After Brown ascended the twelve steps, a white cap was pulled over his face and the hemp rope put around his neck. After a lengthy delay, the trap door fell away from John Brown's feet. His body dropped and made a slight struggle, a few twitches.

Doctors pronounced the old man dead; his spinal column had been ruptured. Yet the body still had a pulse, so it was left hanging. The "loathsome carcass" dangled so long it "stenched the atmosphere," reported the *Richmond News*. Some say it hung for thirty-five minutes, others say thirty-eight. One witness claimed it was precisely noon when Brown's body was lowered, suggesting it was forty-five minutes.[25]

After placing the body in a coffin, it was taken back to the jail and examined by physicians. The eyes were fully open and possessed their natural luster. The limbs were flexible with no rigidity of death, and the body was quite warm. The conclusion: John Brown should not leave Charles Town until his life was "entirely extinct." One observer wanted to administer arsenic; others wanted the head cut off. Instead, liquid ammonia was applied to his eyes. A lighted candle was held near his nose. Nothing. The physicians pronounced him "quite dead."[26]

Now that Brown's life had ended, the *Richmond News* said, "Take him away!" They did not want "such filth" to contaminate Virginia soil. "Horse

Figure 9.3. "Execution of John Brown" in Charles Town with soldiers surrounding the field, December 2, 1859. *Source:* Library of Congress. Public domain.

manure and guano would reject association with it; grass would refuse to sprout in the bosom of the fertile fields of the valley, and that scavenger of our country, the noble buzzard, would be driven from our State by the pestiferous stench of the carcass."[27]

Another Virginia paper claimed, "we vex not his ghost." But if Brown's execution brought him martyrdom and if that should bring bloody results to the South, "Virginia will meet the results with ropes, for which South Carolina grows the cotton, and Kentucky the hemp."[28]

> Let them beat their drums in triumph,
> While the martyr, Brown,
> Living bravely, dying nobly,
> Wears the victor's crown.
> Summoned to his home celestial,
> From their brief control,
> All the hemp of ruthless tyrants
> Could not hang his soul. (G. W. Light, "John Brown's Final Victory")[29]

Virginians believed they had extinguished John Brown's breath and silenced his voice. However, during the hour of John Brown's execution, the bells of Northern churches rang and thousands of voices, white and black, were lifted in speeches and prayers in honor of John Brown. "He triumphs by the gallows," said Thoreau. "He is not Old Brown any longer; he is an angel of light." "In teaching us how to die," John Brown and his men "taught us how to live."[30]

Many black communities closed the doors of their businesses and held meetings on the day of Brown's execution. "I never thought that I should ever join in doing honor to or mourning for any American *white* man," said black abolitionist Charles H. Langston, but in John Brown he found "a lover of mankind—not of any particular class or color, but of all men." Langston felt that Brown fully believed in the equality and brotherhood of man and in the practical application of those words, not as flourish or platitudes. "He is the only American citizen who has lived fully up to the *Declaration of Independence*."[31]

The black community of New Bedford, Massachusetts, adopted a resolution: "Resolved, That the memory of John Brown shall be indelibly written upon the tablets of our hearts, and when tyrants cease to oppress the enslaved, we will teach our children to revere his name, and transmit it to the latest posterity, as being the greatest man in the 19th century."[32]

A Utica, New York newspaper reported that although Brown erred deeply, "the target of his conspiracy is itself a conspiracy against justice and the rights of man. He seized the fire-brand of the revolutionist; but it was to burn down an edifice which is by general acknowledgment the scandal and reproach of the age." The moral heroism and calm defiance he exhibited after his arrest made the reporter ponder: "Who knows but that the death sigh of John Brown may prove the knell of American slavery?"[33]

While abolitionists drafted articles and made speeches, the Brown family members in North Elba felt overwhelmed with sorrow and frustration. News came to them so slowly; the waiting seemed endless. John's last letter to his family did not reach North Elba before his December 2 hanging. "Let me entreat you all to love the whole remnant of our once great family. Try and build up again your broken walls, and to make the utmost of every stone that is left. Nothing can so tend to make life a blessing as the consciousness that your life and example bless and leave others stronger."[34] On December 2, Annie Brown did not know with certainty if her father had been hanged. "His only crime," she said, "was that of being a human being and not a devil." She felt proud to have his blood run in her veins and hoped to always "act in a way to be worthy of such a Father." Annie also longed for her mother's return to North Elba, "for 'home is not sweet home' when Mother is gone."[35]

The Transit of the Body

Mary Brown waited in Harpers Ferry, anxious to begin her journey home. Unfortunately, the bodies of her sons would remain in Virginia. Surgeons took Watson's corpse for dissection and refused to give it to the family. Oliver's decomposing body had been thrown in a trench with other raiders' bodies and was not identifiable. Only John's body would be delivered to her for interment in Adirondack soil.

At about five o'clock in the evening, Virginia authorities brought his body to Mary in Harpers Ferry. But was it John Brown's body? A rumor hinted that his body would be thrown out on a "dung-heap" and a black man's corpse put in the coffin. Mary's escort, Hector Tyndale, asked for the coffin to be opened before he accepted delivery, but the soldier in charge refused to open the lid. Tyndale persisted until the lid was finally lifted, and the body identified as John Brown.

Early the next morning Mary Brown, Tyndale, and the McKims boarded a train and headed northward with the coffin. At Baltimore, they lifted the lid again. They had learned of a plot to throw the coffin from the train before it reached Baltimore and substitute a fake one. It was not to be. Allegedly, the railroad conductor failed to execute the act due to "sickness" or "flinching."[36]

John Brown's body was finally safe and away from Virginia. Final destination: North Elba. Or was it? Other destinations swirled in the mind of James Miller McKim. He tried to persuade Mary to take her husband's body to Boston where it could be buried with fanfare, pomp, and ballyhoo in the illustrious Mount Auburn Cemetery at Cambridge.

As the burial site was debated, the funeral train approached Philadelphia. The entourage planned to spend two nights there, allowing time for Mary to rest and for John's body to be placed with an undertaker. But newspapers had announced the plan, and a mob greeted the train. Tyndale managed to escort Mary through the crowd to a friend's house without either of them being recognized. Back at the depot, policemen tried to mollify the mob by *pretending* to give them what they wanted—Brown's body. Men wrapped a deer skin around a work box, put it in a wagon, and policemen escorted it out of the depot. The mob followed the bogus coffin down the street.

Though the crisis was averted, the mayor of Philadelphia insisted that Brown's body leave the city immediately. After the street cleared, men took Brown's real coffin out the side door of the depot and loaded it onto a furniture wagon. The hoax was seen by boys who had climbed the fence, and as the wagon rolled down the street, a small crowd chased it. No one could keep pace with the wagon, and it reached Walnut Street wharf untouched. McKim accompanied the coffin aboard a boat headed to New York City.

To avoid publicity in New York, a wagon quickly carried the precious cargo from the boat to a nearby coffin manufacturer at No. 163 Bowery. A Brooklyn undertaker arrived and removed the body from the southern coffin and placed it on ice. By the next afternoon, the body was frozen enough to be laid out in a neat white shroud and a white cravat and placed in a plain coffin. City records logged the presence of John Brown's body as age fifty-nine; place of death, Charles Town, Virginia; disease, hanging.[37]

The *Brooklyn Evening Star* reported that "Mrs. Brown gave her consent" to take the body to Albany, where the whole Brown family would view it and then send it to Mount Auburn as the people of Boston insisted. This report came from Boston abolitionist Wendell Phillips who had arrived in New York to accompany the funeral party. However, Mary had *not* agreed to Phillips's plan. The next day, the Brooklyn paper printed a retraction, stating the body would not go to Boston. Instead, John Brown's dying request, to be buried at his North Elba homestead, would be honored.[38]

Phillips tried a new strategy of keeping the body in New York City as long as possible. He claimed at least 20,000 sympathizers wanted to view it. On the other hand, Mary wanted to get back to her children in North Elba with as little publicity and delay as possible. Eventually, Phillips conceded, but he knew an occasion for publicity and fundraising had been squandered. "Ten years of Brown's life had been lost by not having the body remain over a day in New York."

Of course, in public, the abolitionists tried to spin it, appearing to be sensitive to Mary's wishes. The press commended "the perfect propriety and good taste" shown in obeying John Brown's last wishes and avoiding any "public manifestation whatever." The abolitionists received credit for their "great reserve" from holding demonstrations and processions in the cities. Privately, they cringed, knowing that a speedy burial in the relatively unpopulated and isolated town of North Elba meant another bungled opportunity. "We have lost it: a worse loss than the battle of Harper's Ferry," wrote abolitionist Thaddeus Hyatt. "Another John Brown it seems was needed to take charge of John Brown's mortal remains."[39]

Another John Brown had taken charge—*Mrs.* John Brown. She refused to let the abolitionists exploit her husband's corpse and funeral. Amid grief and chaos, Mary stayed true to her word and stood firm. She adhered to her husband's wishes and to her agreement with Governor Wise for interment among family.

Final Miles of the Trek

Bells tolled and people gathered in the streets as the funeral party headed farther north. A "Special Reporter" from the *New York Tribune* accompanied them and described their arrival at the American House in Troy, New York. "They came without notice, but news of their arrival soon spread, and some of the most respectable people of the place called to express their condolence with Mrs. Brown. . . . a large number of persons, including not a few of the colored class, sought and found an opportunity of shaking Mrs. Brown's hand, in token of their sympathy."[40] Since the New York side of Lake Champlain did not have train service, the funeral party boarded a train for Rutland, Vermont. At five o'clock the next morning, they rode in carriages to Vergennes, where they stopped at the Stevens Hotel. Again, a

Figure 9.4. Sail Ferry at Barber's Point near Westport, New York. *Source:* Westport (New York) Library website (https://www.westportnylibrary.org/photos). Public domain.

crowd gathered to express their respect and sympathy. When it came time to leave, local men led the funeral procession to the edge of town and then halted. They formed a double line and removed their hats as the carriages with John Brown's body, his widow, and his friends passed between the columns. "It was a spontaneous tribute, and an affecting sight."[41]

From Adams Ferry (Arnold's Bay) on the Vermont side of Lake Champlain, a sail ferry carried Mary and her friends down the Oxbow River and across the lake to Barber's Point near Westport, New York. Sleighs carried them into the village as heavy rain turned the fallen snow to slush. The sleighs were abandoned for carriages with wheels for the trip to Elizabethtown. The party appealed to get the man in charge of the Westport hearse to haul Brown's body to North Elba, but he refused because the roads were bad (and the hearse wagon was said to be aged and in disrepair). An old spring wagon carried Brown's corpse from Westport to Elizabethtown.[42]

Late that afternoon, during a torrential rainstorm, the cortege arrived in Elizabethtown and stopped to spend the night at the hotel kept by Sheriff Elijah A. Adams. The sheriff offered to keep the coffin at the Essex County Courthouse and Mary agreed. Within a few minutes, John Brown's body rested securely for the night in a second-story room of the courthouse. Several young men sat in the room all night guarding the body.[43] Meanwhile, Adams's hotel filled with people, including the prominent attorneys of Elizabethtown—Judge Augustus C. Hand, Orlando Kellogg, Byron Pond, and Robert S. Hale. Most had known Brown and respected and admired him as a friend and neighbor. They found it hard to comprehend that their fellow citizen had been put to death; they had not thought that "Virginia would do the bloody deed."[44]

The townspeople waited eagerly for Wendell Phillips to speak, and they were not disappointed. For two hours, Phillips provided details about the results of the attack at Harpers Ferry, calling it "a God-send in disguise" and predicting it would be "the entering wedge" to split the Union. He assured the citizens that tomorrow they would consign Brown's lifeless body to the cold earth, but his principles would live on.[45]

The town quieted for the night, then just before daybreak, Sheriff Adams's son Henry started off on horseback for North Elba to notify the Brown family of the party's impending arrival. However, during the night the wind had shifted, and the temperature fell below freezing. Henry found the mountainous country road almost impassable.

At daylight, the funeral procession left Elizabethtown on their final twenty-five-mile trek. Due to the weather, it took about four hours to

Figure 9.5. "1858 View of Court House and Clerks Office of Essex County," Elizabethtown, New York. The courthouse had two floors and an outdoor staircase, which have since been removed. *Source:* Wikimedia Commons. Public domain.

travel the first eight miles to Keene. They paused for a brief stop and meal at the house of abolitionist Phineas Norton. He expressed disbelief about the execution of his good friend and "the proof furnished by the coffin containing the dead body quite overcame him."[46]

From Norton's house, the group began the slow climb up and along the northern face of Pitchoff Mountain. By the time they descended to the other side, the sun had set, and darkness slowed their progress along Old Mountain Road. Soon men with lanterns approached from the other direction. These friends had been waiting at the farm all afternoon in anxious expectation and had come to investigate the cause of the delay. Guided by the lights, the weary troop proceeded in silence to the Browns' house.

When they finally arrived, Mary stepped out of her carriage and a sharp, low cry of "Mother!" broke the silence. "O! Annie!" came the reply in a tone of agony mingled with tenderness. The mother and daughter locked in a long embrace. The scene was repeated with daughters Sarah and Ellen. Then came the widowed daughters-in-law and "there went up a wail, before which flint itself would have softened. It was a scene entirely beyond description."

Figure 9.6. "Arrival of the Body at North Elba. A Moonlight View." John Brown funeral party arriving at the farmhouse, December 7, 1859. The house actually had an upper loft with windows, and the mountains were not as looming as depicted. From *New York Illustrated News*, December 14, 1859. *Source:* West Virginia State Archives. Used with permission.

After a few moments, all were composed and quiet. The strangers and neighbors entered the house and carried the casket upstairs. Mary took Ruth up to open it. "I never saw my father look more peaceful," recalled Ruth. "There was a smile upon his face, and the features were as composed as though he had died surrounded by his friends and in the course of nature. . . . I felt that I would gladly lie down beside that still figure, and be buried in the grave with him, for in his death, justice seemed to perish from the earth and wrong to reign triumphant."[47]

After supper, McKim gave an account of all that had happened since Mary arrived in Philadelphia in early November. It had been "an honor and a privilege," he said, to serve as her escort to Harpers Ferry in "so holy and solemn a mission." Then he described the kindness shown by many Southerners but omitted the indignities, such as a bullet whizzing past him outside the Harpers Ferry hotel. Phillips continued the narrative in a manner that replaced the family's tears and grief with "a holy, pensive joy." At a late hour, the party finally sought rest. Accommodations were found for all the guests, and though the night was intensely cold, all kept comfortable in "good, warm bed-clothing."[48]

The Errand of Rev. Joshua Young

Upon hearing news of the John Brown funeral party passing through Vermont, Unitarian minister Joshua Young and his fellow Underground Railroad collaborator Lucius H. Bigelow decided to go to the funeral.

"Joshua, is it wise?" asked his wife.
"It may not be wise, but I am going anyway."

Figure 9.7. Rev. Joshua Young of Burlington, Vermont. Unitarian minister who performed the funeral service of John Brown. *New York News*, December 24, 1859. *Source:* Wikimedia Commons. Public domain.

Young and Bigelow took a train from Burlington to Vergennes where they learned that the funeral procession had passed through the previous evening. Confident that they could reach North Elba in time for the services, they hurried to the ferry landing. By then, it was raining hard, and a storm threatened to become a "North-Easter." The two men told the ferryman that they desired to cross Lake Champlain as soon as possible, but he did not want to cross with the sail ferry so late in the evening during a storm. Besides, the ferryman said he thought John Brown deserved his fate.[49]

"Why, do you know any evil of him?"

"No, but a great deal of good," replied the ferryman. "I knew John Brown well. He has crossed this ferry with me a hundred times, and a more honest, upright, fair man does not exist. We all like him, but he had no business meddling with other people's n——s."

For three hours, the travelers pleaded with the ferryman to take them across, yet he refused to budge. Suddenly the sky brightened, the wind veered to the west, and the clouds broke up. "See, Mr. Ferryman," exclaimed Young, "God's full-orbed moon has thrown a bridge of silver across the lake: he bids us go, and who shall hinder?"

Within minutes, they were boarding a large scow, and though the wet sail was "as stiff as sheet iron," they managed to hoist it up the mast. A strong wind hastened the three-mile crossing and Young and Bigelow soon stood near Westport, New York. They were drenched from the flying spray. Wet and cold. On an utterly desolate shore. And it was past midnight. Now what?

They saw a glimmering light at a house in the distance and "hailed it as a bright, propitious star." A young man answered the door and was willing to take them to North Elba. Young said, "In less time than I can repeat the pious sentiment that came to my mind—'The Lord will provide'—we were putting the ten miles to Elizabethtown behind us with as rapid pace as the roads would permit."

At two o'clock in the morning, they changed horses at Elizabethtown and then continued to Norton's house in Keene before resting. Upon resuming their journey at daylight, they "entered a region of the grandest and most majestic scenery." Young thought it was the famed Indian Pass, but it was just the Old Mountain Road running north of Pitchoff Mountain. As they made their way over rocks and stumps, the two men clung to their seats, "lest the swaying of the wagon from side to side, pitching like a ship in a heavy sea, or its frequent plunge from a surmounted stump, should throw us out."

A pitching, plunging wagon ride after a freezing ferry crossing. "Oh, what a night was that!" wrote Young, "On such an errand!"

The men came out of the forest onto a broad table land and after turning south off the main road, they soon emerged into a clearing and saw the home of John Brown. The two stiff and half-frozen men entered the house and were greeted by genial welcomes and a hot fire. Wendell Phillips approached Young, and after confirming that he was a minister, said: "It would give Mrs. Brown and the other widows great satisfaction if you would perform the usual service of a clergyman on this occasion."

At that moment, Young knew why God had sent him through the storm. Though Young had never met John Brown, and the family knew nothing of Young, Providence brought them together for this solemn occasion.

In his jail cell, John Brown had refused to be consoled by or prayed over by any minister who preached proslavery or accepted slave owners as Christians. However, Rev. Young was an ardent abolitionist, a member of the Boston Vigilance Committee, and a station keeper on the Underground Railroad in Burlington. He shared the principles of John Brown. After witnessing the forced return of escaped slave Anthony Burns in Boston in 1854, Young railed against slavery and the Fugitive Slave Law. Like John Brown, Young believed that no human law could be compulsory if it conflicted with the commands of Heaven. "There is a Power superior to Congress," said Young, "a Law higher than any human constitution. . . . God's government is higher than man's government, and the Divine law broader than human law." Despite parishioners' disapproval of his sermon and the danger of losing his reputation, his friends, or his life, Young vowed to continue to speak against this sin, "American Slavery," until its abolition or the dissolution of the Union.[50]

Rev. Joshua Young was precisely the kind of man John Brown would have chosen to oversee his funeral.

Chapter 10

Buried Among Kin and Neighbors

> Blow ye the trumpet, blow—
> The gladly solemn sound;
> Let all the nations know,
> To earth's remotest bound,
> The year of Jubilee has come . . .
> Return ye ransom sinners home.
>
> —Charles Wesley, "Blow Ye the Trumpet, Blow,"
> John Brown's favorite hymn

On December 8, guests at the John Brown Farm rose to greet a zero-degree morning, yet the sun shined brilliantly and made a dazzling display on the mountains. "On opening the front door," wrote the *New York Tribune* reporter, "a glorious sight saluted me. . . . a ragged chain of the Adirondacks; broken, jagged, massive, and wonderfully picturesque." Off to the left, the towering pyramid of Whiteface rose "in solitary grandeur;" on the right, the loftiest pinnacles of the Adirondack range. "Just the country for the heroic soul of John Brown."[1]

In the shadow of the great rock, men dug in the frozen ground for a considerable time to make a six-feet-deep grave. Throughout the morning, neighbors, friends, and acquaintances arrived at the farm. In all, about 250 people gathered in the freezing cold for the funeral, which began with the Epps family singing "Blow Ye the Trumpet, Blow." Brown often sang the song to his children, and its page in his hymn book was well thumbed.

As Ruth listened to the sweet voices of the Eppses—Lyman leading with his tenor voice, Lyman Jr. singing the bass line, and Albertine and Evelene adding alto and soprano—it seemed as though her father was there in spirit and singing along.[2]

Rev. Joshua Young delivered a glorious prayer, made even more remarkable since it was entirely spontaneous. Afterward, Young could not recall the words he spoke, "I only know I prayed."[3] Thankfully, the *New York Tribune* reporter recorded his words.

> Almighty and most merciful God! we lift our souls unto thee. . . . Thou art speaking unto us; as in those grand and majestic scenes of nature, so in the great and solemn circumstances which have brought us together. Our souls are filled with awe and are subdued to silence, as we think of that great, reverential, heroic soul, whose mortal remains we are now to commit to the earth, "dust to dust," while his spirit dwells with

Figure 10.1. "The Burial of John Brown, North Elba, December 8, 1859." Notice some carriages with wheels, some sleighs with runners, and a mixture of oxen and horses near the barn. *Source:* West Virginia State Archives. Used with permission.

154 | John Brown in New York

God who gave it, and his memory is enshrined in every pure and holy heart.

At his open grave, as standing by the altar of Christ, the divinest friend and Savior of Man, may we consecrate ourselves anew to the work of Truth, Righteousness and Love, forevermore to sympathize with the outcast and the oppressed, with the humble and the least of our suffering fellow-men.

We pray for these afflicted ones—this sadly bereaved and mourning family. O God, hear our prayers . . . we supplicate thy special blessing upon God's despised ones—the poor enslaved, for whom our brother laid down his life. O God, cause the oppressed to go free; break every yoke and prostrate the pride and prejudice that dare to lift themselves up; and O! hasten on the day when no more wrong or injustice shall be done on the earth; when all men shall love one another with pure hearts . . . Amen.

James McKim spoke next. Even though he had not known Brown in life, McKim said he honored, loved, and admired him in ways words could not express. "These mountain peaks, this weeping group, the body of the martyr for liberty—what could be added to their eloquence?" Yet he felt he should say something to comfort those whose hearthstones had been left desolate. He spoke not only of John Brown, but also of the other four fallen men from North Elba.

Your father, your husband, your brothers not only died bravely, but they died usefully; they were all benefactors; they were all martyrs in a holy cause. . . . Oliver Brown, Watson Brown, Dauphin Thompson, William Thompson, all were attested to be—with the exception of this one act, the assault on Harper's Ferry—without reproach, as well as without fear. Don't weep for them, then, as though their lives had been spent in vain, and their death would prove of no effect. The world will yet acknowledge itself debtor to them, and history will embalm their memory.

McKim assured the families that through their sacrifices they had made contributions to the cause of freedom and humanity. In this respect, "the hearts of tens of thousands beat in the deepest sympathy." Though the outcome at Harpers Ferry may have been disastrous in some respects, it was "in no respect a failure." With his sword of steel, Brown "struck the hollow shell of Southern society, political and social, and revealed its emptiness," said McKim. When his steel sword was taken away, Brown used the sword of the spirit. "His utterances . . . have gone out to the world and are doing their work."

Wendell Phillips spoke next, continuing to praise the "Marvelous old man!" and his works.

> One and another of you, his neighbors, say, "I have known him five years," "I have known him ten years." It seems to me as if we had none of us known him.
>
> How our admiring, loving wonder has grown, day by day, as he has unfolded trait after trait of earnest, brave, tender, Christian life! . . .
>
> He has abolished Slavery in Virginia. . . . History will date Virginia Emancipation from Harpers Ferry. True, the slave is still there. So, when the tempest uproots a pine on your hills, it looks green for months—a year or two. Still, it is timber, not a tree. John Brown has loosened the roots of the Slave system; it only breathes—it does not live—hereafter.
>
> . . . How truly he may say "I have fought a good fight, I have finished my course." Truly he has finished—done his work. . . .
>
> Surely such a life is no failure. How vast the change in men's hearts! Insurrection was a harsh, horrid word to millions a month ago. John Brown went a whole generation beyond it, claiming the right for white men to help the slave to freedom by arms. And now men run up and down, not disputing his principle, but trying to frame excuses for Virginia's hanging of so pure, honest, high-hearted, and heroic a man. Virginia stands at the bar of the civilized world on trial.

Phillips also remembered Watson, Oliver, Dauphin, and William as part of "that score of heroes" who fought alongside John Brown. "How resolute each looked into the face of Virginia, how loyally each stood at his forlorn post, meeting death cheerfully. . . . those brave young hearts, which lie buried on the banks of the Shenandoah." Phillips felt honored to stand under such a roof as they dwelled, to stand with weeping children and widows who seemed "consecrated by long, single-hearted devotion" to freeing the slaves.

The speech was unforgettable. Phillips's words rose into a high atmosphere and painted a sublime vision of hope and prophecy for all to embrace.

> Hereafter you will tell children standing at your knees, "I saw John Brown buried—I sat under his roof."
>
> ... God make us all worthier of him whose dust we lay among these hills he loved. Here he girded himself and went forth to battle. Fuller success than his heart ever dreamed God granted him. He sleeps in the blessings of the crushed and the poor, and men believe more firmly in virtue, now that such a man has lived.

Another hymn was sung while men placed the coffin on a table by the door. Friends and neighbors stepped forward to take a last look at the face of John Brown. Then the family took their final leave of husband and father. Finally, the coffin was carried across the yard and lowered into the grave. Only then did the family burst into sobs of grief, and Rev. Young came forward to comfort them with the words of Paul: "I have fought a

Figure 10.2. "The Last View of John Brown's Body." Family and friends taking a last look at Brown in his partially opened coffin. Tombstone (far right) not yet inscribed with the names of John, Watson, and Oliver. From *New York Illustrated News*, December 24, 1859. *Source:* West Virginia State Archives. Used with permission.

good fight; I have finished my course; I have kept the faith; henceforth there is laid up for me a crown of righteousness." The sobs quieted, and the family and guests withdrew from the grave.

Mementos

Joel Benedict Erhardt, a teacher in Upper Jay, traveled to the funeral with ten or twelve companions in an open wagon. Even though one of his ears froze in the intense cold, Erhardt felt it was worth it to hear the "beautiful oration" of Wendell Phillips. After the funeral, Erhardt wanted a memento, so he asked Phillips if he could get a lock of John Brown's hair. "It would be rather a very delicate matter for me to ask for it," explained Erhardt, as he did not know Mrs. Brown. Phillips went into the house and came back with a lock of hair, which he wrapped in some papers and handed to Erhardt.[4]

Later, Erhardt placed the portion of hair in a mat with an India ink portrait of Brown. Underneath these, he placed the papers that the hair came wrapped in—the notes used by Wendell Phillips for his oration at John Brown's funeral. Erhardt framed the arrangement and presented it to the Union League Club of New York.

It was common for locks of hair to be kept as mementos in the 1800s. Before popular photography, hair provided a keepsake (easily accessible and obtainable without any special skill or tools). Because hair does not decay, it was a way to make loved ones immortal. These objects were emblems of love that acted as personal records of family and friends, both living and deceased.

In mid-December of 1859, another lock of John's hair was placed in a gold locket and mailed to black abolitionist William Still of Philadelphia, one of the most active agents of the Underground Railroad. Mary Brown had promised the memento during her visit to Philadelphia, perhaps in part to thank Still for the assistance he gave to escapees of the Harpers Ferry raid. The locket and hair became part of the William Still Collection at the Philadelphia Historical Museum.

Several museums and historical associations added wisps of John Brown's hair and beard to their collections during the decades after his death. Today, his locks still command attention and fetch large sums of money. A recent eBay listing offered five strands of John Brown's hair for $1,500. Perhaps that explains why a janitor at the Historical Society of Pennsylvania stole artifacts, including Brown's rifle and hair. In another incident, someone snipped two inches from Brown's hair on display at the West Virginia State Capitol.

Where did all this hair come from?

Annie Brown said the hair sent to William Still was clipped from John Brown's head on December 3, 1859, one day after his hanging. The undertaker in New York City cut more hair from Brown's head and beard. And when the body arrived home, family members clipped a few locks for friends, such as Joel Erhardt. Other snippets of hair came from a silly lark. During John's last visit home in June, Mary trimmed his hair and beard. Five-year-old Ellen Brown used the clippings to make birds' nests, which she placed in hollow stumps near the house. After her father's death, her sisters Sarah and Annie made her destroy the nests so they could have the hair to offer as mementos.[5]

Mary gave a different sort of memento to neighbor Bill Nye. He helped receive Brown's coffin at the farmhouse and carry it upstairs. When Mary expressed concern about the condition of the body after coming over the rough roads from Westport, Nye made it presentable for viewing. The next day, he helped dig his friend's grave and then attended his funeral. When Nye went back to visit Mary a few days later, she thanked him for his sympathy and kindheartedness by giving him the collar taken from John's neck. Nye gave the collar to his sister for safekeeping, and she "laid it away so carefully" she never found it.[6]

John Brown of North Elba

Elizabethtown Post (hereafter *EP*) editor David Turner summed up Brown's funeral: "Thus was ended the earthly pilgrimage of John Brown of North Elba." Turner was among the many locals at the funeral on December 8. Erhardt and his friends came from Jay; Daniel Braham and Dr. George T. Stevens from Wadhams; and Judge Robert S. Hale, Mr. Hale, Mr. Livingston, Mr. Nicholson, Milo Durand, and Jay Brown from Elizabethtown. Phineas Norton came from Keene, and Bill Nye, the Thompsons, and the Eppses came from North Elba. The press mentioned those names, but undoubtedly, many other black and white neighbors attended the funeral.[7]

What did these Essex County neighbors think about John Brown? Long after his death, when Brown served as a symbol and local celebrity of sorts, everyone in the county had some blurry recollection or tall tale about their old neighbor. Those accounts are tainted by hindsight and often contain exaggerations and impurities. However, after weeding out the unreliable sources, there are articles in old *EP* newspapers, personal testimonials in Adirondack guidebooks, and miscellaneous chitchat in personal letters and diaries that are authentic nuggets—local attitudes about North Elba, John Brown, and his family.

In early June of 1859, an Essex County resident sent a letter to the *EP* and signed it "ob't serv't" (obedient servant). He had attended John Brown's final Sunday service in North Elba and heard about his activities in Kansas and his slave-snatching in Missouri. The obedient servant asserted: "[John Brown] wholly disregards all laws that he does not consider the laws of the Scripture." Neighbor Robert Scott attended the same service and reported that Brown "boldly advocated the doctrine that it was right to kill the slaveholder to liberate the slave." The listeners "revolted at the doctrine," yet Scott considered Brown "a kind and upright man," despite his abolition politics.[8]

After Brown was captured in Harpers Ferry, authorities sought information about Brown and his conspirators from Elizabethtown lawyer Samuel C. Dwyer. He had known John Brown and seen him frequently. Dwyer said the Brown family came to live there to aid in settling "colored persons" whom Gerrit Smith had given "a large tract of Wild land of little value." Most of the blacks left after a short time but Brown, his wife, and children still resided on their farm. The property was not of much value, but Brown always had money, "sometimes in considerable amounts," said Dwyer, though he did not speculate on the source of the funds or provide names of possible conspirators. Instead, Dwyer declared that Brown had no "confidants" in the region beyond his family and their connections. The Brown family "sustained the character of good citizens" apart from John's "Kansas operations and his political views." Regarding them, John Brown was deemed "deranged."[9]

There were no surprises or incriminating statements in Dwyer's letter, yet it received special recognition. Virginia authorities placed it into evidence at Brown's trial and it was preserved and eventually added to the collections of the Historical Society of Pennsylvania.

Accounts in the *EP* confirmed Dwyer's narrative. "A Citizen of North Elba" described Brown as a kind and affectionate husband and father, a "strictly honest" man, supporter of Christianity, and helpful neighbor "who goes in for all general improvements for the good of community." However, the citizen had always differed from Brown regarding political views, particularly his "insane" notions on slavery. Having his son "murdered in cold blood" in Kansas seemed to have turned Brown into "a monomaniac" and led to the Harpers Ferry attack. Even though he said Brown was wrong and committed a "great crime," the citizen found the penalty of death hard to swallow since Brown "in his wild imagination" had good motives.[10]

David Turner of the *EP* held a *slightly* less favorable opinion. He considered Brown "somewhat respected" and "not a bad man," but he called the raid on Harpers Ferry a "miserable and horrid scheme" and an "inglorious and wretched finale to this deluded man's insane schemes of revolt." As a Democrat, Turner believed each state was an independent sovereignty and should determine its position on slavery, however, unlike most Democrats, he opposed slavery "upon principle." Yet, he still despised Republican abolitionists and blamed them for Brown's "ultra views" on slavery. "In an evil hour," declared Turner, "he [Brown] listened to those false men, who love not the Union, who disregard and condemn and . . . would trample upon our glorious Constitution . . . And this is the fruit of his delusion."[11]

Historian Winslow Watson, also an Essex County Democrat, agreed that "the evil influence of others" aroused Brown into committing deeds of violence and treason and "consigned a band of gallant sons to bloody shrouds." Although Watson had not known Brown well, his friends told him that Brown's natural impulses were "honorable and just," and his education and abilities "of a superior order;" but his mind was distorted and his passions inflamed "by a mad delusion." Watson lamented that Brown had turned to "a career of violence" instead of continuing to apply "the intelligence and zeal" he displayed in husbandry.[12]

As president of the Essex County Agriculture Society, Watson had admired Brown's prize-winning livestock at the 1850 county fair. Shortly afterward, Watson wrote a letter asking Brown for more information about his cattle. The reply letter impressed Watson so greatly that he saved it and commented about it in 1859. "[Brown's] letter is written in a strong and vigorous hand," observed Watson, "and by its orthography, accurate punctuation and careful arrangement of paragraphs, evinces far more than ordinary taste and scholarship. I consider it remarkable, not only for its force and precision of the language, for a business letter, and for the distinction of its statements, but equally for its sound sense and honesty of representation." Although several scholars have criticized Brown's spelling and punctuation, here was a prominent Democrat politician and lawyer (in addition to being a historian and agriculturalist) extoling the virtues of John Brown's penmanship.

Unfortunately, Brown had left his farming life, and Watson denounced the course the old man had taken. Still, "the bold and heroic bearing of the man, his inflexible zeal and devotion, and the appalling end of his schemes," wrote Watson, "assert a claim that we scarcely can resist to our pity and commiseration." (Less than nine months later, in accepting a nomination for a political position, Watson referred to John Brown as a "traitor and murderer.")[13]

Watson thought Brown would meet an ignominious death, while fellow Democrat, *EP* editor Turner hoped that would not happen. On November 12, 1859, the *EP* published a formal appeal to the governor of Virginia for the "Pardon, or Commutation of the sentence, of John Brown." The appeal for mercy assured Virginia that "there has been no political sympathy" with Brown and "no ground for bias on our part, in his favor," but asserted that Brown's case did not require "the utmost rigor of the law." Surely, Virginia was not fearful or in any danger, for thousands in the North "would hasten to aid their Southern brethren," if necessary. "Neither the honor or safety of Virginia demand his life as a sacrifice." Brown's failure proved that such schemes were doomed, thus the main motive of punishment (as a warning) did not exist. In a final plea for sympathy, the *EP* appeal noted that death and desolation had already visited Brown's woe-stricken household, and there was "weeping and wailing of widows on the hearth-stones of the desecrated homes."[14]

Not everyone in Essex County agreed with the appeal for mercy. Hard-shelled Democrats believed Brown deserved hanging. "I certainly shall not subscribe to pardon John Brown . . ." wrote a local citizen identified as K. "Why should Brown breathe while dear friends moulder in the grave." He also criticized the *EP* for claiming slavery was a sin; K asserted that the Bible and its teachings "do not condemn relation of master and slave."[15]

On December 2, 1859, K got his way. All the editorials, letters, and appeals made no difference; John Brown was hanged and taken to moulder in the grave. *EP* editor Turner deplored the result, but instead of faulting Governor Wise or Virginia, he continued to blame the abolitionists. He lampooned the local "abolitionists of Keene" who held a meeting in memory of John Brown and resolved to dedicate December 2 "as a day of prayer in all time to come." Turner joked that he did not want to complain about "any movement by which there will be praying in Keene." Then he gave the men a serious scolding for "meddling" politics with "the Cloth." He believed Brown deserved condemnation, not martyrdom. "The Evil Spirit had already been let loose—'Gog and Magog,'" he wrote. "This is a most fearful epoch to this country."[16]

On the whole, in the aftermath of the raid and John Brown's execution, neighbors testified to his character; he was a good husband and father, an honest man, a community-spirited citizen, a firm Christian, and a first-rate farmer and cattle breeder. They did not judge him by his activities in Kansas, Missouri, or Virginia (though they knew about them). Even those who opposed his political views and violent methods did not describe *him* as cruel, dishonest, fanatical, violent, or bloodthirsty, though they deemed his *ideas* regarding slavery to be crazy or deranged. Many of the Essex County citizens acknowledged his actions as crimes, yet believed his motives were good. However, they did not talk of heroism or martyrdom in the way Wendell Phillips and James Miller McKim did. Notably, no one said much of Brown's relationship with the black grantees, except Willis Hodges, the former leader of Blacksville.

Hodges was not present for the funeral since he had moved back to Brooklyn. Instead, he attended the funeral service held for Brown by the black congregation at the Apostolic Baptist Church. Rev. William Hodges (Willis's brother), who served as pastor, said, "John Brown was emphatically a man of God." When the pastor ended his remarks, Willis gave a more personal account—"a glowing eulogy" on the "amicable qualities of the martyr." He talked of the days he spent working with John Brown in establishing "colonies of colored people" in Franklin and Essex counties. Willis concluded: "The character displayed by the old man in Kansas and Virginia, as a hater of oppression and slavery, a lover of justice and mercy, and a man of exact propriety of conduct, was in strict keeping with his life in Northern New York."[17] Here was the voice of a black friend, a radical abolitionist, unabashedly calling John Brown a martyr and praising his care, generosity, and friendship with the black settlers. Hodges regarded Brown's personal character in the Adirondacks, including his antislavery zeal and brotherhood with blacks, to be exemplary. According to the *New York Tribune*, ten of Brown's neighbors—brave men of "Old Essex County"—subscribed to a John Brown fund, thus showing that they also sincerely sympathized with Brown and possessed like-minded views "in relation to Freedom."[18]

The people of North Elba demonstrated that the North was not of one mindset. Varying opinions existed between, and within, political parties, and even within an individual. For example, *EP* editor Turner claimed he opposed slavery, and, on the same page, he published a *happy slave* article. A Virginia slave named York escaped and made his way to Canada, then ten months later voluntarily returned to Virginia and his "old Missus." This act by York was exhibited as evidence that "the poor deluded fugitives" who escaped to the North were worse off than they were in the South, "and many of them anxious to get back."[19]

Furthermore, Turner asserted that "every consideration of economy and public welfare is on the side of manumission."[20] That is, owners would free their slaves if the North would quit harassing them. The hypocrisy of this claim was palpable; instead of moving toward emancipation, some Southern legislators were making efforts to extend slavery westward—and to reopen the international importation of slaves. During the 1850s, the slave population grew by more than 30 percent, from 3,000,000 to 4,000,000. Slavery was not receding, even though many people wanted to believe it was.

In the Lincoln-Douglas debates of 1858, Abraham Lincoln said he had no doubt that emancipation would occur "in God's own time." He did not think it would happen in a day or a year or even two years. "I do not suppose," said Lincoln, "that in the most peaceful way ultimate extinction [of slavery] would occur in less than a hundred years at the least." He was willing to let slavery continue for another one hundred years, as long as it appeared to be moving toward cessation.[21]

Abolitionist Rev. James Freeman Clarke of Boston attacked the untruths often spoken from Southern pulpits. Ministers recited the verses about Abraham having slaves and Paul sending the runaway slave Onesimus back to his master. They used this as proof that it was "no violation of the golden rule to work negroes to death on the rice plantations of South Carolina and the sugar coast of Mississippi." According to Clarke, ten thousand editors, orators, and philosophic professors had been using "statistics, ethnology and anatomy" to prove the same theory. "But here comes old John Brown, believing slavery a sin, and believing it so much as to fling his life away; and in their hearts and souls the reverend and learned arguers feel that they are sophists, with no truth in them."[22] Yet even those who opposed slavery were often willing to tolerate it. They failed to comprehend their responsibility in its perpetuation. Thoreau pronounced the nation guilty of having a "coffle of four millions of slaves" and working to keep them in this condition. From France, writer Victor Hugo foresaw that the hanging of John Brown would be "an irreparable fault." It would create a "fissure" in the Union and "convulse the entire American Democracy."[23]

In contrast, a United States college student recalled, on the day of John Brown's hanging, his history professor declared "the raid and the execution were of no national importance whatever." Another man predicted that "in six months the world will scarcely remember him or his action."[24]

> Already the corpse is changed, under the stone,
> The strong flesh rotten, the bones dropping away.

Cotton will grow next year, in spite of the skull.
Slaves will be slaves next year, in spite of the bones.
Nothing is changed, John Brown, nothing is changed. (Benet, *John Brown's Body*)

Slaveholders tried to convince themselves that nothing had changed. Brown's men came "to liberate the black race," yet the first man they killed was a "respectable free negro" who was running away from them. The slaves freed by the so-called liberators refused to take up arms. Those actions assured many Southerners that slaves were still slaves, and there was no danger.[25]

Southerners had a great fear that Northerners would make a big fuss and hullabaloo with Brown's funeral. Instead, it was a simple affair with "no vast assemblage . . . no pompous parade; no gorgeous processions." The *New York Daily Tribune* called attention "to the perfect propriety and good taste with which the friends of the late John Brown have obeyed his last wishes as to the disposal of his remains."[26]

The funeral service conducted by Unitarian minister Rev. Joshua Young of Burlington, Vermont, was also quite simple and spur-of-the-moment. However, upon returning to Burlington and delivering his usual Sunday sermon, he sensed "a sort of sea-turn had set in and a chilling mist hung on the air." The *Burlington Sentinel* criticized Young's motives and principles in speaking the words of Paul, "over the grave of a *felon*," and applying them to the "blood-marked *corpse* of one of the most noted brutal murderers of the present age." Supposedly, Young had brought shame upon himself, embarrassment upon his friends, and reproach upon the church of which he was pastor. Some parishioners exited and joined another church. Soon, widespread public rebuke began; Young was called "an anarchist," "a traitor," "an infidel," "a blasphemer," and a "vile associate of Garrison and Phillips." Even honorable men of Vermont suggested that they would not cry at the sight of Young "dangling at the end of a rope from the highest tree on the common, swinging and twisting in the wind."[27]

The funeral of John Brown transformed the beloved pastor into a social outcast. It had "threatened *literally* to shut the door of the church against me," Young wrote to the Anti-Slavery Society. He supposed they might be surprised to hear that from "a voice from the Green Mountains," but the old thinking had not yet passed. "Was there ever an iniquity like the white man's oppression of the black!"[28]

Brown's corpse lay in the frozen ground of North Elba, and it seemed like nothing had changed. Not even in Vermont. Yet some things had changed. Brown was a volcano beneath the snow. His words trumpeted and echoed from the mountainsides. His enemies had allowed him to use his potent pen to preach to them from his jail cell. "He could afford to lose his Sharps rifles," said Henry David Thoreau, "while he retained his faculty of speech, a Sharps rifle of infinitely surer and longer range."

> Where is our professor of belles-lettres, or of logic and rhetoric, who can write so well? . . . I do not know of such words, uttered under such circumstances, and so copiously withal, in Roman or English or any history. What a variety of themes he touched on in that short space!
> . . . Literary gentlemen, editors, and critics think that they know how to write, because they have studied grammar and rhetoric; but they are egregiously mistaken. The *art* of composition is as simple as the discharge of a bullet from a rifle, and its masterpieces imply an infinitely greater force behind them.[29]

According to Thoreau, the greatest rule of composition was "to *speak the truth.*" Sheets of a thousand newspapers carried Brown's truth into every hamlet, fireside, and remotest part of the country. According to a *New York Tribune* article by "A Countryman," millions of people read Brown's words and in the heart of each person lived "a higher law"—a law implanted by nature, a law higher than "the law of Virginia or of Congress," a law of humanity. He predicted that Wise's execution of John Brown would bring slave emancipation in America "fifty years sooner than if John Brown had not perished on the gallows."[30]

President James Buchanan refused to speak of the details of Harpers Ferry in his State of the Union address to Congress on December 19. However, he did express fear of "the demon spirit of sectional hatred and strife" that might cause open warfare. "Let me implore my countrymen, North and South, to cultivate the ancient feelings of mutual forbearance and good-will toward each other." The president attempted to play peacemaker by promoting the premise that there was no need for a national conflict over slavery. If the slaveholding states had not been "ruthlessly assailed by the Abolitionists," some of the Southern states would have discussed emancipation and proceeded in that direction. This was a convenient spin for politicians; the problem was abolition, not slavery.[31]

Abraham Lincoln had a slightly different opinion. "Old John Brown has just been executed for treason against the state. We cannot object," said

Lincoln on December 3, 1859, "even though he agreed with us in thinking slavery wrong. That cannot excuse violence, bloodshed, and treason. It could avail him nothing that he might think himself right." Regarding those who threatened to break up the Union if a Republican was elected president, Lincoln said, "it will be our duty to deal with you as old John Brown has been dealt with."[32]

Something had changed.

In December of 1859, Lincoln and Buchanan already foresaw an impending crisis as a consequence of the Harpers Ferry rebellion, John Brown's execution, and reactions in the North and South. When he spoke in Elizabethtown before Brown's burial, Wendell Phillips called it "the entering wedge" that would split the Union. David Turner of the *EP* felt the tremor, too. "We fear that more progress has been made in disunion by this unfortunate business than by any other event that has ever happened to this nation." In the next week's editorial, Turner claimed that freeing the slaves would bring "incalculable dangers" such as "murder, arson, robbery, rape and torture, universal death and desolation" to men, women, and children of the Southern states. It could lead to the "annihilation of both races" or produce "anarchy and national hatred" and "dissolve this Union."[33]

Remarkably, before the end of December 1859, this editor of a small-town newspaper foresaw what was coming. He realized that the citizens of Essex County knew Brown's personal character, but people in the South saw him only as their "bitter and determined enemy." South Carolina had already proposed the idea of a Southern Confederacy and Turner feared other states would be ready to join her. He advocated for "patriotism and good faith" and for an end to fanaticism and sectionalism and "the machinery of politics." Otherwise, "the splendid legacy of our brave and wise fathers" would come to nothing. Our glory would become a mockery, and "the prosperous and happy self-government of a great people be forever buried in our miserable end."[34]

Instead of trying to calm the crisis, other slavery sympathizers in the North drove the wedge harder and deeper. Charles O'Conor, Esq., head of the New York State Bar, not only believed slavery was ordained by nature and "not unjust," but also said it was the constitutional duty of the North to aid in maintaining and extending slavery. O'Conor claimed that if slave owners were not allowed to continue their "traditions," the country would split. The North would lose the grave of George Washington to Virginia, and the abolitionists would try to comfort people with the grave of John Brown.[35]

"Shall we erect a monument in North Elba among the wilds of the interior," asked O'Conor, "and make pilgrimages there to console us for the loss [of the tomb of Washington]?"

"No," he said.

The ghost of John Brown haunted his enemies; his grave had turned into an icon, a national symbol. Yet it remained uncertain whether "this new sepulcher" would eventually be honored or condemned. Again, in Essex County, the *EP* editor decided to tread lightly. Brown's supporters would likely make his tomb "the shrine to which the friends of liberty will make pilgrimages." On the other hand, "the darkest obloquy" might settle upon his memory, "and all good men condemn him." The editor concluded that the final judgment would be made, not by man, but by a "higher tribunal."[36]

Would the higher law of God be the final judgment? Or would the tribunal of Man (that is, the ballot box and the press) judge John Brown?

Even though North Elba was majority Republican, the Democratic candidates won many of the local elections in the spring of 1860. According to a witness, the ballot box had been overwhelmed with Democratic votes by "outsiders from lumber jobs" armed with "slung shots, which were exhibited, and flourished with threatening aspect." It was largely the "intoxicating drinks, bulleyism, and border ruffianism" that won the elections. The witness said he had never observed in Kansas "a more perfect specimen of such power" than he had seen in North Elba. "As in Kansas, so in North Elba," he declared.[37]

The win by Milote Baker for North Elba Supervisor was especially satisfying for the Democrats because they won by a wide margin (51 to 29). The win was even more glorious because they had defeated John Thompson, whose two brothers had joined John Brown and killed in the raid. The Democrats claimed they had crushed "John Brown Republicanism" and shouted, "Six cheers and a tiger for the democracy of North Elba!"[38]

The national press grabbed hold of the election results favoring Democrats in North Elba and throughout Essex County. Newspapers from Tennessee, Louisiana, and Ohio concluded, "Brown's neighbors do not approve of that [Harpers Ferry] raid."[39]

Political tensions in North Elba had escalated and some residents expressed their disapproval of the Browns. A neighbor claimed that Henry Thompson and two of the Browns came to a town meeting with knives open and ready to use. "The trouble at Harper's Ferry is nothing more than could have been expected," wrote the neighbor, "for wherever they are there is trouble." John Brown always meddled in other people's affairs and was "a brute" and "an old heathen." After Kansas, he thought he could "conquer the whole world," so he went to Harpers Ferry and committed an "outrageous act." This North Elba neighbor believed John Brown got what he deserved. "Gov. Wise did nobly and manfully. . . . If men will not obey the laws of our land, let them abide the consequence." The writer felt proud to mention "Old Virginia" and proud to have relatives who lived there.[40]

While abolitionists often called Mary Brown a noble woman, the neighbor considered her "an ignorant, superstitious, weak minded woman" who wanted "nothing to do with any one that does not think just as she does." According to the writer, few people in North Elba sympathized with the Browns; "indifference was manifested by their neighbors."

Chapter 11

Suffering, Stone Inscriptions, and School

> Belonging to the race your dear husband reached forth his hand to assist, I need not tell you that my sympathies are with you. I thank you for the brave words you have spoken. A republic that produces such a wife and mother may hope for better days. . . . Enclosed I send you a few dollars as a token of my gratitude, reverence and love.
>
> —Frances E. Watkins (Harper) to
> Mary Brown, November 14, 1859

Three weeks following John Brown's funeral, the young son of John Brown Jr. slipped at his Ohio home and broke his leg in three places. John Jr. summed up the situation, writing, "It does seem as if misfortunes never come single."[1]

Troubles also tumbled into Mary Brown's New York household two, three, or more at a time. The ordeal of bringing John's remains to North Elba left Mary in grief and poor health. Other women at the farm became ill, too, leaving seventeen-year-old Martha Brewster Brown to manage all the housekeeping as she also dealt with pregnancy and the loss of her husband and friends. Despite her misfortunes, Martha held onto one hope—that she might give birth to a living child. Her duty as mother to Oliver's baby would force her to find the strength to carry on. But if the infant died, "I shall die too," she said, "as I shall have nothing to live for, then."[2]

Sixteen-year-old Annie Brown understood Martha's feelings; she, too, had gone to Maryland and knew the men from the Kennedy Farm.

While people praised the two girls for "the honor and glory" of the work they did for the cause, it did not ease their suffering. "[It] did not fill the aching void that was left in my heart after losing so many loved ones and friends," said Annie.

The family also worried about Owen Brown, who had managed to escape Harpers Ferry. Early in November, they heard that "one whose name begins with a round O" was safe. A few weeks later, Owen sent a letter telling his family that he and fellow raider Charles Tidd were in the care of George Delamater (Owen's cousin) in Crawford County, Pennsylvania. But the Browns did not know Owen's recent whereabouts. "*One* is wandering somewhere," wrote Ruth in January 1860, "and our anxiety for him is very great."[3]

Mary Brown was busy managing the farm and household matters, in addition to writing letters. A lot of letters. The family received twenty-six letters a week, so they had plenty of responses to write. People throughout the country, especially black citizens, wrote to the family and sent money to Mary, her young daughters, and those made widows by the Harpers Ferry affair.

Contributions from the black citizens of Philadelphia totaled $100 (the equivalent of about $4,000 today). New Haven sent $12.75. Detroit sent $25, "not as an act of charity, but as a heartfelt offering of gratitude from those for whose cause you are now so sadly bereaved." A sum of $16 came from Columbus, Ohio, which had been collected at a meeting "to offer up prayers and supplications to the Almighty" on the day of Brown's execution. Black friends in Boston sent $59 as a token of their love for the great hero and "in behalf of the slaves." Five black women in Elmira, New York, held a festival and gathered $30. "If for our sake his family must lose a husband and father, we cannot help doing our little share in caring for them."[4]

Frances E. Watkins (Harper) sent a few dollars along with words of sympathy. "May God, our own God, sustain you in the hour of trial," wrote Watkins. "If there is one thing on earth I can do for you or yours, let me be apprized."[5] The black community on the whole evidenced great support for John Brown and sympathy for his family.

Mary Brown wrote many thank-you letters expressing her gratitude for the compassion and benevolence given to "the widow and fatherless." She sent thanks "to all lovers of equal rights" in Detroit, who had remembered her family. As characteristic of Mary, she said they did not need much of worldly goods, as "contentment with Godliness is great gain." In addition to

Figure 11.1. Abolitionist, suffragist, poet, speaker, and writer Frances Ellen Watkins Harper, circa 1890s. *Source:* Library of Congress. Public domain.

aid sent directly to Mary, James Miller McKim gathered funds in Philadelphia and James Redpath raised funds by authoring a book. Proceeds from his 400-page biography, *The Public Life of Captain John Brown*, were to be distributed equally between the four widows: Mary Brown, Belle Brown, Martha Brown, and Mary Thompson. Aid came from so many sources, each with special stipulations, that Mary asked Wendell Phillips to take charge of her money affairs.[6]

There was also concern that the other raiders' widows, children, and mothers should not be overlooked, especially the families of the black men. Annie sent the names and addresses of some of the raiders' families to Higginson, so he could aid them. Regarding Dangerfield Newby, she explained that his wife and nine children were the property of some gentleman in Virginia. "Oh! A free country this is," Annie commented sarcastically, "where cradle robbers can take men and *murder* them for doing right."[7]

Following John Brown's hanging on December 2, four raiders were hanged on December 16, 1859. The white men, Edwin Coppoc and John Cook, were hanged separately from the black men, John Copeland and Shields Green. On the way to the gallows, Copeland said, "If I am dying for Freedom, I could not die for a better cause—I had rather die than be a Slave!"[8]

Two prisoners remained in jail, Aaron Stevens and Albert Hazlett, and friends feared they would meet the same fate as the others. When Higginson asked for permission to use some of Mary's funds to free the jailed raiders, Annie replied that her mother approved of using the money for that purpose because the men deserved to be set free. Unfortunately, the escape failed, and Hazlett and Stevens were hanged on March 16, 1860.

The Old Stone Marker

In addition to other tasks, Mary Brown had to deal with her husband's grave marker. The day before his hanging, John Brown wrote the wording for new inscriptions for himself, Watson, and Oliver to be placed on the family stone. He loved the old stone for its age and homeliness and imagined it as a memorial for generation after generation to look upon and remember their ancestors and their fight for liberty. He believed that in a hundred years, it would be "a great curiosity."[9] If he only knew.

The stone is an instigator of oodles of opinions and mountains of misperceptions. People generally call it John Brown's tombstone, but that does not tell even half of the story. The inscription names two John Browns and three other members of the Brown family, thus commemorating a total of five men who died for "adherence to the cause of freedom." People with puzzled faces try to figure out the relationship of the two John Browns, the correlation of names to graves, and the reason for three styles of lettering.

The long history of the stone begins in 1776. It originally stood in a cemetery at Canton, Connecticut, as a memorial to John's grandfather, Capt. John Brown, who served as an officer during the American Revolution. He died of illness at a Continental Army camp near New York City, and his body was never recovered, so the family erected the memorial stone at the cemetery in Canton. When Capt. Brown's widow died in 1831, the family set aside the stone and placed a larger headstone for the couple.

During a visit to Canton, Connecticut, in 1857, John Brown saw the unused marker and noticed that Capt. Brown had died—almost to the day—eighty years before the death of his great-grandson Frederick Brown in Kansas. It seemed fitting for the two men to share a memorial stone; both having died for the cause of freedom and neither being buried in a family graveyard. John shipped the eighty-year-old stone to Westport, New York. James Allen, owner of the steamboat wharf, remembered its arrival and its presence in the freight room for a long time. At some point, John composed an inscription in memory of his son Frederick and arranged to have it carved on the back of the stone.

When John left for Kansas in 1857, he told Mary that if he did not survive, he wanted the plain stone—and "no other monument"—used to mark his grave. Since John survived the Kansas war, he did not need the grave marker at that time. Good thing, because Mary had not even brought the stone to the farm. John wrote to her twice in 1858, and again in May of 1859, reminding her to retrieve it from Westport and to "have the stone handled very carefully."[10] Later that year, the tombstone was finally hauled to the farm.

When Thomas Wentworth Higginson visited in late October, he saw it and noted: "There is one decoration which at once takes the eye"—the "old, mossy, time-worn tombstone" leaning against the house. Higginson imagined how the early morning light must gild the stone and the red reflection of sunset glow back on it. "Its silent appeal has perpetually strengthened and sanctified that home." Yet Higginson also felt the location of the stone was strange, not set in the ground at the head of a grave but resting against the house "as if its time were either past or not yet come."[11]

Both were true. It had a past duty as a memorial, bearing the names of Capt. Brown and Frederick (both dead but neither buried at the farm). It also had a forthcoming function for John, Watson, and Oliver. For the young men, it would serve as a memorial stone and later, in 1882 and 1899, as a gravestone (when their bodies were recovered and buried at the farm). It became a grave marker for John in 1860.

There was no time to have the stone inscribed before John's funeral. A few weeks later, Mary Brown met marble cutter Benjamin Albert Barrett at an oyster supper in Wadhams (Falls) and hired him to come to the farm and cut the inscriptions. When he arrived in early January of 1860, it was so cold he brought the stone into the kitchen to work on it. "The Brown family—what was left of it—watched me work all the time," Barrett said. The women excelled as hosts and cooks. "Never had better eating in my life." However, he found no beauties among them. "As a whole, I never saw a more ugly lot of women, but they were kind in disposition and that covered a multitude of shortcomings."[12]

Since there was no verse on the stone, Mary wanted to add one, but after Barrett measured the space for the names and dates, there was no room for additional text. On the front side, below the original inscription, Barrett added the records of John and Oliver. On the back side, below Frederick's inscription, he placed Watson's record. Barrett completed the work in a week, but the stone monument could not be set into the frozen ground. When the spring thaw came, the stone was placed at the head of John Brown's grave. For some people, the slab and its five inscriptions were a puzzle. For others, granite chips from the stone were treasured keepsakes. A "great curiosity," as John had predicted.

Schooling for Annie and Sarah

Besides dealing with the tombstone and correspondences of sympathy and aid, Mary Brown mulled over a batch of letters about schooling arrangements for Annie and Sarah. Rebecca Spring had broached the subject to John Brown back in early November when she visited him in jail. Spring wanted the girls to attend her school, the prestigious Eagleswood School in Perth Amboy, New Jersey, whose teachers included Theodore Weld, Angelina (Grimke) Weld, and Sarah Grimke. Despite Spring's plea, John said the decision would be made by their mother.

Although he left the choice to Mary, John relayed to her that the girls should have "a very plain but perfectly practical education." He wanted them trained to handle business transactions and develop good business habits, thus preparing them "to be useful, though poor, and to meet the stern realities of life with a good grace." From his experiences and observations, he believed early training of the plain, practical kind was preferable to one of the "more popular and fashionable" kind. He had always felt that "the music of the broom, washtub, needle, Spindle, loom, axe, scythe, hoe, flail, etc." should be learned before the piano. "I put them in that order as most conducive to health of body and mind."[13]

Mrs. Spring told Mary that she had already raised $350 for Annie and Sarah to attend Eagleswood School. However, other people made offers for Mary to consider. Edwin Bullard proposed enrollment at a new school in Ballston, New York. Boston abolitionists wanted the girls to go to Franklin Sanborn's school in Concord, Massachusetts. Strangest of all, a man in Winchendon, Massachusetts, offered to adopt one of the girls and teach her telegraphy. To encourage Mary to choose Eagleswood, Mr. and Mrs. Spring proposed purchasing a nearby property for $5,000 to $6,000 for the Brown family. The house would allow the girls to live at home rather than board at school. Mr. Spring felt the climate in New Jersey would be much better than the cold Adirondacks. He saw no value in the North Elba farm and thought it should be given away.[14]

Friends in Concord and Boston were not happy about the girls going to Mrs. Spring's school. Wendell Phillips was particularly irate and said he would never consent to sending either of the Brown girls to Eagleswood. Soon, Boston abolitionist George Stearns made a visit to North Elba to promote the merits of Sanborn's school. Having been one of John Brown's most intimate friends and wealthy supporters, Stearns succeeded in persuading Mary to send the girls to Concord. It also helped that Sanborn provided free tuition and Stearns paid for room and board in a private house.

Just days after Stearns's visit to North Elba, Salmon's wife, Abbie, gave birth to a daughter, whom the couple named Cora. Another baby girl arrived within three weeks. On February 3, 1860, Oliver Brown's widow, Martha, gave birth to a little girl as pretty as a baby doll. Martha named her Olive, in memory of Oliver.

Two days later, Franklin Sanborn stopped at the Brown's house to make schooling arrangements for Annie and Sarah. (He was on his way to Canada to escape seizure by authorities seeking to interrogate him regarding Harpers Ferry.) Sanborn arrived during a snowstorm and from his bed in the loft, he heard the storm murmuring and moaning all night. In the morning, he found snow had sifted through the roof and made two small snowdrifts, one on his coverlet and one on the floor near the bed. After he descended from the frosty loft, Sanborn learned the sad news. During the night, baby Olive passed away.

Martha tried to be brave and did not shed a tear until Annie held the infant's lifeless body at her bedside. A few great teardrops fell from Martha's eyes onto the babe's pale, little face as she kissed her goodbye. Olive was laid to rest in the North Elba Cemetery and her tombstone inscribed:

> Olive, daughter of O. and M. E. Brown,
> Died Feb. 5th, 1860, Aged three days.
> The lamb of Jesus rests
> In his kind arms of love;
> The flower that drooped upon the breast
> Hath fairer bloomed above.

Martha grieved so terribly that she came down with a raging fever. Mary cared for her day and night, leaving her side just once, in mid-February, to accompany Annie and Sarah to Vergennes, Vermont, on their way to school in Concord. Despite Mary's attentive nursing, Martha declined in health and expressed a willingness to leave this world of sorrow to be reunited with her baby and her husband. Martha died on March 2, 1860, and was buried in the North Elba Cemetery. Once again, the Browns had to drink deep from the bitter cup. They missed Martha dearly and considered her a heroine of the Harpers Ferry tragedy.

Annie was miserable, even before she knew of Martha's death. She never had a desire to go to school but had obeyed her mother's wishes and gone to Concord. Sometimes she would lock herself in her room "and lay and roll on the floor in the agony of a tearless grief for hours at a time." Annie said, "My memory was effected so I could not commit school books. The harder I studied the less I seemed to know." Her teachers did not understand that she still suffered from the terrible shock of Harpers Ferry.[15]

In early April, she left school and returned to North Elba, bringing along some plants from Mrs. Stearns's greenhouse. Annie treasured the plants and cared for them, but they wilted. Ruth felt sorry for Annie and thought, "Ah, is such to be her fate? Are these once beautiful plants, now withered and dead, emblematic?"[16] To Ruth's surprise, new sprouts grew, and the plants lived, helping to draw Annie's mind away from her troubles.

Sarah Brown remained at Sanborn's school and came to know her father's friends and Concord's renowned citizens such as Ralph Waldo Emerson, Henry David Thoreau, Nathaniel Hawthorne, and Amos Bronson Alcott. In late May of 1860, Mary Brown, Belle, and baby Freddy visited Concord, and the Alcott family held a tea in their honor. The notoriety of the Brown family was evidenced by forty people arriving instead of the twenty invitees. According to Louisa May Alcott, the little meal turned into a "tea fight." The uninvited guests started to "eat fast and drink like sponges," so Louisa quickly filled a big plate with food, made two cups of tea "strong enough for a dozen," and handed them to Emerson and her uncle, Samuel May. She then served the rest of the invited guests and let the uninvited wait and *"moan* for tea."[17]

Amid the mayhem, the guest of honor, Mary Brown, sat silent and calm. Louisa described her as a tall, plain, stout woman having "a natural dignity that showed she was something better than a 'lady,' though she *did* drink out of her saucer and used the plainest speech."

Louisa said Belle Brown's nine-month-old son, Freddy, acted like a little king and had serious eyes that looked about as if saying: "I am a Brown! Are these friends or enemies?" Louisa and her allies kissed him "as if he were a little saint" and felt honored when he sucked their fingers or walked on them "with his honest little red shoes."

Figure 11.2. Isabelle (Belle) Thompson Brown, wife of Watson, with their son Freddy, circa 1860. *Source:* Ella Thompson Towne Scrapbook, the Huntington Library, San Marino, California. Used with permission.

As for Freddy's mother, her face appeared "heartbroken . . . a whole Harpers Ferry tragedy in a look." When Louisa's mother read aloud a letter telling news of a wedding, the widowed Belle sat with tears rolling down her face. Freddy laughed and crowed at her feet as if there was not an ounce of trouble in the world.

The Brown women and children had been thrust into the national spotlight, and the soon-to-be famous author Louisa May Alcott was there to observe it: the noble antics of young Freddy and the dignity and calm heartache of the Brown women, but also, Mary's uncouthness in sipping from her saucer and the plainness of the women's looks and speech.

People of a more urban society often characterized the Brown women as lacking sophistication, particularly in their mannerisms and fashions. The previous winter, when Annie and Sarah arrived for school, women in Concord immediately supplied them with new dresses. Remarks about Mary's shabby dress were made by Boston ladies when she visited in 1859, and when Mrs. Spring purchased a fine suit for John to be buried in, Mary made her return it for a plainer brown suit. She insisted that John would not want money wasted on clothing of no use. On the same principle, Mary made dresses last as long as possible, so funds could be used to help the cause of freedom.

The simple, frugal lifestyle in North Elba was so stark in contrast to society's standard that people often considered the Browns impoverished and destitute. Even activities such as berry picking morphed into pitiable tasks. Thomas Higginson reported that one winter the family had no money for postage, "except a tiny treasury which the younger girls had earned" by picking and selling berries during the summer. Although he presented the task as forced on the children, berry picking was part of Adirondack culture, a festive tradition practiced by youths, rich and poor. The same was true of mapling, fishing, and hunting.[18]

Yet Higginson stuck with the poverty narrative. "It is too cold to raise corn there; they can scarcely, in the most favorable seasons, obtain a few ears for roasting." The family had enough to eat, he said, "namely, bread and potatoes, pork and mutton—not any great abundance of these, but ordinarily enough." They also had enough to wear, "at least of woolen clothing," spun from sheep wool. But they almost never had anything extra to sell from the farm, so money was scarce. Higginson emphasized that he did not mean they had "no superfluous cash to go shopping with," he meant they had almost none. He recalled one young widow was spoken of as "not totally and absolutely destitute," because her husband had left her five sheep. At $2 per head, her estate amounted to $10.

Mary Brown also found $10 to be a hefty sum of money. An impending tax bill of $8 to $10 was a "formidable" amount and caused her great anxiety. She had saved money for the tax, but then loaned it to a poor black woman, with little hope of repayment. Such acts of generosity frequently left the Browns in hardship, but duty to those in need overruled personal necessity. While Higginson created an impression of financial distress (perhaps in part to help raise funds for the Browns), he also noted that their poverty was "the noble result of years of self-devotion." Prior to moving to the Adirondacks, John Brown praised his wife, Mary, for being the sharer of his "poverty, trials, discredit, and sore afflictions," as well as the "comfort and seeming prosperity" that had come to him. Frederick Douglass described the Brown's home in Springfield, Massachusetts, as plain, outside and inside, as "might have pleased a Spartan." In the Brown house, "stern truth and solid purpose breathed in all its arrangements."[19]

It was the same with all the comforts of life: fine clothes, fancy food, and elegant furniture. The Browns did not strive for money or glory. It was always *duty* with them. They shored up their households and lived by the Golden Rule and the Bible. How could they enjoy luxury while others suffered under the lash?

During her visit to Concord, Mary Brown attended the New England Anti-Slavery Convention in Boston and mingled with prominent abolitionists such as Wendell Phillips, Maria W. Chapman, Lydia Maria Child, Abby Kelley Foster, Aaron M. Powell, Samuel May Jr., and Henry C. Wright. Just before adjourning the morning session, William Lloyd Garrison announced that John Brown attended the convention the previous year and his widow, "truly a noble woman," was on the platform this year. The mention of Mary Brown's presence "induced a general spontaneous expression of the deep sympathy felt for her and her children."[20]

Mary served her duty as John Brown's proxy but made no address to the audience. As a woman of few words, she rarely spoke in public. Such actions (or lack of actions) dumbfounded many observers and historians, thus, they often described Mary as something far from noble. "Mary Brown was simply a peasant woman who, never having had anything but children—and plenty of them—had no reason to expect much," wrote David Karsner in 1934. "If Brown taught her that it was the lot of woman to keep pregnant, to keep the kettles bright, and the home fires burning, then Mary Brown learned her lessons very well. Perhaps your modern woman will resent her because she did not fly into a divorce court."[21]

History often tried to force Mary into established molds—impoverished, dim-witted, obedient wife or acclaimed, sophisticated reformer.

However, she did not fit any stereotype, nor did she meet the expectations of abolitionists or critics. In her letters, public statements, and actions, Mary demonstrated that she was a loyal wife and loving mother imbued with Christian faith and abolitionist values. Her sudden thrust from a plain, hardworking pioneer into public celebrity placed her into a role for which there was no script.

Mary spoke and acted when necessary. Was it imperative for her to add to her husband's noble words? John Brown still spoke, and so did plenty of abolitionists. On July 4, 1860, Rev. Luther Lee stood atop the boulder above the grave of John Brown and said the following:

> He, being dead, yet speaketh: his death speaks, his blood speaks, and there goes forth a voice from his grave and from this rock that overhangs it; and that voice, from year to year, shall:
>
> Go forth with a trumpet's sound,
> And tell to the nations round,—
> On the hills which our heroes trod,
> In the shrines of the saints of God,
> In the ruler's hall and the captive's prison,
> That the slumber is broken, the sleepers are risen;
> That the day of the scourge and the fetter is o'er,
> And earth feels the tread of her freedom once more.[22]

Fourth of July

Old-timers say there are only two seasons in the Adirondacks: winter and Fourth of July. The funeral of John Brown was in the winter season when snow, rain, and ice made travel conditions unpredictable. Few people from outside the region traveled to North Elba for the burial service. Abolitionists hoped to hold a larger event during the other Adirondack season. They soon announced plans for a "great meeting" at the John Brown gravesite on July 4, 1860. Specifically, Ruth said the meeting would be held "on and around" the big rock, and if her brothers Jason and John Jr. attended, they would "stand on that rock."[23] Evidently, climbing to the top of the boulder was a familiar act for the Brown children. On the Fourth of July, it became a ceremonial tradition to stand on the ancient rostrum overlooking Brown's grave and deliver words to awaken, incite, and uplift audiences.

Figure 11.3. Old Family Tombstone on John Brown's Grave. The stone was inscribed and placed in early 1860. Wooden steps (left) used for scaling the big rock (served as pulpit for speakers). *Source:* Sketch from Edwin R. Wallace, *Descriptive Guide to the Adirondacks* (New York: American News Company, 1875). Public domain.

Summer weather wasn't the only consideration in choosing the date. July 4 marked the anniversary of American independence as established by the Declaration of Independence, which held great significance for abolitionists. On that day, they reaffirmed the self-evident truths set forth by the nation's forefathers: "that all men are created equal, that they are endowed by their Creator with certain unalienable rights; that among these are life, liberty, and the pursuit of happiness." Abolitionists also pointed to the faults of those truths and decreed slavery to be "in utter disregard and violation" of those natural, unalienable rights. They advocated a duty to oppose tyranny and argued for a rebirth of independence. In originally planning the raid on Harpers Ferry for July 4 and preparing the "Provisional Constitution" and "Declaration of Liberty," John Brown attempted that rebirth. He tried to change the meaning of July 4, to declare and enact independence and equality for all.

July 4 was not a day of celebration for enslaved blacks and free blacks; it was a day of protest against the hypocrisy of slavery existing within the republic. In 1852, Frederick Douglass said, "Your celebration is a sham. . . . a thin veil to cover up crimes which would disgrace a nation of savages. There is not a nation on the earth guilty of practices more shocking and bloody than are the people of the United States, at this very hour."[24]

Douglass spoke those words to a crowd of six hundred people in his hometown of Rochester, New York, in his famous speech "What to the Slave Is the Fourth of July?" He said that more than any other day of the year, July 4 revealed the "gross injustice and cruelty" of slavery. The sounds of whites rejoicing for "liberty and equality" were empty and heartless. "This Fourth of July is yours, not mine. You may rejoice, I must mourn." "You profess to believe, 'that, of one blood, God made all nations of men to dwell on the face of all the earth,' and hath commanded all men everywhere to love one another; yet you notoriously hate (and glory in your hatred) all men whose skins are not colored like your own." Despite the inconsistencies and hypocrisies that America was built on, Douglass remained hopeful. He believed the Declaration of Independence embodied the great principles of freedom and justice, and the Constitution was "a glorious Liberty document," *if* it was interpreted as it ought to be interpreted. "The conscience of the nation must be roused," said Douglass.

In 1852, he had called for "the storm, the whirlwind, and the earthquake" to expose the hypocrisy and startle the nation. Yet, in 1859, he did not join Brown at Harpers Ferry, deeming the plan to be doomed. Despite the outcome, Douglass admired the efforts of Brown and his brave associates for they had done more "to upset the logic and shake the security of slavery, than all other efforts in that direction for twenty years." Perhaps the slaves learned more from "the eight-and-forty hours of *John Brown's school in the mountains* of Virginia" than a half century could have taught them otherwise.[25]

Five black men helped teach that lesson; only one of them survived. Osborne Anderson was born a free black in Pennsylvania in 1830, and later attended Oberlin College in Ohio. At the age of twenty, he moved to Chatham, Ontario, Canada. He became a printer and met John Brown at the Chatham Convention of 1858. He joined Brown's army and was glad to come out of Harpers Ferry alive, but being an escaped raider with a price on his head was horrific. Old friends turned him away and his own father

Figure 11.4. Osborne Perry Anderson, fought at Harpers Ferry and escaped. *Source:* New York Public Library. Public domain.

rejected him. Some threatened his arrest, which forced him into hiding under a stairway for weeks. Feeling friendless and alone, he went to North Elba to visit John Brown's last resting place in late June of 1860.

Annie Brown looked out the farmhouse window at a tall, handsome black man weeping and praying at her father's grave. Thinking she might know him, she went outside and immediately recognized him as Osborne Anderson, one of her "brothers" from the Kennedy farm. After chatting with Annie, Anderson said, "God bless you, you dear girl" and started to

Suffering, Stone Inscriptions, and School | 185

leave. Annie stopped him and insisted that he meet her mother and Watson's son, Freddy.[26]

"I might not be welcome," Anderson said. "I have seen you and the Captain's grave, and now I'll go." Annie assured him that he was welcome in the Browns' home, and the family convinced him to stay for a few days, through the Fourth of July.

Chapter 12

July Fourth at North Elba

THE AMERICAN INSURRECTIONS. The believers in the doctrines of the Declaration of Independence, and of that Method of proclaiming them inaugurated by Gen. Warren at Bunker Hill, and continued by Capt. Brown at Harpers Ferry, are requested to meet at NORTH ELBA, Essex Co., N.Y., on the FOURTH OF JULY next, to re-affirm, over the grave of THE MARTYR OF VIRGINIA, their unabated faith in the truth of these principles, and the wisdom of that time-honored policy.

—*Liberator*, June 29, 1860

The July 4, 1860, celebration was the first major memorial event held at the John Brown Farm. As the day approached, few of the advertised speakers had yet accepted the invitation to attend. Even James Redpath, the major promoter, was unable to be there. Ruth Brown Thompson hoped the replies of her brothers would be more affirmative. Though visiting the old homestead might make them miss "the dear ones that are departed," Ruth deeply longed for their "scattered and broken family" to be reunited.[1]

Organizers intended to use the event to raise funds for the Brown family but abandoned the plan when John Jr. respectfully protested it "as derogating from the well-earned traditional reputation of the family for entire disinterestedness." Some family members accepted financial aid to pay their expenses to attend the event. Thus, the Brown family was able to reunite.[2]

The summer season definitely made the journey to North Elba doable, even pleasurable. One group of travelers crossed Lake Champlain from

Burlington to Port Kent and then went by stage to Keeseville. They rented an open wagon with a pair of horses and began riding into the "enchanted land of the Adirondacks." After passing through Wilmington, the road cut through the side of a sheer precipice with barely room enough to pass. "Words cannot paint the wild grandeur of the scene." Fifty or a hundred feet below, the river roared. Above, overhanging masses of rock looked ready to fall on someone's head.[3]

Even though it was near sundown when the party reached the John Brown Farm, they immediately visited their hero's grave, "a simple turfed hillock, carefully banked and tended." In the fading sunlight, they read the words on the old gravestone—*murdered for adherence to the cause of freedom*. "How unpretending! how touching! yet how significant the inscription!" remarked one of the guests. "What a commentary!"

On the morning of July 4, the weather was clear and bright, as nearly a thousand people arrived for the celebration. The meeting began with Rev. Nathan Wardner of Wilmington, New York, being chosen president, after which he mounted the rock, called the meeting to order, and made a few introductory remarks. The Declaration of Independence was read, a prayer given, and then the Epps family sang. In repeating their performance from John Brown's funeral, the Epps established another tradition—the singing of John Brown's favorite hymn, "Blow Ye the Trumpet, Blow!" The music stirred and swelled in the summer air until "the listening hills seemed to echo back the strains."

The orator of the day, Rev. Dr. Luther Lee of Chagrin Falls, Ohio, had been a conductor for the Underground Railroad in Syracuse for many years and a prominent lecturer for the New York State Anti-Slavery Society. Notwithstanding his many famous speeches, Dr. Lee said his July 4 address was the oration of his life, "the most radical and, probably, the most able I ever delivered." A reporter summed up the masterful speech: "From exordium to peroration it was one continued chain of solid material. Idea after idea, argument after argument, were presented in a clear, direct, and forcible manner. Nail after nail was driven and clinched just when and where it ought to have been."[4]

Dr. Lee presented, argued, and nailed for nearly two hours. Yet, the entire crowd listened "with marked attention"—except for "a few whining Democrats, who writhed and fretted beneath the well-directed blows of the orator."

After making eloquent statements on the principles of the Declaration of Independence and their application to the institution of slavery, Dr. Lee turned his attention to John Brown. He affirmed the opinions of Brown's neighbors that all evidence declared him a good citizen, a true friend, and an exemplary Christian. "The only charges that have been filed against him in the Court of Public Opinion relate to his public life, commencing in Kansas, and ending at Harpers Ferry," said Dr. Lee. After commenting on the warlike conditions in Kansas, he concluded that Brown used his sword in defense of liberty, "and I thank God today that he drew it not in vain . . . and Kansas became free."[5]

Dr. Lee considered governments that suppressed liberty and denied rights to be "without binding force." They were not sanctioned by God or founded in the law; thus, they had no claim for obedience or support. Dr. Lee admitted that Brown may have erred in his invasion of Virginia regarding timing and manner and circumstances. "But the principle involved, I defend upon the ground of the Declaration of American Independence."

> All men have an inalienable right to liberty; slaves are men, and therefore slaves have an inalienable right to liberty. . . . therefore John Brown had a right to invade Virginia for the purpose of helping the slaves to obtain their liberty. . . . the only fundamental question, on which the whole turns is, have men the right to defend liberty by the sword.
> . . . John Brown had just as good a right to go to Virginia, with the heaven-granted bill of human rights in his hand, and demand the surrender of the bondmen, as Ethan Allen had to go to Ticonderoga and demand the surrender of the fort in the name of the great Jehovah and the Continental Congress; and if the former deserved to be hung for his act, the latter should have been hung for his.
> But Capt. Brown did not succeed. True, and there are at least a few who deeply regret his failure. But success or defeat does not determine or change the right or wrong of the cause. Had Washington and his compatriots failed, they would have been hung as high as John Brown was, and their names would have been sent down to posterity disgraced as traitors and rebels; but it would not have changed their real character, nor altered the justice of their cause. But a better future awaits the name of John Brown; his name goes down as that of a patriot, a hero, a martyr and a saint.

Dr. Lee told the audience to ignore the "fossil divines and politicians" who told them to stay still and be quiet. As lovers of human rights and human liberty, they had a part to play in the battle against slavery. "The rallying cry shall again be, 'Give me liberty, or give me death!'" He concluded with a promise to return to the farm when the day of liberty came. The day when the Declaration of Independence became a practical reality. When the bondman's chains were broken, and liberty proclaimed through all the land and to all the inhabitants. When all of that occurred, and if his heart was still beating, Dr. Lee promised to come back and stand on the rock rostrum. "Then let freedom rally," he said, "and let the freed slave come and wave his unmanacled hands here, and we will raise one long loud hallelujah over the grave of Freedom's first martyr, and the nation shall respond in a loud Amen."

The speech ended with a resounding "Hallelujah!"

When Dr. Lee came down from the rock, he shook hands with members of the Brown family. Upon taking Dr. Lee's hand, one of the sons said, "It electrifies my arm clear up to my shoulder and makes my heart jump to take hold of your hand."[6]

More Letters and Speeches

After the close of the oration, the Epps family sang another hymn. Then Richard Hinton read letters from distinguished speakers who were unable to attend. Franklin Sanborn wrote that he considered the July 4 celebration at North Elba to be the only proper one in the nation. Most people had no right to read the Declaration of Independence, for it held only "glittering generalities" for them. But to the Brown family, "it is the true charter of liberty," to which John Brown "added some marginal notes."[7]

Next came a letter from "a humble representative of the race for whom John Brown died," John Sella Martin, Pastor of the Eleventh Baptist Church in Boston. He lamented that his vows could not be offered with those who carried on the work. "I regret that my tears cannot mingle with yours over his grave. . . . I hope fresh glory will go out and renewed strength be given."

Frederick Douglass also regretted being absent from the assembly, but he knew there was little anyone could do "to add lustre" to Brown's fame.

> His name is covered with a glory so bright and enduring, as to require nothing at our hands to increase or perpetuate it. Only

for our own sake, and that of enslaved and imbruted humanity, need we assemble. To have been acquainted with John Brown, shared his counsels, enjoyed his confidence, and sympathized with the great objects of his life and death, I esteem as among the highest privileges of my life.

In the past, Douglass had opposed the use of violence, now he expressed little hope in ending slavery by peaceful means. Slaveholders would continue to quote the Bible and invoke falsehoods to justify their wrongs. "The only penetrable point of a tyrant is the *fear of death*," wrote Douglass. "The outcry that they make as to the danger of having their *throats cut*, is because they know they deserve to have them *cut*."

A letter from James Redpath continued the theme: "Slavery must be abolished by force." He was done with "advocacy of the *doctrines* of the Declaration;" henceforth, he would regard them as "self-evident truths" that required no argument. It was time to spread information on the "methods of abolition," wrote Redpath, and perhaps even "engage in the work itself."

After reading the letters, Hinton introduced John Brown Jr., "a noble son of a noble sire." John Jr. relayed the family's thanks for the presence of so many friends. His brother Owen came forward, too, and kept the assembly in a roar of laughter with his quaint speech and oddball descriptions. Afterward, someone made a motion to adjourn but Hinton blocked it; he had something more to say.[8]

Hinton pointed out that Brown not only died *for* the black man but also died *with* black men in the form of Lewis Leary, Dangerfield Newby, John Copeland, and Shields Green. A fifth black man, Osborne Anderson, bravely acted his part at Harpers Ferry and escaped. To the surprise of the crowd, Hinton announced that Anderson was present. Though Virginia offered a reward of $1,500 for the return of Anderson, the crowd at the celebration pledged, "we have good revolvers and strong arms, wherewith to defend our friends." Hinton deemed Anderson "worthy to stand on this rock and speak for his race," and called him forward.[9]

Anderson said he had always considered the day to be "a lie and a juggle," but "Thank God, it was no longer so!" Anderson declared that it was the first occasion in his life when he felt that *he* could stand on a Fourth of July platform. He stood on the rock rostrum and looked down at Brown's grave knowing the Declaration of Independence held more than "glittering generalities." Because of John Brown, Anderson had gone to Virginia "not as a mulatto, but as a *man*," and now he wore "the proud mark of manhood."

After Anderson and a few others spoke, the meeting concluded, and the crowd adjourned to a field where Mary Brown provided a hearty meal, at her expense. Admiration and sympathy for the John Brown family flowed forth. "Long may they live in prosperity and peace," wrote a Vermont reporter. "May they live to see that cause triumph for which they have sacrificed a husband, father, and a friend."[10]

When all had feasted, the wagons and carriages came forth and guests turned homeward. There was hope that the words of the day would sink deep into the hearts of the audience, "and may the seed there sown spring up and produce abundant fruit." The metaphor was an echo from Thoreau's famous speech, "A Plea for Captain John Brown," in which he said: "When you plant, or bury, a hero in his field, a crop of heroes is sure to spring up."[11]

One reading by Hinton spread seeds most abundantly. On his way to the meeting, Hinton had been handed a manuscript in Concord, Massachusetts. It came from that "fearless, truthful soul," Henry David Thoreau. The text was fresh from his pen, not a repeat of the plea he made after John Brown's capture or his "Remarks" made on the day of Brown's execution. This was the first public reading of what became famously titled "The Last Days of John Brown."

> John Brown's career for the last six weeks of his life was meteor-like, flashing through the darkness in which we live. I know of nothing so miraculous in our history. . . . For my own part, I commonly attend more to nature than to man, but any affecting human event may blind our eyes to natural objects. I was so absorbed in him as to be surprised whenever I detected the routine of the natural world surviving still, or met persons going about their affairs indifferent. It appeared strange to me. . . .
>
> When a noble deed is done, who is likely to appreciate it? . . .
>
> Editors persevered for a good while in saying that Brown was crazy; but at last they said only that it was "a crazy scheme," and the only evidence brought to prove it was that it cost him his life. . . . They seem to have known nothing about living or dying for a principle. . . .
>
> On the day of his translation, I heard, to be sure, that he was *hung*, but I did not know what that meant; I felt no sorrow on that account; but not for a day or two did I even *hear* that he was *dead*, and not after any number of days shall I believe

it. Of all the men who were said to be my contemporaries, it seemed to me that John Brown was the only one who *had not died*. . . . He is more alive than he ever was. He has earned immortality. He is not confined to North Elba nor to Kansas. He is no longer working in secret. He works in public, and in the clearest light that shines on this land.[12]

The July 4 gathering consisted of more than glorious letters, speeches, and music. The meeting of John Brown supporters also produced meaningful resolutions, written by a committee consisting of Judge W. F. M. Arny of Kansas; Wendell Lansing, editor of the *Press Republican*, of Keeseville, Essex County; and Rev. Lyman Prindle of West Chazy, Clinton County. In the first resolution, the men and women of Essex County extended a hearty welcome to Thaddeus Hyatt, who had withstood incarceration in "a prison and slave pen at Washington City," for refusing to testify before the Committee investigating the Harpers Ferry raid. The second resolution extended a warm greeting to those of the "immortal twenty-one" raiders who survived Harpers Ferry. As if ordained by Providence, five comrades from the Kennedy farm were reunited that day: Osborne Anderson, Annie Brown, Owen Brown, Francis Meriam, and Barclay Coppoc. The last resolution declared a pledge of all attendees—to reaffirm their faith in the principles of Universal Freedom and reiterate their determination to aid slaves "by ALL and EVERY means" to become free. In what manner and at what time actions should take place was left to "each individual conscience."

On July 4, 1860, abolitionists established the North Elba farm as a place of vigilance and Universal Freedom. They also had an opportunity to meet the Brown family. Thaddeus Hyatt remained with the Browns for several days after the July 4 meeting and observed: "It is something to have 'looked into the eyes of John Brown!' It is something to have 'looked into the eyes' of his noble family—illustrious survivors of an illustrious sire!"[13]

As Hyatt wandered about the farm one day, he heard a little boy yell, "I'll stab him!"

The words startled Hyatt and he looked in the yard for the child. He found a grandson of John Brown (the son of John Brown Jr.). Unable to imagine what the young lad was thinking, Hyatt said, "Oh no, my little boy; you wouldn't stab any one, would you?"

With a defiant air, the boy replied: "Yes, I would stab them if they hurt my grandfather!"

Here was the son of the son. Charles Town had not extinguished John Brown. "His fires still live and burn in his descendants, burn in the seething blood of the third generation," said Hyatt. ". . . . Behold, oh! Virginia! The blood of the martyr is already bearing its fruit!"

He concluded, "God and the Adirondacks still stand."

National Election of 1860

Not all Northerners praised the July 4 gathering in North Elba. An article titled "The Fanatics at Their Orgies" mocked the attendees, saying: "All of the Browns, and some of the blacks, were to be on hand." Another account depicted the event as a "sickish and disgusting performance" by white men and "cullud" men, including "one ignoramus [Osborne] Anderson," taking turns on the platform "speculating as to the most effectual method of carrying out the bloody work which their defunct fellow-treasonists had begun."[14]

Even some Essex County citizens criticized their neighbors for endorsing "murder and treason" and desecrating the Fourth of July. They considered John Brown's attack on Harpers Ferry a disgrace to Essex County and the State of New York. Their concern was holding the Union together, so these citizens voiced support for Stephen A. Douglas, the Democratic candidate for president of the United States in the upcoming national election.[15] Part of their criticism of the July 4 gathering was sparked by abolitionist Gerrit Smith's entry into the presidential race.

Despite Smith's release from an insane asylum just six months earlier, attendees of the Anti-Slavery Convention in Boston nominated him as their candidate for president of the United States. In late June, the press referred to his supporters as "insurrectionary abolitionists of the John Brown genus" and expected them to reassemble and endorse Smith at the "grand pow-wow which is to take place over the grave of Old John Brown" on the Fourth of July. That did not happen; there was no mention of Gerrit Smith in accounts of the celebration at North Elba. Even so, the Browns and the July 4 attendees were pulled into political banter—labeled "a mixed up and motley throng of malcontented abolitionists" who held a "pow-wow" over their "departed chieftain."[16]

The 1860 federal election proved to be contentious and combative, with several candidates seeking the presidency: Republican (or Black Republican) Party, Abraham Lincoln of Illinois; Northern (or National) Democracy Party, Stephen A. Douglas of Illinois; Southern Accession (or State Rights)

Democracy Party, John C. Breckinridge of Kentucky; Independent Democracy Party, Sam Houston of Texas; National Union Party, John Bell of Tennessee; and Abolition (or John Brown or Insurrectionary) Party, Gerrit Smith of New York.[17] When ballots were counted, Lincoln was elected to serve as the sixteenth president of the United States. Almost immediately, without even waiting for Lincoln's inauguration, South Carolina seceded from the Union on December 20.

Within a few days, Northern abolitionists reacted by calling for every patriot and every antislavery man to take up arms. "We tell you plainly and frankly—you of the Slave States, you slaveholders, while we disclaim any personal enmity or malice towards you—we hate your institutions," wrote *Liberator* correspondent J.H.C. "We declare uncompromising hostility against slavery." Some men might try to retard the antislavery movement and reverse the engine of human progress, but "the swelling tides of truth" were rolling in and slavery must retreat. "Let us do our duty."[18]

According to J.H.C., even if things did not go well and the enemy drove the patriots from Washington, it would cause little concern. Even if proslavery forces threatened to take Philadelphia, New York City, and Boston—even if they reached Bunker Hill and set up tents in Newburyport—all would not be lost. J.H.C. had a plan: "Friends of liberty . . . and others taking up the Ark of Freedom, will retire to North Elba, that Calvary of our cause, and there, over the grave of its martyr, we will inaugurate by our death, if need be, a conflict which shall end only in universal emancipation." A great conflict and more deaths seemed inevitable. Holding the nation together proved implausible when Mississippi, Florida, Alabama, Georgia, Louisiana, and Texas followed the path of South Carolina. The seven states established a provisional Confederate government on February 8, 1861, with Jefferson Davis as president of the Confederacy. A month later, on March 4, Abraham Lincoln took the office of US president.

The Thorny Issue of Disunion

The prospect of disunion had plagued the country for decades. During the formation of the Missouri Compromise of 1820, John Quincy Adams wrote in his journal that "the seeds of the Declaration of Independence are yet maturing. The harvest will be what [the painter Benjamin] West calls the terrible sublime." According to historian John Stauffer, Adams's vision of emancipation encompassed death and dissolution of the Union as well as the rebirth of slaves into citizens and the nation into a free country.[19] Throughout the 1840s and 1850s, *disunion* became a frequent word of both Southern proslavery men and Northern abolitionists. After John Brown's hanging, the splitting of the nation and outbreak of war seemed unavoidable.

For Southerners, Brown was "the embodiment of all their fears—a white man willing to die to end slavery—and the most potent symbol yet of aggressive Northern anti-slavery sentiment," according to historian Paul Finkelman. On the other hand, Brown became "a prophet of righteousness" for many Northerners, "bringing down a terrible swift sword against the immorality of slavery and the haughtiness of the Southern master class." The oppression, cruelty, and tyranny of slavery could no longer be ignored. Three days before Brown's execution in 1859, Rev. Edwin M. Wheelock had asserted that the insurrection in Virginia was not a mistake, it was "necessary, seasonable and right." It was *not* "a beginning" of civil war. Wheelock said it was "a continuance of it in a new phase. In taking up arms, John Brown had only done aggressively what the North would have been compelled to do in a few years in self-defense."[20]

On the one-year anniversary of John Brown's burial, December 8, 1860, Mary Brown recalled the sacrifice made by her husband for the cause of freedom. She also mourned the other lives lost but remained steadfast in her faith in God. She believed justice would prevail, and whatever course the nation took—union or disunion—would benefit the slave.

Not all her neighbors agreed. Timothy (or T. S.) Nash was one of the earliest settlers in North Elba, having moved there in 1840, at age sixteen. As an adult, he held several offices in the town: superintendent of Schools, supervisor, and postmaster. He was also indirectly related to the John Brown family in two ways; Nash's sister was the mother of Martha Brewster (who married Oliver Brown) and Nash's brother was married to Martha's aunt.[21] Given his family ties, it is not surprising that on the day of John Brown's hanging, Nash attended a prayer meeting in Keene. *Elizabethtown Post* editor Turner mistook his presence as proof of his abolitionist status, rather than the actions of a good neighbor and Christian. Nash was not a hero worshiper or an abolitionist; he was a Democrat and opposed John Brown's views on slavery.

In a letter to his sister and brother-in-law, dated April 17, 1861, Nash expressed his belief that the Constitution guaranteed each state "the right to regulate their own domestic affairs in their own way." Each state was essentially "an independent sovereignty" and abolitionists of the North had no right to interfere with other states. Nash claimed that "most of the conservative men in the North" perceived the abolitionists as having inflicted "great injuries" on the South by making gross insults to slave owners, encouraging slave insurrections, or aiding escaped slaves.[22]

"The Abolition Party in the north are the only disunion party there is," wrote Nash. It irked him that abolitionist Wendell Phillips preached, "Disunion is abolition. . . . All hail disunion. Rest in peace the ashes of the martyr of Harper's Ferry." Though Nash exhibited sympathy for Brown's death, the call to break up the Union because of slavery was too rash and coming "a little too fast." Nash believed the closely connected interests of the states made preserving the Union paramount. There was no need for disunion; it would "look very foolish."

As Nash sat in North Elba finishing the letter, the bombshell news about Fort Sumter, South Carolina, interrupted his narrative. When he resumed, he wrote: "We have just received the intelligence that Sumter is taken. We hope the report is not true. We shall hate to see the Great pillars of our blessed Constitution pulled down. . . . A civil war of a nation of a Republican government . . . is like brother fighting against brother." South Carolina troops had fired shots at Fort Sumter on April 12, 1861. They took possession of the fort, stripped away the American flag, and raised the Confederate flag. Within the time span of writing a letter, the news reached Essex County and speculation turned into certainty—Nash envisioned brother fighting brother in a civil war.

In addition to Nash's foresight into the impending conflict, his letter provided a rare, firsthand account of a North Elba resident at the outbreak of the Civil War. Its contents were enriched by a later account, in which Nash gave his recollections of John Brown. In April of 1900, Nash admitted that in the 1850s he had considered his neighbor to be "frank, genial and gentlemanly," and to hold "wild ideas" on slavery. The call to duty that Brown heard was not from God; it "originated in his own brain," according to Nash. However, in 1900, he acknowledged he had misjudged the man—Brown's predictions turned out to be correct. Nash now referred to Brown as a good citizen and neighbor, and as "a Christian, an abolitionist and a warrior."[23]

The narratives of T. S. Nash documented the evolving opinions of John Brown in the North, particularly in North Elba. Many Northerners who sympathized with Southerners thought the hanging noose around Brown's neck would allow them to settle back into their old way of life, but subsequent events forced them to adjust their attitude. Initially, though, many people considered the Civil War to be about preserving the Union, not ending slavery.

On April 15, 1861, President Lincoln called for troops to suppress the rebellion and "save the Union." Bostonians acted wholeheartedly ready for battle. "The whole North is a unit," wrote Henry Ingersoll Bowditch. "We allow no treason. Newspapers that have been preaching Southern sentiments are gagged and compelled by an insulted people to stop their vile treasonable talk." When drums and fifes summoned men to volunteer, support for the Union cause was undeniable in Boston, and in North Elba. The *Liberator* reported that seventy men enlisted in the Town of North Elba, which had only eighty voters. "Truly, John Brown's soul is marching on."[24]

In Harpers Ferry, the legacy of John Brown played out in a different way. The town was a strategic military location and hotly contested during the Civil War, changing between Union and Confederate occupation more than a dozen times. The fight for control of the town began immediately after the first shots at Fort Sumter. On April 16, the day after President Lincoln called for Union troops, Henry Wise ordered Virginia troops to seize the arms at the Federal Arsenal in Harpers Ferry. Wise was now the ex-governor and had no official power to give an order to Virginia troops. Nor did he have any right to appropriate government property, but he was determined to steal or destroy the stockpile of weapons before federal troops arrived to claim them. Wise was committing the same crime (treason) at the same US government facility for which he had ordered the hanging of John Brown only eighteen months earlier.

The seizure was part of Wise's effort to force the State of Virginia to withdraw from the Union. As the unauthorized seizures were occurring on April 17, Wise stood at the Virginia Secession Convention and announced that, by his command, there was "a foot-race" underway between Virginia soldiers and Federal troops, and likely, "before the sun sets this day," Virginia would be at war with the federal government. Accounts claimed Wise displayed his huge horse pistol and said that if anyone wished to shoot him for treason, they would have to wrestle away his pistol. He forced indecisive minds to choose between assassination and secession from the Union.[25]

In essence, Wise's actions (even without the drama of a horse pistol) sealed Virginia's fate. There was little debate; the convention passed the Virginia Ordinance of Secession that day. Two weeks later, Wise told his fellow countrymen: "Get a spear—a lance. Take a lesson from John Brown, manufacture your blades from old iron, even though it be the tires of your cart-wheels." Wise had already duplicated Brown's crime, now he was encouraging his neighbors to follow the example of Brown. The hypocrisy and belligerence of Wise's words and actions laid bare for all to see.

He captured Harper's Ferry, with his nineteen men so few,
And frightened "Old Virginny" till she trembled through and through
They hung him for a traitor, themselves a traitor crew.
   (Version of the "John Brown Song," 1862)

Chapter 13

Wartime in Essex County and Concord

> Fire must be met with water, darkness with light, and war for the destruction of liberty must be met with war for the destruction of slavery.
>
> —Frederick Douglass, *Douglass' Monthly*, May 1861

In Essex County, New York, the Town of Elizabethtown furnished a whole company of soldiers, led by Captain Samuel Dwyer (the attorney who had provided testimony for John Brown's trial). Company K of the Thirty-Eighth New York Volunteers headed south and fought at the First Battle of Bull Run on July 21, 1861. Anxious fathers, mothers and sweethearts sought news of their beloved soldiers, and when Quakers from Philadelphia arrived in Elizabethtown, a crowd swarmed to them, inquiring of any word from the warfront. The Quakers managed to escape to the Mansion House where Sheriff Elijah Adams and his wife gave refuge. After devouring mounds of broiled trout and corn bread, the guests assembled in the parlor to exchange pleasantries with their hosts and other friends. Before long, the conversation turned to the causes and consequences of the war. To the surprise of the visitors, the inhabitants of the rural town provided a "thorough and subtle analysis" such as rarely experienced anywhere.[1]

The next morning, the Quakers jumped aboard a makeshift stagecoach loaded with fishing rods, bait boxes, knapsacks, blankets, and camp equipment to begin their wilderness adventure. Along the road to Keene, the wagon driver stopped at a new log cabin where a young woman sat spinning her wheel in the doorway. She sang merrily as she made yarn for warm winter stockings for her newlywed husband who had enlisted and gone off to war.

The driver delivered the news to her as gently as possible. Her husband and a comrade had stood together fighting hour after hour when suddenly a rifle ball went through her husband's chest and struck him dead. Upon hearing the terrible news, the wife did not sob, but as she gradually comprehended the words, "the color left her cheek, the brightness fled from her eye, [the] elasticity from her muscles." It was a scene of desolation and "speechless heart-breaking agony."

The wagonful of travelers left the young widow and continued to North Elba where they spent several days hiking, boating, fishing, and sightseeing. On Sunday afternoon, the Quakers paid their respects at John Brown's grave, and then Mary Brown invited them into the house. The visitors examined John's bookcase and admired a well-worn Bible. Then the youngest daughter, Ellen, proudly exhibited the Bible given to her by her father and inscribed by his hand.

Daughters Annie and Sarah were not at the farm to greet the Quakers that day. Annie felt ready to return to her studies for the spring 1861 term, so the sisters were attending Sanborn's school in Concord, Massachusetts. They boarded with the Alcott family, which displeased twenty-nine-year-old Louisa. "Stories simmered in my brain," she said, "demanding to be writ; but I let them simmer, knowing that the longer the divine afflatus was bottled up the better it would be." After seven years of musing, her classic book *Little Women* would win her widespread success, but in the meantime, her parents needed to rent rooms to help support their household.[2]

"John Brown's daughters came to board and upset my plans of rest and writing. . . . ," wrote Louisa. "I had my fit of woe up garret on the fat rag-bag, and then put my papers away, and fell to work housekeeping." After her episode in the attic, Louisa resolved to accept her circumstances. "I think disappointment must be good for me, I get so much of it; and the constant thumping Fate gives me may be a mellowing process; so I shall be a ripe and sweet old pippin before I die."

Here was something she had in common with Annie Brown. Both young women had experienced great disappointments, yet they also possessed determination and wit. In their evenings together, Louisa and Annie played card games, usually Old Maid. One time, Annie asked why Louisa did not marry a man who was quite attentive to her. "Ah he is too blue and too prudent for me," replied Louisa. "I should shock him constantly."

Figure 13.1. Louisa May Alcott, circa 1870. *Source:* Library of Congress. Public domain.

Annie also became friends with other distinguished citizens of Concord, such as Henry David Thoreau. She had an especially pleasant time with him, even spending a school vacation at his house. Annie appreciated that he had been one of the first Americans to make public utterance in defense of her father after the Harpers Ferry raid. Thoreau's words helped John Brown's message spread like fire, spark open conflict at Fort Sumter, and burst into a war between the states.

The town of Concord was in a "high state of topsey turveyness" and everyone was "boiling over with excitement." Particularly the boys, who drilled in the streets, preparing to be soldiers. Louisa's father, Amos Bronson Alcott, being a peace man, would not "kill a mosquito"; nor did he appreciate the boys shouting about shooting the enemy. One day as the boys marched by, Mr. Alcott made them stop and wait while he carried out some plump pumpkins. The boys then expressed their feelings by charging into the orange enemies. Afterward, he gave them a lecture on the "wickedness of such warlike feelings."[3]

Despite her father's opinion, Louisa wanted to take up arms and march off to battle. "I long to be a man," she wrote, "but as I can't fight, I will content myself with working for those who can." Annie Brown also lamented that she could not go to war since she was of the supposed "weaker sex."[4]

The young women watched as the older boys soon left Sanborn's school to join the war. Younger students from the South left to attend schools in the Confederacy. Soon, Annie and Sarah Brown also left and returned home to North Elba.

A Marching Song, A Battle Hymn

Not far from Concord, at Fort Warren on Georges Island in Boston Harbor, soldiers began to sing about John Brown. "I never heard anything more impressive," said Thomas Higginson, "and it seemed a wonderful piece of popular justice to make his name the War song." The simple tune and words spread and quickly became the most famous song of the Civil War. "It was heard everywhere in the streets," wrote music critic Richard Grant White. "Regiments marched to it, and the air had its place in the programme of every barrel-organ grinder."[5]

> John Brown's body lies a-mouldering in the grave
> His soul is marching on.
> Glory, Glory Hallelujah!

The song kept John Brown alive, glorified his gravesite, and inextricably linked him with the Civil War. Yet there seemed to be an odd form of Providence at work. The original lyrics were written about a young soldier, not the hero buried in North Elba. It was all a splendid accident.

On April 29, 1861, the Second Battalion, Boston Light Infantry, Massachusetts Voluntary Militia was ordered to occupy Fort Warren in Boston Harbor. Among the battalion was a young Sergeant named John Brown. "He was among the leading spirits, foremost always in fun making," wrote fellow soldier George Kimball, "and as he happened to bear the identical name of the old hero of Harpers Ferry, he became at once the butt of his comrades."[6]

When Brown was late for roll call, someone would ask, "Where's John Brown?"

Another would answer, "John Brown is not here! He is dead!"

When the soldier arrived, another added, "But he's a pretty lively corpse to go marching around."

Some of the soldiers were fine singers and enjoyed the Methodist hymn, "Say, Brothers, Will You Meet Us!," with its rousing chorus of "Glory hallelujah." Before long the good-natured joshing of John Brown merged with the singing, and ditties were composed of "the most nonsensical, doggerel rhymes." One of the men came up with the line, "John Brown's body lies a mouldering in the grave." Another soldier added "His soul's marching on," and this became the first verse of the song. The second verse, "He's gone to be a soldier in the army of the Lord," came from the chaplain referring to the men as soldiers in the Lord's army. The third verse, "John Brown's knapsack is strapped upon his back," was a jab at the supposedly runty Brown whose backpack dwarfed him.

Although these soldiers were known as the Tigers, they were light-hearted and merry since they had not yet been on the battlefield. Their jolliness continued as they hammered out other verses, such as one about Jefferson Davis, head of the Confederacy. "We'll feed him on sour apples, till he has the di-ar-rhee!" This original line was considered "too crude for delicate Victorian ears" so they decided to "hang Jeff Davis to a tree, as they march along!" Various kinds of trees were inserted until the sour apple tree reclaimed its honor.

At the end of May, the group of singing soldiers from the Tigers enlisted with the Twelfth Regiment of Massachusetts. Two months later, as they left for battle, they created "a great popular furore" as they marched through Boston singing the "John Brown Song." The next day, the soldiers arrived in New York City and sang the song as they marched down Broadway. The press reported: "Seldom, if ever, has New York witnessed such a sight, or heard such strains. . . . Thousands of private citizens, young and

Figure 13.2. Copy of early version of the "John Brown Song," July 16, 1861, six verses and chorus. In folksong tradition, other verses and renditions were crafted. More than sixty-five separate versions were published during the Civil War, with titles such as "John Brown's Body" and "Glory, Glory, Hallelujah." *Source:* Library of Congress. Public domain.

old, on the sidewalks and in crowded doorways and windows, joined in the chorus . . . and many an eye was wet with tears."[7] By altering the music of "Say, Brothers" a little to fit the new lyrics and quickening the tempo, the soldiers created a mighty war march sprinkled with a little humor. However, the public turned Sergeant Brown of Massachusetts into a phantom, replacing him with the mouldering body belonging to abolitionist John Brown of Harpers Ferry fame. The straightforward messages in the song reminded people that John Brown was dead and buried, his soul was alive and marching on, and hallelujah (praise God). His acts of violence became less significant, or even praiseworthy, in a time of open warfare.

The time for mild measures had passed. "They are pearls cast before swine," said Frederick Douglass. Many abolitionists agreed with him—"The simple way, then, to put an end to the savage and desolating war now waged by slaveholders, is to strike down slavery itself, the primal cause of that war." Douglass also wanted to let slaves and free blacks be called to service "and formed into a liberating army, to march into the South."[8]

The radical words of Douglass and the praises of John Brown sung by soldiers made some Northerners uncomfortable. They did not want the war to be about slavery. Even for President Lincoln the war was still about saving the Union. The *Chicago Tribune* worried that Virginians would think Brown was "worshipped as a Northern hero, in spite of all denials, if even [Colonel] Fletcher Webster's Boston troops sing a song as this."[9] The "John Brown Song" would be wonderful if only John Brown could be taken out of it.

"The bugle blasts are sounding, 'tis time to be away," was suggested as an alternative, but all efforts to alter or ban the song failed. Union soldiers refused to let go of John Brown's body.[10]

John Brown's spirit marched on with the song and its offshoots. After hearing soldiers sing the tune, poet Julia Ward Howe felt inspired to write new words. She claimed that as she lay in bed waiting for the dawn, the lines began to form in her mind. "I must get up and write these verses down," she said, "lest I fall asleep again and forget them." She scrawled the verses of the "Battle Hymn of the Republic" almost without looking at the paper.[11] The *Atlantic Monthly* printed the lyrics on the front page of its February 1862 edition. By lengthening the lines and slowing the tempo, Howe shaped the song into a solemn and dignified hymn. She also removed John Brown's name and transformed the war into a holy war. This pleased the Union government and they quickly distributed copies to soldiers.

Although the "Battle Hymn" became a widespread favorite, it did not replace the folksy John Brown Song. The original form and lyrics had worked their way into Union regiments and into parlors back home. Music critic White said, "The alternative jig and swing of the air caused it to stick to the uneducated ear as burrs stick to a blackberry girl." According to prominent essayist and women's rights advocate Gail Hamilton (Mary Abigail Dodge), the music was both simple and magnificent, and the song's lyrics had something for everybody—"a sense of poetic justice and righteous retribution"; "a scorn of grammar, rhetoric, rhyme, and reason"; "a brutality"; and "a patriotism." The John Brown Song was "a song of the people."[12]

The great writers of Concord (Ralph Waldo Emerson, Henry David Thoreau, Louisa May Alcott, and Frank Sanborn) had already immortalized John Brown, yet the simple song stitched together by a few Union soldiers resurrected him in a singular way. John Brown Jr. called it "a revelation." Until he heard the song, he had not understood why his father allowed himself to be captured or why his mission was brought to such a disastrous end. Nor could John Jr. foresee "the moral victory in that appalling defeat."[13]

Hearing soldiers sing "his soul is marching on" made John Jr. realize why his father died as he did.

> [John Brown] headed no party, changed no law, won no large following, suffered an ignominious death. His life went out in tragic gloom and apparent failure. But suddenly he seemed to be, as Thoreau said, "more alive than any man living." The spirit, the moral heroism, in which he had courted the sacrifice, awoke the conscience of a people, and such reparation as was possible was made. There was something like public remorse and shame that a great nation should have shirked its duty, allowed one old man to hurl himself to death against a national wrong.

Buffeted from Pillar to Post

As the national spotlight kept shining on members of John Brown's family, unwelcome strangers pestered them and made visits. John Jr. said his house in Ohio was like "a well patronized Hotel," with many visitors coming from "motives of mere curiosity." Even though the Browns did not seek attention and tried to resume their ordinary lives, "efforts to forget were fruitless," said Salmon. The Browns found themselves despised bitterly by slavery sympathizers and considered "victims of a righteous wrath" by friends of freedom. "Our family was long buffeted from pillar to post."[14]

Even abolitionists sometimes showed disrespect for the Brown family. A month after the July 4 celebration in 1860, Henry C. Wright showed up at the Brown Farm with the intention of digging up John Brown's body. He planned to move it to Mount Auburn Cemetery and erect a monument there. However, as Wright sat by the grave looking at the glorious panorama of Adirondack Mountains, he realized why Brown wished to rest in that spot. "No monument that money could purchase or human ingenuity contrive, or art execute, could so fitly and so grandly perpetuate the memory of such a man."[15]

Wright realized a man-made monument was not warranted. Then he pondered whether Nature's grand tribute was necessary. Did John Brown's body have to rest at the farm "as a finality?" "*Ought* the grave of John Brown be left in North Elba? It would not be difficult to raise the means to remove it, and give it a place and a monument in Mount Auburn. . . . But, *cui bono!*" Who benefits? According to Wright, future generations needed a monument to remind them of John Brown's spirit and tenderness and sympathy. Of his readiness to die for the enslaved. Of his "sublime consistency and moral heroism." If Brown's remains were deposited in the Boston area, his inspiring words would be engraved on a monument, and many thousands would visit each year. Wright asked, "Who shall move in this matter?"

The *National Anti-Slavery Standard* replied, "Let it be done, say we, and with such ceremonies as may be deemed appropriate by the friends of freedom." December 2, 1860, the anniversary of Brown's execution, was proposed as a suitable time for the reburial.[16]

"May it never be!" exclaimed Rev. Joshua Young, who officiated at Brown's funeral. He wanted the body to stay beside the great boulder. "Here Nature's own hand has built for his lasting monument."[17] John Brown's body stayed undisturbed, for the time being.

Another issue faced by the Browns was the distribution and use of funds. Plenty of aid came to Mary Brown, which allowed her to make additions to the house and hire farm helpers. She also gave funds to others who needed them. For example, the widow and young child of John Cook, who was hanged for his participation in the Harpers Ferry raid, lived in a distressing situation with unsympathetic people. Mary sent her money to come and live with them in North Elba, but Mrs. Cook returned the money because the folks she lived with refused to let her go.

Mary felt heartbroken, imagining how dreadful life must be where frowns were cast upon you, and no one was your friend. That was not the case with the Browns, and Mary felt thankful for the many friends and sympathizers in their affliction who helped them "bear up under it." Abolitionist friends brought comfort to Mary, as did their financial aid. After the July 4 gathering, Thaddeus Hyatt distributed $2,600 in gold among Mary, Ruth, John Jr., Owen, Jason, Salmon, Isabelle (widow of Watson Brown), Mary (widow of William Thompson), and "two escaped raiders." In their thank-you letter to Hyatt, the Browns said the funds "could not have been more equitably distributed than it has been by you" and assured him they would forever hold "in grateful remembrance your affectionate regards for us."[18]

While Mary appreciated the aid, it yielded some upsetting consequences. News articles reported that Mary Brown received $30,000 from Haiti. "I have never received one cent from Hayti," replied Mary in July 1860, "neither do I know anything about the contributions of the people of that island." Because of these false reports, people were applying to Mary for loans of money. "If truth was known," wrote Mary, "I think [such requests] would not be sent."[19]

Friends also tried to correct the false report and stop the pesky, disrespectful solicitations. The most forceful repudiation came from Thaddeus Hyatt in *Douglass' Monthly*. He reported that only $6,150 had been raised for the family in this country and he expected the Haitian fund would be much less. "I hope, therefore," wrote Hyatt, "that the sympathizing gentlemen through the country who are mailing to the widow of Captain Brown leather photographs of their interesting faces, with 'offers' to borrow sums of a thousand and downward, will cease tormenting their imaginations with inflammatory pictures of bags of gold! The *widow has no money to loan*! Let this suffice."[20]

Mary stayed in North Elba, knowing it was John's wish, but it required a great deal of money for her to live there. She fixed up the house, having it plastered and finished inside and a wing added to the northern side. She also spent funds to hire men to help with the farm, especially after Salmon moved to his own house. Mary hadn't raised any crops in 1860, and had to buy everything they ate and wore—and pay for delivery as she did not own a horse and wagon. "I don't like to be dependent on others," she wrote. She wanted to raise crops and perhaps some sheep to make the farm profitable. Yet some of the people who raised funds for Mary were indifferent or dismissive of her requests for disbursement.[21]

Salmon Brown tried to establish a sense of normalcy in his life in North Elba. He cleared several acres of forest, built a house near his in-laws (the Hinckleys), and moved his family to their new home in November 1860.

A visit from Col. James Fairman in February 1862 interrupted the couple's simple, happy life. Fairman wanted Salmon to recruit men for Company K of the Ninety-Sixth Regiment of New York at Plattsburgh. Though Salmon had already fought the "hell born law" of the slave power for two years in Kansas, he agreed to fight again, and Fairman promised him a Lieutenant's Commission for his work.

Four feet of snow covered the Adirondack countryside as Salmon and his brother-in-law Alexis Hinckley trekked from house to house recruiting men. When the company was filled, the band of recruits walked nearly sixty miles to their barracks in Plattsburgh. "When we got inside the parade ground," said Salmon, "the soldiers rushed around us and took me off the ground in their arms. Of course I was very proud of my efforts."[22]

The warm welcome ended abruptly. Col. Fairman told Salmon that the regiment officers had raised a fuss because he was the son of John Brown. They submitted a petition stating that they were not against Salmon "as a man or citizen," but they feared his father's notoriety would bring additional risks and attacks to the regiment. The officers asked for Salmon to be removed from his position.

Col. Fairman refused to comply with the detestable petition. "I will resign myself first," he said to Salmon.

"I will step down and out," replied Salmon, "you can do more good than I can."

It felt hard and unfair to Salmon—the best way to serve his country was to resign from the army. He returned to his pregnant wife and young child in North Elba.

Although Salmon settled the matter quietly, L.G.B. of Burlington, Vermont, was outraged by the action of his New York neighbors and wanted their names to be "handed down in history!" He wrote to the *Liberator* and publicized the names of those who had scorned the son of John Brown, a "manly specimen of bodily strength and vigor."[23]

Ohioans considered the petition against Salmon to be a "dirty piece of business." They hoped the Lieutenants of the New York Ninety-Sixth would not meet the brunt of any battle, "for if they are afraid of the ghost of John Brown what will they do when they see a live rebel."[24]

Although Salmon Brown did not remain with the Ninety-Sixth Regiment, other recruits from the region served in the unit, including Alexis Hinckley, Judson Ware, and Idge Welsh of North Elba. The Chaplain of the regiment was Rev. Nathan Wardner of Jay, who had served as president of the July 4, 1860, abolitionist meeting at the John Brown Farm. Acts of benevolence characterized Rev. Wardner; in addition to other duties at his post in Plymouth, North Carolina, he held two Sabbath schools each Sunday in the church of the Methodist Episcopal Society. During the week he ran a day school, for freedmen mostly, with pupils ranging in age from five to eighty. He also received special commendation "for charging with his regiment in the advancing columns, ready to administer the lasting consolation to the dying."[25]

Rev. Wardner resigned his post as Chaplain when he became ill, but before he returned home to Essex County, an escaped slave woman appeared at the Union camp with her three-year-old child. The little girl was as "white as most of the children we see in our streets" and "very pretty and intelligent." Her mother said she would "rather have her took North than South," so Rev. Wardner brought her home to Jay.[26]

Even before the Union allowed black men to join the infantry, some enlisted with white regiments. William Appo Jr. signed up in North Elba in September of 1861, and was assigned the rank of Private with the Thirteenth Regiment of New York Infantry at Troy. He received a promotion to Corporal in February of 1862, and died during the Second Battle of Bull Run in August 1862. Although his body was buried on the battlefield, friends placed a marker for him in the Epps plot at the North Elba Cemetery.

Silas Frazier arrived in North Elba in 1854 and moved to Westport later in the decade. He joined the Second New York Veterans Volunteer Cavalry in December of 1863 with several white men from Westport. William Carasaw (a Timbucto grantee) and Josiah Hasbrook Jr. (the son of a grantee) enlisted in the Twenty-Sixth United States Colored Infantry Regiment and mustered out on September 1, 1864. Several other black men from Essex and Franklin Counties fought in the Civil War, including Stephen Warren Morehouse (the son of a grantee in Vermontville) who served with the acclaimed Fifty-Fourth Massachusetts Infantry Regiment.[27]

Willard Thompson, whose twin brother William was killed in Harpers Ferry, served the Union throughout the entire war. Willard had moved to New Hampshire just prior to the war and enlisted there in April 1861. In a letter to his brothers and sisters in North Elba, he wrote: "God help us in this dilemma and make us victorious." He hoped the Union would "strike at the very rituals of slavery" and send it to "the devil, for that is the place for it." He pledged to serve for a lifetime if he could help establish liberty in the place of slavery. True to his word, Willard Thompson stayed in uniform until July 1865—an amazing feat, especially since he spent time in two Confederate prisons with notorious reputations, Libby Prison in Virginia and Andersonville Prison in Georgia.[28]

Willard placed blame for the war on men such as James Buchanan, Henry Wise, and Jefferson Davis, while some people around him in Washington, DC, blamed John Brown. "But that is a lie," he said. "For it started before John Brown was known in the history of this land of slavery and horror."

The assertion that Brown should receive blame (or credit) for the war existed in the South and the North. The *New York Journal of Commerce* also pointed the finger at the radical press and abolitionists who, instead of condemning Brown, tried to turn a murderer into a saint. "A marching song of a Massachusetts regiment, or a strolling band of abolition songsters, will not . . . restore to salvation the condemned," declared the *Journal*. "For every victim, Northern or Southern, sent from battlefields to the bar of God, John Brown-ism at the North must render part . . . of the fearful account."[29]

The John Brown Song promoted John Brown–ism and threatened to make the war about slavery. As Union soldiers marched southward, they observed the institution close-up and met enslaved people face-to-face. Soldiers sometimes complained when they were required to return escaped slaves to the Confederacy. The policy seemed heartless, and some officers defied it, declaring the slaves to be contraband of war and refusing to return them to their masters. At the same time, Union troops struggled on the battlefield, while France and England seemed ready to support the Confederacy. President Lincoln needed to do something.

While he personally considered slavery to be immoral, Lincoln did not believe that the Constitution gave him power to abolish it in the states where it existed. By July of 1862, events pressured him to reconsider his stance and sign two pieces of legislature. The Militia Act allowed black men to serve in the Union's armed forces as laborers. The Confiscation Act mandated that enslaved people seized from Confederate supporters would be declared forever free. Lincoln also tried to work with the slave states that had not seceded from the Union. He pushed for gradual emancipation in these border states, even offering compensation to their owners. His efforts were unsuccessful, but they indicated a change in policy.

"My paramount object in this struggle *is* to save the Union and is *not* either to save or to destroy slavery . . . . ," said President Lincoln. "What I do about slavery, and the colored race, I do because I believe it helps to save the Union."[30] Finally, a month later, after the Union's victory at Antietam,

Lincoln issued a decree: unless the rebellious states returned to the Union by January 1, 1863, freedom would be granted to slaves within those states. This was the preliminary announcement of the Emancipation Proclamation.

In Western and Central New York, citizens cheered. "The people talk and act as if a load was lifted from their hearts. They sing, they shout over it. They think the day of redemption has dawned." Even in the border state of Maryland, people said, "God bless Abraham Lincoln," and a group of 2,000 soldiers sang the John Brown Song. "My blood fairly jumped in my veins and choked my heart," wrote a newsman, recalling that less than three years before, just a little distance away, John Brown hung between heaven and earth. "Truly, the world moves, and the people move with it."[31]

On January 1, 1863, President Lincoln issued the official Emancipation Proclamation. In making all slaves in rebelling states "thenceforward, and forever free," the proclamation captured the hearts and imaginations of millions of Americans. Abolitionist John Brown did not live to see this glorious day. Neither did the original soldier in the marching song, Sgt. John Brown; he drowned when his boat capsized in the Shenandoah River in June of 1862. Yet their spirit lived on in versions of the song.

> John Brown lives—we are gaining on our foes—
> Right shall be victor, whatever may oppose—
> Fresh thru the darkness the word of warning blows—
> Freedom reigns today!
> John Brown's soul through the world is marching on;
> Hail to the hour when oppression shall be gone!
> All men will sing, in the better age's dawn.
> Freedom reigns today!
> John Brown's body lies mouldering in the grave;
> John Brown lives in the triumphs of the brave;
> John Brown's soul not a higher joy can crave;
> Freedom reigns today![32]

The Emancipation Proclamation made the war about slavery and enabled the liberated to become liberators. After January 1, every advance of federal troops expanded freedom to slaves, and black men could now serve as soldiers in both the Union Army and Navy. "God bless Abraham Lincoln," wrote Mary Brown, "and give God the glory for the day of Jubilee has come." She also cheered the Union Army's recruiting of black men. "I feel that that is just as it should be." Abolitionist friends in Massachusetts held a tribute to John Brown on Emancipation Day. Amos Bronson Alcott, Julia Ward Howe, Ralph Waldo Emerson, and others gathered in the parlor of George and Mary Stearns to unveil a marble bust of John Brown. After admiring the bust, Wendell Phillips praised John Brown and gave him credit for the results of the past three years. "His hand was swaying the President's, and was signing the decree of emancipation."[33]

Mary Brown was unable to attend the event, but she wrote to Mrs. Stearns that she was there in spirit. In a follow-up letter, Mary wrote, "I feel that there is a great deal to be encouraged about, but God only knows where the end is of this terrible affliction that is upon us."[34]

Reality had set in. Though the Emancipation Proclamation had been widely praised, perhaps a bit overzealously, it did not immediately free anyone. It applied only to states that had seceded from the Union and left slavery untouched in the loyal border states. Lincoln's secretary of State, William Seward, called the proclamation a "puff of wind" and pointed out the irony that "we show our sympathy with slavery by emancipating slaves where we cannot reach them and holding them in bondage where we can set them free."[35]

"I long to see the axe of War laid at the root of our troubles," wrote John Brown Jr., "not even sparing the cursed thing in the loyal Slaveholding States." He realized he was an "extreme Radical" and the "better way" was often between extremes. Yet he worried that if Lincoln's statements represented the "average" sentiment of antislavery people, then the nation would have to take "further lessons in the School of Adversity."[36]

As the fighting dragged on through the summer of 1863, Mary Brown lamented, "Oh what a dreadful war this is." Like John Jr., Mary recognized the guilt of the whole nation in perpetuating the sin of slavery. She wrote: "When will this nation be willing to do right, to love mercy, Justice and truth. I feel that we deserve all this punishment from the hands of God but when I read of so much suffering I feel to cry out how long Oh Lord how long shall this people continue in their sins and the innocent have to suffer with the guilty."[37]

Chapter 14

Truly, the World Moves, and the People Move with It

> As I knew I was near some of the peaks of North Elba, under whose shadows sleep the remains of John Brown, I could not but think of him. I learned from all his neighbors he was a sincere and pious man, of the noble old Puritan type. Family worship each day ascended from his hearth, and he lived in these wilds a patriarch of a numerous family, all of whom he educated in simple piety, and a noble love of liberty, such as these mountains always tend to give.
>
> —Henry Ingersoll Bowditch, September 1863[1]

Salmon and Abbie Brown were comfortable in their new cabin in North Elba and blessed with another daughter, Minnie, on March 10, 1863. "We probably would have spent many more years there, if not our whole lives," said Abbie, "if an uncle of mine had not returned from California."[2] Abbie's uncle told such spectacular tales that the couple felt compelled to move to the land of golden opportunity.

In North Elba, "there was six months' winter and the other six months was cold weather," said Salmon.[3] He wanted to go westward, and after the debacle of his army enlistment in 1862, who could blame him? Without hesitation, Salmon and Abbie sold their farm and planned to leave New York in the fall of 1863—to go west to Iowa, and then, in the spring, to California. Ruth and Henry Thompson prepared to move west, too, and by early September, they had sold their farm to Lyman Epps.

What would Mary Brown do? She had spent funds to fix the house and make it comfortable in the winter. But could she run the farm and live happily without family nearby? One of John's final statements was: "I hope you will always live in Essex County." On the other hand, he wanted her to keep the family together, which was only possible by moving.

Mary considered the needs of her daughters Sarah and Annie. The girls were away at school, not in Concord, but at Fort Edward Institute, seventy miles south of North Elba. Besides their basic courses, Sarah studied painting and music while Annie concentrated on painting and penciling. Mary was proud of their progress—the school principal reported, "Sarah is a doing nobly and Annie is doing fairly"—and planned to have the girls stay at school for one more term.[4]

By August of 1863, Mary resolved to move to Kansas or Iowa so her children could have "larger fields for labor and usefulness." In a new place, her daughters could be teachers and her sons would have a better climate for their farms and livestock. However, leaving North Elba created a new quandary: What would Mary do about John's grave? She planned to dig up his remains and carry them with her. Her Quaker friends considered it "an undertaking few women but the widow of John Brown would dream of." Soon another thought came to Mary. Might the Boston abolitionists who swooped and swarmed for her husband's body in 1859 and 1860 like to have it? No, they were busy with the war effort and no longer had an interest in the bones of John Brown.[5]

As Mary pondered her course of action, illness spread through the family. Diphtheria attacked Ellen and some of Ruth's children, but Mary, a convert to the water cure, healed them with cold water and ice. Then, her four-year-old grandson, Freddy, came down with diphtheria and died. The family thought of him as an exceptional and bright boy, and again, they drank deep from the bitter cup. As heart-wrenching as it must have been, Mary walked away from John's grave at the farm and the graves of Freddy and other relatives and friends in the North Elba Cemetery.

In mid-September of 1863, Mary and eight-year-old Ellen took the rails to Ohio, where they stopped to visit Owen, John Jr., and his family. The next day, they continued to Decorah, Iowa, with Salmon, Abbie, and their two daughters, Cora, age three, and Minnie, six months. Ruth and Henry had intended to go with the others to Iowa. Instead, they decided to stay at Put-in-Bay, Ohio, near John Jr. and Wealthy. (Ruth and Henry eventually moved to Pasadena, California, in 1884.)

Annie and Sarah planned to join their mother and family in Iowa at the end of the Fall 1863 term at Fort Edward Institute. To the dismay of the family, Annie headed south instead of west. She was "desirous of going South to Port Royal, Hilton Head, or elsewhere to engage in teaching Contrabands," and William Lloyd Garrison helped her find a position. In October, Annie went to teach at a freedmen's school in Union-occupied Norfolk, Virginia.[6]

Stories circulated about Annie instructing black pupils in reading and writing at the Union-occupied mansion of ex-governor Henry Wise. Supposedly, Wise traveled to his 884-acre plantation one day and Annie refused to let him enter the house. When Wise heard the story, he said it was a rich joke; no incident seemed "so supremely ludicrous and whimsical" as his mansion being converted into a "negro school" and the daughter of the man he hanged for treason not permitting him to cross the threshold.[7] The factual basis for the tale was that Annie taught blacks at the Fortress Monroe Department near Norfolk, about six miles from Wise's former mansion. Annie did not recall ever meeting Wise, but she had visited the estate and found it inexplicable to be standing in the house of the man responsible for hanging her father.

While Annie was in Virginia, the Brown family enjoyed life in Decorah, Iowa. The weather was fine, Salmon earned twelve dollars for a week of chopping cord wood, and his sheep were greatly admired. Many wealthy people lived in the town, and everything seemed so wonderful that the Browns decided they would stay there. Then, the sweet vision turned sour as the latter winter months brought unusually cold weather. After Annie arrived in April of 1864, the family left Iowa and headed to California.

Traveling to California

Mary and the girls rode in one wagon, Salmon's family in another, each pulled by two yoke of steers and one yoke of milk cows. A third wagon carried Salmon's six Spanish Merino sheep. Two young men helped drive the teams in exchange for food and board (basically a blanket in front of a fire). The Browns took a good supply of provisions: baked hardtack, dried potatoes, beef sausage, bacon, fruit, and cows for milk. They had a sheet iron stove for cooking and Salmon had guns for hunting and protection, but they did not carry extras. This made timing crucial. They needed to reach California by October, otherwise they might be trapped in the mountains by snow without supplies.

The Mormon Trail and Oregon Trail were extremely dangerous that year because the regular troops stationed throughout the frontier had been called away to the war and replaced by less experienced soldiers. Hearing stories of "Indian troubles," the Browns joined a small wagon train from Indiana. Abbie recalled "a band of 250 Sioux warriors" approaching them along the way and the white men pulling out their rifles to scare them away.[8]

They had no further trouble until they hitched onto a larger wagon train. A group of Confederate sympathizers joined the group and discovered they were the family of John Brown. Not long afterward, someone poisoned two of Salmon's sheep. The Browns feared the act was only the prelude to a more dastardly deed—killing Salmon, and perhaps the rest of the family. Soon afterward, the *New York Tribune* reported news of "a painful rumor, not yet confirmed," that the Brown family were pursued by Missouri rebels and then captured, robbed, and murdered.[9]

The rumor proved untrue. When the wagon train stopped to fix a wheel, Salmon Brown said his family was going to continue over "the next rise" to camp for the night. The Browns drove over the knoll and kept going until four in the morning, when one of their wagons overturned going down a steep hill. After fixing the wagon, they traveled until noon. Off in the distance, they saw the rebels' wagons were in pursuit.

The Browns continued at top speed for a week, stopping only to eat and sleep. They finally reached safety at the Union post at Soda Springs, Idaho, just three hours ahead of their pursuers. The Union soldiers asked the Missouri rebels if they were Union men or not. Being greatly outnumbered, the rebels answered, "Union men" and swore an oath of allegiance to the United States. In private, one of them said to Salmon, "There would have been some needed blood-letting if we had caught you."[10]

Prior to the threats, Abbie and Annie wrote cheerful letters about wildflowers, golden wheat, and Chimney Rock. Now, as they rested for a few days, they wondered what dangers awaited them on the trail and in California. When the Browns set out from Soda Springs, Lt. Francis Shoemaker and six soldiers accompanied them for two hundred miles to Nevada. From there, the family followed the trail to Humboldt City and entered northern California.

When they reached the tollgate outside of Red Bluff, a collector extended his hand for money. "And what might be your name?" he asked.[11]

Upon hearing they were John Brown's family, he handed back their money, removed his hat, and said, "Pass."

The Browns reached the town of Red Bluff, California, on September 30, 1864, having traveled about two thousand miles from Iowa. "You will ask how I liked crossing the Plains," wrote Annie. "It will do for six months of one's life, but I should hate to waste another by doing it over again."[12]

The family arrived "barefooted" and "very poor," and the townspeople came to their aid. They gave Mary a sack of flour and other groceries, and some furniture. Annie and Sarah passed their "school marms" exams and found teaching jobs while young Ellen attended school. They lived in "a little hencoop of a house," with Annie and Sarah sleeping on the floor, but the people of Red Bluff soon started a subscription to build them a better house.[13]

Abbie Hinckley Brown was given a pair of shoes and cloth for a dress. Salmon got a job grubbing out young oaks and earned forty dollars in eight days. "We felt rich," Abbie wrote. "How I loved California."

A Rebirth of John Brown and the Nation

When the Browns reached California, more than four years had passed since John's death. During that time, the public was turning him into a symbol. That transformation had required the *man* John Brown to die. Henry Ward Beecher grasped this truth even before Brown was sentenced. "Let no man pray that Brown be spared," said Beecher. "Let Virginia make him a martyr. Now, he has only blundered. His soul was noble; his work miserable. But a cord and a gibbet would redeem all that, and round up Brown's failure with a heroic success."[14]

Brown admitted he had erred by waiting too long to leave Harpers Ferry and stoically accepted his fate. However, he did not want to be buried in the land of slaves, or in Boston or Washington, DC, or Philadelphia, where tombs of great American men stood. He did not want an obelisk as high as Bunker Hill Monument. Brown chose to be buried at his humble backwoods farm amid towering mountains, at the side of the boulder where he loved to sit and read God's words. That rugged boulder rose about ten feet high, as "huge and simple as his own great nature."[15]

> John Brown
> Was such a stone—unreasoning as the stone,
> Destructive as the stone, and, if you like,
> Heroic and devoted as such a stone.
> He had no gift for life, no gift to bring

Life but his body and a cutting edge,
But he knew how to die. (Benet, *John Brown's Body*)

The old family stone was important to John Brown, too. The day before his hanging, he finalized his Will and specified that his son John Jr. should have his surveying tools and the "old granite monument." He wanted the stone to remain at North Elba, "so long as any of my children or my wife may remain there as residents." However, when the Brown family moved away in 1863, they knew the great effort undertaken by John to bring the monument to North Elba. It belonged at his grave, representing John's hope that "my posterity should not only remember their parentage, but also the cause they labored in."[16]

In North Elba, he saw himself in the continuum of establishing a nation based on freedom and liberty for all. It began in 1776 with his grandfather, continued through his sons, and ended with his hanging at the gallows. No modern marker could ever outshine the historic and patriotic significance of the old stone that memorialized five soldiers. Capt. Brown died wearing a colonial uniform; Frederick was murdered in Kansas; Watson died of wounds inflicted while bearing a flag of truce in Harpers Ferry; Oliver was killed in battle there; and John Brown hanged by the State of Virginia. Though he was dead and buried, Brown also became part of the ongoing Civil War.

For the North, the war was no longer about saving the Union. Leaders such as President Abraham Lincoln and Frederick Douglass had tied the war to slavery and the founding principles of the republic. In his 1863 Gettysburg Address, Lincoln stated that our forefathers brought forth a new nation, "conceived in liberty, and dedicated to the proposition that all men are created equal." The Civil War tested whether that nation could endure. Lincoln proclaimed that the nation "shall have a new birth of freedom, and that government of the people, by the people, for the people, shall not perish from the earth."

Frederick Douglass stated the mission of the war as he saw it in early 1864: "No war but an Abolition war; no peace but an Abolition peace; liberty for all, chains for none; the black man a soldier in war, a laborer in peace; a voter at the South as well as at the North; America his permanent home, and all Americans his fellow countrymen.... If accomplished, our glory as a nation will be complete, our peace will flow like a river, and our foundation will be the everlasting rocks."[17] From the perspective of Douglass and Lincoln, an end to the war required a remaking of the nation as a place of liberty *for all*, where *all* Americans felt safe and enjoyed fellowship. It required the death of slavery and a rebirth of democracy. It required finishing the task begun by John Brown.

Brown knew the country was engaged in sin and brutal wrongs and evil injustice. He spent twenty years trying, talking, and waiting before deciding that only through rebirth could the United States adhere to its original principles. He did not wait for the consent of politicians or ministers or legal officials or the rich, white ruling class of the North (who often benefited economically from slavery). Brown acted out of personal responsibility and moral conviction, regardless of legal framework and the possibility of innocent bloodshed. He could no longer be complicit in the sins of his country—in its brutal injustice and barbaric war imposed on four million black people.

For men such as Douglass and Thoreau, the end of slavery in America had seemed inevitable as soon as John Brown walked into Harpers Ferry in 1859. For others, the Civil War gave new significance to Brown. "I thought his design foolish and wrong," wrote prominent Boston physician and abolitionist Henry Ingersoll Bowditch, "and how foolish was *my* thought as I consider subsequent events, which made him the leader of our hosts in the Civil War, during which 'his soul was marching on,' and compelled even his enemies to admire him even while they sought his life."[18]

When Bowditch made a pilgrimage to Brown's grave, he said it was marked by a "crumbling headstone" and surrounded by "rosebushes, a little neglected." Yet, the grave impressed him as "a spot associated with valor, self-sacrifice, and a noble life." He felt as if he were "standing on Calvary."

> The sword he wielded for the right
> Turns to a victor's palm;
> His memory sounds forever more,
> A spirit-stirring psalm.
> No breath of shame can touch his shield,
> Nor ages dim its shine;
> Living, he made life beautiful,—
> Dying, made death divine.
> No monument of quarried stone,
> No eloquence of speech
> Can grave the lessons on the land
> His martyrdom will teach.
> No eulogy like his own words,

With hero-spirit rife,
"I truly serve the cause I love,
By yielding up my life." (Louisa May Alcott, "With a Rose,
  That Bloomed on the Day of John Brown's Martyrdom,"
  December 2, 1859)[19]

Noted landscape artist William Trost Richards captured the scene in his painting *John Brown's Grave*, first exhibited in 1864. Contemporaneous viewers of the painting would immediately recognize the horizontal patch of golden wheat symbolizing the Union cause during the Civil War. They would also associate the grave scene with the soldier who sparked the ongoing war against slavery and injustice, the man whose name was voiced by the North in song. They would recall his moldering body and his soul marching on—his death and rebirth.[20]

Those who knew John Brown as a farmer and a man of the Bible would readily grasp the metaphor of sowing and reaping. John 12:20–24 says, "Very truly I tell you, unless a kernel of wheat falls to the ground and

Figure 14.1. *John Brown's Grave*, painting by William Trost Richards, circa 1864. Believed to be painted on the spot at North Elba, New York. Richards used artistic license in turning the tombstone sideways to show the inscription face. *Source:* Courtesy of the Adirondack Experience. Used with permission.

dies, it remains only a single seed. But if it dies, it produces many seeds." In other words, a grain of wheat keeps on being a lone kernel (seed) as long as it remains in the head of a stalk. Only when it is removed and buried in the ground (in a sense, dies) does it have the chance to germinate and produce many more grains (seeds). Hence, wheat is also a symbol of resurrection, of new life and eternal life.

The veiled rainbow in the upper right of the painting suggests Divine hope. A rainbow often serves as a pathway or sky-bridge from earth or to heaven and God (resurrection). The ivy climbing the boulder is another symbol of immortality, transformation, and rebirth. Its leaves often fall off in the winter, but new leaves appear in spring. Ivy suggests that, even in the darkest phases of life, there is always the hope of new beginnings. The leafless tree represents the same theme, while the blooming roses suggest Christian martyrdom.

Richards uses Nature's landscape to convey human morals and emotions—to represent the cycle of life, death, and rebirth of the *man* John Brown, and of a nation. Many scholars perceive *John Brown's Grave* as epitomizing America's grave, showing the sense of loss, loneliness, and grief that prevailed during the Civil War. It also shows a hope for what America can become—when things look dead, there is still promise for new life.

"Every seed bears fruit after its kind," said Frederick Douglass, "and nothing is reaped which was not sowed." He asserted that even if the one who ploughed and sowed was not able to reap, even if decades passed, the harvest would surely come. "The bloody harvest of Harper's Ferry was ripened by the heat and moisture of merciless bondage of more than two hundred years," said Douglass. Brown acts were "the avenging angel" for the invasions "of Christian slave-traders" on Africa.[21]

Likewise, Thoreau extended the metaphor from the physical realm to the moral, and predicted the consequences of Brown's execution. Thoreau said: "Like the seed is the fruit and that in the moral world, when good seed is planted, good fruit is inevitable, and does not depend on our watering and cultivating; that when you plant, or bury, a hero in his field, a crop of heroes is sure to spring up. This is a seed of such force and vitality, that it does not ask our leave to germinate."[22]

Many decades may pass; even the two-hundred-and-fifty-year anniversary of the Declaration of Independence may come and go, before a new crop of heroes of freedom and equality shall spring up and the harvest shall come.

"You Have John Brown"

When the Brown family left New York in 1863, they left behind John's grave, the old family stone, and the farm, which Mary Brown was unable to sell. For the meantime, she rented it to Alexis Hinckley, who had been discharged from the Ninety-Sixth Regiment because of illness. He was considered family, being Abbie's brother, Salmon's best friend, and Henry Thompson's cousin. Yet Mary regretted that she "ever spent a cent on that farm in North Elba," repairing and enlarging it. "I am in hopes of selling it sometime," she wrote in 1864, "so as to get back a part that I spent there."[23]

Two years later, Alexis purchased the farm for $700. Finally, Mary recovered part of her capital. Perhaps more significantly, she inserted a provision in the deed that retained ownership of the graveyard plot (about one-quarter-acre) for the Brown family and their descendants.[24]

After the close of the war, Col. Francis L. Lee, who had commanded the Forty-Fourth Regiment of Massachusetts Volunteers, hired a stonecutter to engrave the boulder beside John Brown's grave with "JOHN BROWN 1859." Each letter and figure was cut one-foot high, one-foot wide, and one-inch deep into the rock. A friend called it "a touching tribute from a gallant soldier to the memory of a man whose fame will live forever."[25]

Alexis Hinckley and his family lived at the farm until the winter of 1868, when his wife died. "Deciding to sell, and wishing to leave it in friendly hands," said Alexis, "I thought of John Brown's antislavery friends, thinking they might be glad to secure the place if they knew it was going to be sold." He offered it to Gerrit Smith, who replied that it was not important who owned it; Smith suggested letting a farmer have it. "This was a very practical view of it," said Alexis, "but it did not coincide with my views."[26]

The house sat unoccupied when journalist Kate Field came along in the summer of 1869. Upon hearing the property was for sale, Field found nineteen co-sponsors and they purchased it for $2,000 in January of 1870. The group leased it to a local farm family, and the John Brown Farm became a tourist site—a historic attraction and dining-lodging business. However, the owners recognized the historical importance of the property and the need for preserving it beyond their lifespans. In 1896, Field and her friends donated the farm to New York State, with the provision that it be kept forever as a reservation or park. During the celebration of the ownership transfer, a Civil War veteran donated a US flag, which was raised over Brown's grave, and soldiers fired a military salute to John Brown.

Figure 14.2. Home of John Brown, North Elba, New York, circa 1880s. The house was greatly expanded from 1870 to 1896, when it functioned as a private tourist attraction with dining and lodging facilities. In 1959, New York State restored the house to its original 1850s configuration. *Source:* Library of Congress. Public domain.

New York State. Essex County. North Elba. "You have John Brown." As Dick Gregory said, "This man is real and you have him." His body was planted *here*.

People come to see where John Brown of Kansas and Harpers Ferry fame "lies amouldering in the grave." What they discover is John Brown of North Elba. The man who believed in the words of the Bible and the Golden Rule and the Declaration of Independence. He was a family patriarch, good Christian, common farmer, and helpful neighbor with extraordinary egalitarianism and moral virtues. He hated oppression, injustice, and slavery. He loved family, God, and country and was willing to sacrifice comfort, safety, and life to execute his duty and responsibility. Wealth, fame, and power held no appeal for him.

John Brown was not confused or duplicitous or erratic; his conscience was clear. The difficulty he poses is within us. "Heaven help us!" said Frederick Douglass. "When our loftiest types of patriotism, our sublimest historic ideals of philanthropy, come to be treated as evidence of moonstruck madness. Posterity will owe everlasting thanks to John Brown for lifting up once more to the gaze of a nation grown fat and flabby on the garbage of lust and oppression, a true standard of heroic philanthropy, and each coming generation will pay its installment of the debt."[27]

When viewed in his time and place, the *man* John Brown is not difficult to understand. Who he is in the Adirondacks is who he is.

Appendix A

John Brown's Family

John Brown. Born May 9, 1800, in Torrington, Connecticut. Died December 2, 1859, in Charles Town, Virginia. Buried at John Brown Farm, North Elba, New York.

Dianthe Lusk. Born January 12, 1801. Married John Brown on June 21, 1820. Died August 10, 1832. Buried in Richmond, Pennsylvania.

CHILDREN OF JOHN BROWN AND DIANTHE LUSK BROWN

John Brown Jr. Born July 25, 1821, in Hudson, Ohio. Married Wealthy Hotchkiss in July 1847. Fought in Kansas and was captured, beaten, and put in chains. Died May 3, 1895, buried in Ohio.

Jason Brown. Born January 19, 1823, in Hudson, Ohio. Married Ellen Sherbondy in July 1847. Fought in Kansas. Died December 24, 1912, in Akron, Ohio.

Owen Brown. Born November 4, 1824, in Hudson, Ohio. Died January 9, 1889, in Pasadena, California. Owen had a withered arm but was able to be as active as any other person. Fought in Kansas. Took part in Harpers Ferry raid and escaped.

Frederick Brown (1). Born January 9, 1827, in Richmond, Pennsylvania. Died March 31, 1831.

Ruth Brown. Born February 18, 1829, in Richmond, Pennsylvania. Married Henry Thompson on September 26, 1850. Died January 18, 1904, in Pasadena, California. Children born in North Elba: Johnny (named after John Brown) and Ella Jane. Henry fought in Kansas and was wounded.

Henry and Isabelle Thompson are siblings, and cousins of Abbie and Alexis Hinckley.

Frederick Brown (2). Born December 21, 1830, in Richmond, Pennsylvania. Went to Kansas and killed there. Died August 30, 1856. Buried in Kansas.

Infant son, unnamed. Born August 7, 1832. Died that day.

༄

Mary Ann Day Brown. Born April 15, 1816, Granville, New York. Married John Brown on July 11, 1833. Died February 29, 1884. Buried in Madronia Cemetery, Saratoga, California.

CHILDREN OF JOHN BROWN AND MARY ANN DAY BROWN, HIS SECOND WIFE

Sarah Brown (1). Born May 11, 1834, in Richmond, Pennsylvania. Died of dysentery September 23, 1843. Buried in Richfield, Ohio.

Watson Brown. Born October 7, 1835, in Franklin Mills, Ohio. Married Isabelle (Belle) Thompson in September 1856. Died October 19, 1859, in Harpers Ferry, Virginia. Skeleton preserved, taken to Indiana, then buried at North Elba farm, October 13, 1882. Son, Frederick, born August 1859. Died August 1863, buried in North Elba Cemetery.

Salmon Brown. Born October 2, 1836, in Hudson, Ohio. Married Abigail (Abbie) C. Hinckley on October 15, 1857. Fought in Kansas. Did not go to Harpers Ferry. Died May 10, 1919, in Portland, Oregon. Children born in North Elba: Cora and Minnie Eliza. Wife, Abbie, was daughter of Horatio and Amanda Hinckley; Abbie and Isabella Thompson were first cousins; their mothers were sisters in the Jenkins family.

Charles Brown. Born November 3, 1837, in Hudson, Ohio. Died of dysentery, September 11, 1843. Buried in Richfield, Ohio.

Oliver Brown. Born March 9, 1839, in Franklin Mills, Ohio. Married Martha Brewster on April 7, 1858. Fought in Kansas. Died October 17, 1859, in Harpers Ferry, Virginia. Buried along Shenandoah River, body was later moved and buried at John Brown Farm on August 30, 1899. Daughter, Olive, born February 2, 1860. Died two days later, buried in North Elba Cemetery. Wife, Martha, died March 2, 1860, buried in North Elba Cemetery.

Peter Brown. Born December 7, 1840, in Hudson, Ohio. Died of dysentery, September 22, 1843, Buried in Richfield, Ohio.

Austin Brown. Born September 14, 1842, in Richfield, Ohio. Died of dysentery, September 21, 1843. Buried in Richfield, Ohio.

Annie Brown. Born December 23, 1843, in Richfield, Ohio. At age fifteen, served as lookout at Kennedy farm in Maryland. Married Samuel Adams. Died October 5, 1926, in Shively, California.

Amelia Brown. Born June 22, 1845, in Akron, Ohio. Died from accidental scalding, October 30, 1846. Buried in Akron, Ohio.

Sarah Brown (2). Born September 11, 1846, in Akron, Ohio. Died June 30, 1916, in Saratoga, California.

Ellen Brown (1). Born May 20, 1848, in Springfield, Massachusetts. Died April 30, 1849, in Springfield, Massachusetts. Buried in North Elba Cemetery.

Infant son, unnamed. Born April 26, 1852, in Akron, Ohio. Died three weeks later (May 17) of whooping cough. Buried in Akron, Ohio.

Ellen Brown (2). Born September 25, 1854, in Akron, Ohio. Married James Fablinger in 1876. Died July 25, 1916. Buried in Saratoga, California.

Appendix B

Timeline

1846   Gerrit Smith announces land giveaway to free blacks. Most of the lots lie in the Adirondacks.

1847   Brown family moves to Springfield, Massachusetts. John operates wool business.

1848   April 8: John visits Gerrit Smith in Peterboro, New York, and offers to join the black settlers.

October: John visits black settlers in Essex and Franklin County (Timbucto and Blacksville).

1849   Mid-May: Family moves to rented house in North Elba (Flanders farm on Lot 110).

June 28: Richard Henry Dana Jr. visits the Browns.

August: John goes to Europe to sell wool. Mary goes to Water Cure.

November: John and Mary return home. John and two sons contract with Gerrit Smith to buy Lot 95 (future site of John Brown Farm).

1850   January: Town of North Elba forms (previously part of Town of Keene).

September: John exhibits cattle at Essex County show. Ruth marries Henry Thompson. New Fugitive Slave Act goes into effect.

1851   March: Brown family moves to Akron, Ohio. Ruth and Henry remain in North Elba.

1854   Missouri Compromise is repealed by the Kansas-Nebraska Act, which enacts popular sovereignty.

1855   Five of Brown's sons and their families settle in Kansas Territory. The war in Kansas is underway.

June: John Brown and his family move back to North Elba to new house on Lot 95.

August 13: John and Henry leave for Kansas and Oliver joins them along the way.

October 7: John, Henry, and Oliver arrive in Osawatomie, Kansas.

1856   May 24: Pottawatomie Creek slayings take place.

June 2: Battle of Black Jack occurs.

August 30: John Brown becomes famous at Battle of Osawatomie.

1857   January to February: John visits North Elba.

March: John discovers grandfather's memorial stone and sends it to Westport, New York.

Mid-March: John speaks in Concord.

April 30 to May 12: John visits North Elba.

August: Franklin Sanborn visits North Elba to complete transfer of Lot 88—half to Mary, half to Ruth.

1858   March 23 to April 1: John visits North Elba.

April to May: John is in Canada and holds conference in Chatham.

Early June: John visits North Elba.

December 20: John and other men enter Missouri to liberate eleven slaves.

1859   April 19 to May 5: John visits North Elba.

May 8: John speaks at Concord Town Hall.

June: John visits North Elba for last time.

Early July: John moves to Kennedy farm in Maryland.

Mid-July: Annie and Martha go to Kennedy farm.

Early August: Watson and Dauphin and William Thompson come to Kennedy farm.

September 29: Anne and Martha leave Kennedy farm.

October 16 to 18: Harpers Ferry raid occurs.

November 2: John makes famous speech in court. He is sentenced to hang.

November 3: Mary leaves North Elba with Higginson.

December 1: Mary visits John in jail.

December 2: John Brown is executed and Mary receives his body in Harpers Ferry.

December 7: Mary arrives at farm with the coffin.

December 8: John is buried in grave at the North Elba farm.

1860 Early January: George Stearns visits Brown family in North Elba.

February 5 to 7: Franklin Sanborn visits Brown family in North Elba.

Mid-February: Annie and Sarah attend school in Concord. Annie returns home after a month.

May: Tea party given by Alcott family in Concord, Massachusetts, for Mary, Isabelle, and little Frederick.

Late June: Osborne Anderson visits the John Brown Farm.

July 4: Abolition celebration is held at the John Brown Farm.

1861 Annie and Sarah return to Sanborn's school and board with Alcott family.

April 12: Civil War begins when South Carolina troops fire on Fort Sumter.

Appendix B | 235

Annie and Sarah come back closer to home for school (Fort Edward Institute).

1862 February: Salmon Brown recruits Union soldiers and then forced to resign his officer post.

September 27: Mary Brown visits Boston and then visits family in Meadville, Pennsylvania.

1863 January 1: President Lincoln issues Emancipation Proclamation.

Mid-September: Families of Mary Brown, Salmon and Abbie Brown, and Ruth and Henry Thompson leave North Elba. Thompsons stay in Ohio, while Browns proceed to Iowa for the winter.

October 1863 to March 1864: Annie teaches at freedman's school in Norfolk, Virginia.

1864 April: Browns leave Iowa for California.

September 30: Browns reach Red Bluff, California.

Notes

Introduction

1. Professor Ebenezer Emmons in New York State Assembly Document 200, February 20, 1838; Emmons believed that the "Adirondacks" (or Algonquins) "resided in and occupied a part of the northern section of the state" before they were "expelled by the superior force of the Agoneseah, or Five Nations." This "historical fact"—the original inhabitants of the region were the Algonquins—induced Emmons to propose the name Adirondack for the High Peaks region in 1838. Soon after, the name Adirondack came to refer to the entire mountain region.

2. Edna Dean Proctor, "The Virginia Scaffold," in Edna Dean Proctor, *Poems* (Hurd and Houghton, 1867), 51–53. Poem read at a meeting in New York on December 2, 1859.

3. Douglass, *Life and Times*, 339.

4. "Sunday Reading," *Daily Appeal* (Carson City, NV), December 2, 1877.

5. Charles Dudley Warner, *The Press* (Hartford, CT), November 24, 1866.

6. Thomas Wentworth Higginson, "A Visit to John Brown's Household in 1859," in Ruchames, *Reader*, 219–23.

7. Louis A. DeCaro Jr., "John Brown's Grave," John Brown Today blog, December 9, 2018.

Chapter 1

1. "The John Brownites in Council," *New York Daily Herald*, December 16, 1859; Watson, "Supplement to Survey of Essex County," 705.

2. *Elizabethtown Post*, December 24, 1859. New York State Census data of 1855 confirmed the claims of large quantities of crops and farm items produced. The town also had a blacksmith, a potato starch mill, and two lumbering operations.

3. J.C., a correspondent, "North Elba and the Fourth of July Next," *Burlington Weekly Free Press*, June 1, 1860.

4. *Elizabethtown Post*, December 24, 1859. *New York Herald*, December 16, 1859. Watson, *A General View of the County of Essex*, 721, 879–80. Watson, "Supplement to Survey of Essex County," 710–11. Watson also said (as in any new colony), among the virtuous and worthy of Essex County, there drifted a few of the loose and reckless. *A General View*, 714.

5. Charles Day (1777–1852) married Mary "Polly" Gould (1780–1813) and they had six children: Orson, Martha, Horace, Elizabeth, Sarah, and Permelia. After Mary's death, Charles married Mary Ann Little (1787–1882) and they had five children: Mary Ann (who married John Brown), Nancy, John C., Charles A., and Diantha. Some records indicate that Mary Ann Brown's mother's name may have been Crossett but her gravestone inscription says Mary Ann Little Day. "Ancestry of Mary Ann Day," compiled by Elizabeth Thew McDonald, Glens Falls, New York, 1984–1985; "George Delamater letters," transcribed by Elizabeth Thew McDonald, August 1984. Martha Day's husband Thomas Delamater was from Whitehall, New York.

6. Ernest C. Miller, "John Brown's Ten Years in Northwestern Pennsylvania," *Pennsylvania History* (January 1948), 24–29; Sanborn, *Life and Letters*, 90.

7. Hon. Zenas H. Ellis of Rutland, Vermont, "Writes of Impressions Here at Unveiling of John Brown Memorial," *Lake Placid News*, June 21, 1935. This important Brown-Delamater-Day connection is rarely noted by historians. Accounts generally refer to the Delamaters as friends, not family, and describe Mary as an empty shell, molded (or forced) by John into accepting his views.

8. JB to brother Frederick, November 21, 1834, in Sanborn, *Life and Letters*, 40–41.

9. "From the Philadelphia Observer," *Alton (IL) Observer*, December 28, 1837.

10. Emerson, in Sanborn, *Life and Letters*, 54.

11. JB to MB, March 7, 1846 (misdated 1844), in Sanborn, *Life and Letters*, 60–61.

12. Oates, *To Purge This Land*, 17; Sanborn, *Life and Letters*, 92; RBT recollections in Sanborn, *Life and Letters*, 38; Villard, *Fifty Years After*, 19. Historian Sean Wilentz uses this to describe Brown as "a beaten child as well as a child-beater" and a man "capable of cruelty to his family." Writer Daegan Miller claims, "Brown's system was the exact same one used by Southerners—they called it the pushing system—to drive their slaves to pick ever more cotton." However, the occasional use of the switch to punish a child's bad behavior (and improve morals) is not "the exact same" as repeatedly inflicting brutal lashes of a whip as punishment for working too slowly, talking back, trying to read, or other reasons (or no reason at all). Historian John Stauffer says Brown often did the thrashing "with tears in his eyes" and one time he insisted on taking half of the lashes himself, commanding his son to whip his bare back. Sean Wilentz, "Homegrown Terrorist," *New Republic*

Online, October 27, 2005; Miller, *This Radical Land*, 271 note 112; Stauffer, *Black Hearts of Men*, 91.

13. Douglass, *John Brown, An Address by Frederick Douglass*, 1881.

14. JB, "Provisional Constitution and Ordinances for the People of the United States," May 8, 1858, in Stauffer and Trodd, *Tribunal*, 26–37; Frederick Douglass, "Editorial Correspondence," *North Star*, February 11, 1848.

15. RBT recollections in Sanborn, *Life and Letters*, 100.

16. Gerrit Smith to Rev. Charles B. Ray, Rev. Theodore S. Wright, and Dr. James McCune Smith, August 1, 1846, in Frothingham, *Gerrit Smith*, 102–5; "National Convention of Colored Americans and Their Friends," *Liberator*, September 24, 1847. The objects of meeting on October 6, 1847, in Troy included: to urge "the necessity of acquiring Property as a means of destroying prejudice, and of elevating the character of the colored people to a high and honorable position in society." *Proceedings of the National Convention of Colored People . . . Troy, NY . . . 1847*.

17. Gerrit Smith to Dr. James McCune Smith, Elder Charles B. Ray and Rev. T. Wright, November 14, 1846.

18. Gerrit Smith, "To the Colored People of the Northern States," *North Star*, August 4, 1848.

19. Frederick Douglass, *North Star*, February 18, 1848. The agents made lists of the first 2,000 grantees in 1846, but most of those deeds were not completed until the spring of 1847 or later. Smith wrote to his agents on September 9, 1846, that he had made out 2,000 deeds and it would take "perhaps a couple of years" to award the other 1,000 deeds. (It took until 1853.) Frothingham, *Gerrit Smith*, 105–6.

20. "Gerrit Smith's Land," *North Star*, February 25, 1848, from *Ram's Horn*.

21. *Brooklyn Daily Eagle*, March 10, 1848.

22. "The Smith Lands," *North Star*, April 14, 1848.

23. Extract of Sermon by Henry Highland Garnet, *North Star*, May 12, 1848.

24. Willis A. Hodges and Charles B. Ray, Agriculture Committee, *Proceedings of the National Convention of Colored People . . . Troy, NY . . . 1847*; Gatewood, *Free Man of Color*, 80.

25. James Henderson to Henry Highland Garnet, January 29, 1849, in *North Star*, February 16, 1849.

26. Gerrit Smith to Rev. Charles B. Ray, Rev. Theodore S. Wright, and Dr. James McCune Smith, August 1, 1846, in Frothingham, *Gerrit Smith*, 102–5.

27. Rev. Charles B. Ray, Rev. Theodore S. Wright, and Dr. James McCune Smith to Friends (grantees), September 9, 1846, in *An Address to the Three Thousand Colored Citizens of New York Who Are the Owners of 120,000 Acres of Land . . . Given to Them by Gerrit Smith Esq., 1846*.

28. "Convention of Colored People," *New York Tribune*, March 20, 1851.

29. J. W. Loguen to James McCune Smith, in *North Star*, March 24, 1848.

30. "From the *Model Worker* New York, May 18, 1848," *North Star*, January 12, 1849; "Gerrit Smith's Land," *North Star*, January 12, 1849; "Wait J. Lewis,"

North Star, December 8, 1848; "Essex County," from *Northern Star and Colored Farmer*, in *North Star*, February 2, 1849. It is difficult to make general judgments from the various accounts. There were some good lots and plenty of bad lots (many of which have never been inhabited). There were unscrupulous surveyors and there were overexaggerations of the land quality. For example: J. W. Loguen visited many of the granted lots in Franklin and Essex County in September of 1847. He concluded that, in Essex County, "the farms given by Mr. Smith, with very few exceptions, are as good land as any man can need." Regarding the lands in Franklin County, he said they were "first-rate" (either for farming or valuable timber) and "not one that is worthless." Loguen to McCune Smith, in *North Star*, March 24, 1848. Loguen overstated the potential of the lands; many of the granted lots were worthless, inaccessible mountain or swamp lands.

31. Garnet preaching to Smith grantees in Troy, New York, in *North Star*, May 12, 1848.

32. Frederick Douglass, "The Smith Land," *North Star*, February 18, 1848.

33. Hinton, *John Brown and His Men*, 16–17. Various versions of what Brown said are given in Redpath, *Public Life*, 59; Sanborn, *Life and Letters*, 87; and others. Brown might have read about Smith's project in *Ram's Horn* or *North Star* or heard about it from Willis Hodges or Frederick Douglass in person.

34. Mary MacKenzie, "History of the Northwest Bay-Hopkinton Road," *Franklin Historical Review* (1992–1993–1994), 9. This old route was precipitous and hazardous. In 1858 a new road was built through Cascade Pass, but the old road was still passable in the early 1900s.

35. JB to Hodges, October 28, 1848, in "John Brown in Essex County," *Evening Post*, December 20, 1859. Brown bought the supplies using all the funds he had; Hodges had to pay the freight charge when the supplies arrived.

36. "Movements of the Grantees of the City of Troy," *North Star*, November 10, 1848.

37. JB to Hodges, January 22, 1849, in "John Brown in Essex County."

38. JB to his father Owen Brown, January 10, 1849, in Ruchames, *Reader*, 67.

39. JB to Hodges, March 30 and May 7, 1849, in "John Brown in Essex County." Accounts often fault Brown for his delay in arrival, ignoring the tragic reason for his delay.

40. RBT recollections in Sanborn, *Life and Letters*, 44.

41. AB recollections in "Our Weekly Boston Letter," *Springfield* (Massachusetts) *Daily Republican*, June 6, 1908. Inscription recorded by Clarence Gee in a letter to Velma West Sykes, September 4, 1967. Sykes.

Chapter 2

1. William Lloyd Garrison, "The Colored Population of the United States, No. 2," *Liberator*, January 22, 1831; Gatewood, *Free Man of Color*, Preface, 4. Quoted

text written by Willis Hodges on his thirty-fourth birthday, February 12, 1849, in Blacksville, Franklin County, New York. Hodges was referring to an incident with slave catchers in the North in 1829. As a free black in Virginia, Hodges observed slaves being compelled to labor in sickness as well as health, and without wages or sufficient food or clothing. Runaways were hunted with blood hounds and shot, with large rewards given by their masters to their killers.

2. Henry Highland Garnet, "The Past and Present Condition, and the Destiny, of the Colored Race," address made to the Female Benevolent Society of Troy, New York, January 10, 1848; "Farming," the *Colored American*, December 4, 1841.

3. James Henderson to Henry Highland Garnet, January 29, 1849, in *North Star*, February 16, 1849.

4. Alfred Lord Tennyson, "Timbuctoo," in J. C. Thomson, ed., *The Suppressed Poems of Alfred Lord Tennyson 1830–1868* (Sands, 1910), 9–20. "Timbuctoo" was one of Tennyson's first poems (written while he studied at Trinity College) and it won the Chancellor's Medal at the Cambridge Commencement of 1829.

5. "John Brown in Essex County." The article stated that John Brown named Timbucto. James Henderson to Henry Highland Garnet, January 29, 1849, in *North Star*, February 16, 1849; RBT to MB, September 7, 1849, Sykes; JBJr, October 15, 1849, in Cotter to Gee, July 31, 1967, Stutler. Brown's May 22, 1849, letter was misdated 1848; other historical records confirm the family moved to Essex County in May of 1849 (not 1848). More recently, a few writers changed the spelling to "Timbuctoo" (with two *o*'s). John Brown and Henderson spelled Timbucto with one *o*. It was not a misspelling; it was an accepted alternate form of the name of the Africa city and appeared in several newspaper accounts at that time. Timbucto did not refer to the entirety of the Town of North Elba, nor to the entire Gerrit Smith land giveaway of 120,000 acres. The residences of the John Brown family were not considered part of Timbucto. Ruth and John Jr. clearly state that Timbucto was separate from the Flanders farm, and Ruth refers only to black people as residing there. Regarding the historic farm on Lot 95, the Browns did not move there until 1855, years after the term Timbucto went out of use. Perhaps after "North Elba" became an officially designated Town with physical boundaries in late 1849, there was no longer a need for the vague, ill-defined terms "West Keene" or "Timbucto."

6. Douglass, *John Brown, An Address by Frederick Douglass*, 1881.

7. George Delamater to JBJr., July 23, 1849, in Cotter to Gee, July 31, 1967, Stutler. The family came by way of Whitehall to visit their Day family relatives. George heard from "Jay the Day" of Whitehall that the family stopped on their way to the "colony in Northeastern NY."

8. RBT recollections in Sanborn, *Life and Letters*, 100; John Brown's statement quoted in Jason Brown to JBJr, February 15, 1853, in Kristin L. Gibbons, *Extracts of Letters of the John Brown Family 1849–1863: Pertaining to Life at North Elba, Essex County, New York* (New York State Parks and Recreation, Division for Historic Preservation, 1979), 13.

9. RBT recollections in Sanborn, *Life and Letters*, 99–100. Many accounts erroneously call this the Cone Flanders farm (Cone was Chapin's son). The photo of the Flanders house in Donaldson's *A History of the Adirondacks* is not the correct house. The Chapin Flanders house burned in 1900. A historical marker on Route 73 indicates the approximate spot where the house once stood.

10. "John Brown in Essex County."

11. RBT recollections in Sanborn, *Life and Letters*, 100.

12. Lucid, *Journal of Dana*, 364.

13. Lucid, *Journal of Dana*; RBT recollections in Sanborn, *Life and Letters*, 101–2. Dana stayed at (Iddo) Osgood's Inn, which had opened in 1833 and became the local post office in 1849. Later, Osgood's son Dillon ran the place, followed by Martin and Amanda Lyon, until it eventually became the Stagecoach Inn. Nearby, Robert Scott began to take in visitors on a regular basis, circa 1850.

14. This and subsequent references to Dana's article/account in this chapter refer to "How We Met John Brown," *Atlantic Monthly* (July 1871). Dana felt confident that the dwelling was a "log-house," but since others described it as a frame building, he suggested Brown "may have put up a frame house afterwards." Though many houses in the area were built of logs, neither the Flanders house nor the Browns house were log cabins. Almost immediately after Dana's 1871 article appeared, an article by E. M. Sears in the *Religious Magazine and Monthly Review* (July 1871) pointed out, "There are two houses in North Elba in which John Brown lived, neither of them a log cabin." Dana also described the site as a "mere recent clearing," but the Flanders farm had existed for decades. Again, Dana made his 1871 narrative agree with accounts written about the John Brown Farm.

15. Charles Francis Adams, *Richard Henry Dana, A Biography* (Houghton Mifflin, 1890); Wilbur H. Siebert, *The Underground Railroad from Slavery to Freedom* (Macmillan, 1898), 113, 126–27; Alexander C. Flick, ed., *History of the State of New York*, vol. 7 (Columbia University Press, 1935), 68; Tom Calarco, *The Underground Railroad in the Adirondack Region* (McFarland, 2004).

16. It was improbable that John Brown was manning a station since he had arrived just weeks prior and was absent from home with great frequency. There was no reason to make the difficult, out-of-the-way journey of twenty-five-plus miles through the mountains westward from Westport or Elizabethtown into the wilds of North Elba. Upon reaching North Elba, there was nowhere to go except back northeastward. Reaching North Elba from the south through Indian Pass was even more problematic. Even local guides got lost trying to trek through Indian Pass.

17. Smith gave grants to a few fugitives, such as John Thomas who settled in Franklin County. There may have been a fugitive among the North Elba grantees in Essex County, but no reliable record has been found. The claims of an established route of the Underground Railroad in North Elba are based on assumptions, later recollections, or articles known to be erroneous. These include Dana, "How We Met

John Brown," *Atlantic Monthly* (July 1871); Donaldson, *History of the Adirondacks*, 1920; recollections by Lyman Epps Jr., such as Mary Lee, "John Brown Rests Amid the Mountains," *New York Times*, October 20, 1929; and Charles A. Wardner, *Footprints on Adirondack Trails*, unpublished manuscript (memories recalled by his father James M. Wardner at an old age), Adirondack Experience Library, Blue Mountain Lake, New York.

18. *Proceedings of the Anti-Slavery Convention of American Women, Held in Philadelphia, May 15th, 16th, 17th, and 18th, 1838* (Merrihew & Gunn, 1838).

19. Gatewood, *Free Man of Color*, 78, 80, 56. Hodges and Brown exchanged forty-seven letters, but most of them were destroyed after Harpers Ferry. Yet Hodges left impressions of John Brown in his autobiography, written in Franklin County in 1848–1849, with an introduction added by his grandson.

20. JB to Gerrit Smith, June 20, 1849, Stutler. The forty-acre lot given to James Henderson was in Lot 83, but it was wilderness and unfit for farming, so he settled (squatted) on better land Lot 93. The land contract was never completed, and the grantees were leery of making improvements on the lot. Brown's payment for Lot 93 was transferred toward the purchase of Lot 95.

21. James McCune Smith to Gerrit Smith, February 6, 1850, in C. Peter Ripley, *The Black Abolitionist Papers*, vol. *IV*, 42–45. While in North Elba, McCune Smith attended a religious service at the house of "old Deacon" Iddo Osgood.

22. The 1850 census undercounted the black population in North Elba. Several settlers were not listed and Thomas Brown was listed as white. Based on McCune Smith's letter and other data, the black population in 1850 was about fifty to sixty. Given the inherent inadequacy of census taking and the frequent comings and goings of residents, these numbers are only estimates, yet they make it clear that the black population was always quite small. See Manchester, *The Plains of Abraham*, chapter Twenty-Three, for more information on the settlers.

23. *Enterprise and Vermonter* (Vergennes, VT), November 26, 1851; T. S. Nash, "Personal Recollections of John Brown," *Plattsburgh Republican*, April 27, 1900; *Semi-Weekly Standard* (Raleigh, NC), November 18, 1858.

24. Gerrit Smith, "To the Liberty Party," May 7, 1846, online at loc.gov. Black men had been seeking the vote for many years. At an 1840 convention in New York City, they were asked, "Are you willing to leave your children no better public inheritance than to be among the disenfranchised—the politically oppressed?" Black men answered, "O no! . . . We can redeem ourselves. . . . That we shall eventually triumph is sure and certain." "Address of the New York State Convention to their Colored Fellow Citizens," *Colored American*, November 21, 1840.

25. Miller, *This Radical Land*, 72.

26. "Free Soil Nominations," in *Council Grove (KS) Republican*, September 23, 1848. The Free Soil Party merged into the Republican Party in 1854.

27. "Free Soil Nominations;" Gerrit Smith to Charles B. Ray, November 16, 1848, in *North Star*, January 12, 1849.

28. JB to Willis Hodges, January 22, 1849, in "John Brown in Essex County;" Godine, *The Black Woods*, 188. Three others voted sporadically in the Town of Franklin starting in 1860. The 1855 New York Census indicated that eleven black men qualified as voters in North Elba.

29. Watson, *General View of County of Essex*, 726.

30. "To the New York State Convention Assembled in the City of Troy," *The Colored American*, August 28, 1841; Henry Highland Garnet sermon, *North Star*, May 12, 1848.

31. In 1834, Brown asked his brother Frederick to join him in forming a black school and to bring some first-rate abolitionist families from Ohio with him. However, as with many of Brown's ideas, the undertaking never materialized. In 1847, John tried to interest his nephew George Delamater in going to Canada to start an African school but having recently passed the bar exam, George was eager to practice law and declined the teaching offer.

32. Moore, *History of the A. M. E. Zion Church*, 307–14; Deed, Gerrit Smith to Christopher Rush, 160 acres in North Elba, recorded on September 23, 1847. Indenture, Christopher Rush to Trustees for Rush Academy, 160 acres, written 1847, recorded 1849, Essex County Deed Book CC, 245–46. Trustees were Jas. P. Thompson, J. S. Smith, Ed. V. Clark, Samuel J. Howard, John Tappan, J. W. Loguen, William Sanford, John Thomas, John Darnell, Henry Travis, Christopher Brown, and Jas. Stokley. The Manual Labor School movement promoted the practice of agriculture or mechanic work along with academic studies. Despite the detailed plans and Constitution (with 14 articles), there was no umpf to the Rush Academy project. Minimal funds were collected, and no building plans were developed. It seems likely that John Brown knew about the plan, since he traveled in the same circle of friends and cities as the AMEZ organizers.

33. Watson, *General View of County of Essex*, 725–26.

Chapter 3

1. Brown references Bible passages from Galatians and Deuteronomy. The final quote, "but let us resolutely trust in God, and keep our *powder dry*," is generally attributed to Oliver Cromwell.

2. JB to JBJr, September 21, 1849, in Sanborn, *Life and Letters*, 72–73.

3. JB to Sons, December 4, 1850, in Sanborn, *Life and Letters*, 77.

4. Christopher Clark, *The Communitarian Moment* (Cornell University Press 1995), 199. Regardless of the effectiveness of the water treatment itself, the clean water, sanitary conditions, and rest probably cured many ills, especially for women who did dangerous, toilsome housework and birthed several children. Mary Brown gave birth eleven times in her first fourteen years of marriage.

5. JBJr to JB, September 18, 1849, Gee.

6. RBT to MB, September 7, 1849, Sykes.

7. RBT to MB, September 7, 1849, Sykes; RBT to MB, October 31, 1849, in "John Brown's Family," *The Collector* XLIV, no. 7 (June 1930): 74.

8. JBJr to MB, October 15, 1849, in Gibbons, *Extracts of Letters of the John Brown Family*, 1. The Epps and Dickson houses were on Bear Cub Road, south of the Hinckley farm.

9. Gerrit Smith and wife (of Peterboro) to John, Jason, and Owen Brown (of Keene) for $244, the parcel of land Lot 95 of Township Number 12, Old Military Tract, Thorne Survey containing 244 acres more or less. Indenture written November 8, 1849, signed November 9, 1849, and recorded in Essex County, New York, on December 13, 1849. Essex County Deed Book GG, 265. A note was written on the back of the Lot 93 agreement, saying John Brown no longer wanted his $225 payment applied toward that contract. Instead, the money would be credited toward the purchase of Lot 95. Cotter.

10. MB to JBJr, November 8, 1849, Stutler; JB to MB, November 28, 1850, in Sanborn, *Life and Letters*, 106–7.

11. JB to Sons and Daughters, December 4, 1850, in Sanborn, *Life and Letters*, 75–77; "John Brown's Grave," Lake Placid letter to *New York Tribune* in *Iowa State Register*, December 12, 1886.

12. JB to Sons and Daughters, December 4, 1850.

13. RBT to Wealthy Brown, August 6, 1850, in Mary McKenzie, *Placid Pioneer* (Spring 1968).

14. DeCaro, *Fire from the Midst of You*, 187.

15. JB to MB, November 28, 1850; JB to MB, December 15 and 22, 1849; JB to MB, September 28, 1850, Cotter.

16. "The Fairs," *Essex County Republican*, October 5, 1850; "Agricultural Fair," *Essex County Republican*, September 28, 1850; "John Brown as a Farmer," *Evening Star*, November 14, 1859.

17. RBT to Wealthy Brown, August 6, 1850.

18. Byron Brewster, "Reminiscences of John Brown of North Elba," *Saranac Lake News*, February 4, 1911; JB to JBJr, November 4 and December 4, 1850, in Sanborn, *Life and Letters*, 75–77.

19. JB to MB, November 28, 1850.

20. "Essex County. N.Y.," *Liberator*, August 11, 1837; "Anti-Slavery Convention," *Keeseville Argus*, June 14, 1837; Lewis Lott, "Interesting Reminiscences," *Essex County Republican*, June 9, 1887.

21. "Meeting in Jay," *Essex County Republican*, October 26, 1850. James Kimball, chairman, E. P. Newell and N. C. Boynton, secretaries. Resolution Committee representing Jay: Daniel Blish, Hiram Newell; Wilmington: Wendell Lansing, Rogers Hikok (Hickok); Keene: U. D. Mihills, Joseph Hillman; North Elba: Iddo Osgood, Roswell Thompson; and St. Armand: D. C. Skiff, E. G. Titus. Addressed the meeting: Rev. W. Kingsley, R. C. R. Chase, Esq., and Wm. W. Finch, Esq.

22. RBT recollections in Sanborn, *Life and Letters*, 131–32.

23. JB to Mary, November 28, 1850.

24. JB to HT, March 15, 1851, in Sanborn, *Life and Letters*, 107–8.

25. Judge Robert S. Hale, as told in 1878, in Vincent Y. Bowditch, *Life and Correspondence of Henry Ingersoll Bowditch* (Houghton, Mifflin, 1902), 82.

26. JB to RBT and HT, October 6, 1851, in Sanborn, *Life and Letters*, 108; RBT recollections in Sanborn, *Life and Letters*, 104.

27. JB to RBT and HT, January 1852, in Sanborn, *Life and Letters*, 148 and 45. Four children of Mary and John had been taken by dysentery in 1843, one scalded by hot water in 1846, one gave way to consumption in 1849, and one lost to whooping cough in 1852.

28. JB to RBT, August 10, 1852, in Sanborn, *Life and Letters*, 152; JB to RBT and HT, October 6, 1851, in Sanborn, *Life and Letters*, 108; JB to MB, December 27, 1852, in Sanborn, *Life and Letters*, 108–9; RBT recollections in Sanborn, *Life and Letters*, 104.

29. S. R. Stoddard, *The Adirondacks Illustrated* (Weed, Parsons, 1874), 69. Stoddard said: "It is a well-known fact that some unused to the woods will become so effectually 'turned around' that they will be certain that something is the matter with the compass to make it point wrong, and even distrust the sun itself if it happens to be in a different position from that which they think it ought to be." Another version of the Henderson story is told by John G. Fay in his "Letter to the Editor," *Lake Placid News*, December 11, 1942.

30. Watson, *A General View of the County of Essex*, 725–26; MacKenzie, *Lake Placid and North Elba*, 8; Manchester, *The Plains of Abraham*, 151–52.

31. Manchester, *The Plains of Abraham*, 131. Lyman Epps passed away in 1897 and it was said, "He will be long remembered as a music teacher of rare natural ability and as a man of frankness and gracious manners." "John Brown, His Raiders and Their Last Resting Place," *Post and Gazette*, August 31, 1899. Lyman's son, Lyman Epps Jr., stayed in Lake Placid and was the last survivor of Timbucto, dying in 1942.

32. William Appo was listed as part of Mary Brown's household in the 1860 census. After William's death, his Lot 87 property passed to Albertine, who sold parts of it to her brother Lyman Epps Jr. and Anna Newman in 1900, and part to Edward Brewster in 1903. The part of the lot (with a house and barn where Albertine lived in 1888) was deeded to Anna Newman in 1906.

Chapter 4

1. JB to JBJr, June 1854, in Sanborn, *Life and Letters*, 105.

2. JB to MB, December 27, 1852, and JB to John Jr., December 15, 1852, in Sanborn, *Life and Letters*, 105–9.

3. Jason Brown to JBJr, February 1, 1852, and RBT to Wealthy Brown, February 22 and September 27, 1852, in Gibbons, *Extracts of Letters of the John Brown Family*, 8, 11.

4. JB to RBT and HT, April 6, 1853, in Sanborn, *Life and Letters*, 109.

5. JB to RBT and HT, April 6 and June 30, 1853, in Sanborn, *Life and Letters*, 109–10; JB to Children (RBT and Henry), May 10, 1853, Stutler.

6. JB to JBJr, June 1854, in Sanborn, *Life and Letters*, 105; DeCaro, *Fire from the Midst of You*, 210; Jason (and Owen) Brown to Brothers, February 15, 1853, in Gibbons, *Extracts of Letters of the John Brown Family*, 12–13.

7. JB to sons, August 21, 1854, in Sanborn, *Life and Letters*, 191.

8. JB to RBT and HT, September 30, 1854, in Ruchames, *Reader*, 86. Historian David Reynolds claimed the black settlers voted for Brown's return and "affected the course of American history by helping him decide upon the direction of his anti-slavery activities. . . . Largely because of a decision made by black colonists at North Elba, Brown deferred his [Allegheny] plan." Although it is quite probable that the black settlers encouraged Brown to return, there is no evidence of their response. Also, Brown's return to North Elba did not defer Brown's plan, the Kansas war did. Reynolds, *John Brown*, 132.

9. JB to RBT and HT, February 18, 1854, and May 7, 1855, in Sanborn, *Life and Letters*, 192–93. To finance the venture, John attempted to sell cattle in Illinois.

10. "Among the Adirondacks," *New York Times*, August 5, 1867; "John Brown's House and Grave," *Terre Haute Daily Gazette*, September 22, 1870; Donaldson, *History of the Adirondacks*, vol. II, 7; New York State 1855 census; North Elba, Essex County Tax Records, 1855. The shorter John Brown Road, which starts opposite the horse show fields, did not exist at that time. The log cabin confusion was caused by erroneous statements such as, "the logs of the original building have been covered by clap boards." "An Excursion to the Adirondack Mountains, in the Summer of 1861," *Friends' Intelligencer*, 743.

11. JB to Children (RBT and HT), May 10, 1853, Stutler.

12. W. R. Lethaby, *Architecture, Mysticism and Myth* (Macmillan, 1892), 53–69; Gene Logsdon, "Why the Midwest is Square," *The Old Farmer's Almanac* (1987).

13. JBJr recollections given November 1883, in Sanborn, *Life and Letters*, 190; SB to Father, May 21, 1855, in Villard, *Fifty Years After*, 82.

14. Villard, *Fifty Years After*, 82–84. Letter written May 20 and 24, 1855.

15. JB to MB, June 28, 1855, in Sanborn, *Life and Letters*, 193–94; "Great Anti-Slavery Convention," *Frederick Douglass' Paper*, July 6, 1855.

16. Du Bois, *John Brown*, 132; JB, told to Richard Hinton in 1858, in Sanborn, *Life and Letters*, 117.

17. Chamberlin, *John Brown (The Beacon Biographies)*, 48–49.

18. Lyman E. Epps, *Frederick Douglass' Paper*, July 12, 1854.

19. *Proceedings of the Colored National Convention, Held in Rochester, July 6, 7 and 8, 1853* (Office of Frederick Douglass' Paper, 1853), 33–38. Douglass proposed

the establishment of an Industrial College to teach the mechanic arts as a superior alternative to farming initiatives.

20. Thomas Addison Richards, *The Romance of American Landscape* (Leavitt and Allen, 1855), 235–36.

21. Gerrit Smith, "Letter from Mr. Gerrit Smith," *New-York Tribune*, August 10, 1857.

22. "Letter from Mr. Gerrit Smith," *New-York Tribune*, August 10, 1857; "John Brown as Farmer," *Syracuse* (NY) *Daily Courier and Union*, November 10, 1859; A Virginian, *The Two Rebellions*, 38.

23. Frothingham, *Gerrit Smith*, 112–13.

24. Godine, *The Black Woods*, 453n19.

25. Donaldson, *A History of the Adirondacks*, vol. I, xix; vol. II, 3–6.

26. "Anniversary of Birth of John Brown Observed Here," *Lake Placid News*, May 12, 1922; O. Byron Brewster, "Brown, the Man Manifest," in *John Brown in Bronze, 1800–1859* (John Brown Memorial Association, 1935), 20–25. Brewster insinuated that Freeman's Home (not Timbucto) was *the* black settlement in North Elba.

27. Donaldson, *A History of the Adirondacks*, vol. II, 6.

28. "The John Brownites in Council," *New York Daily Herald*, December 16, 1859; "Brooklyn. Colored Peoples' Funeral Services—Honors to John Brown in Essex County," *Evening Post*, December 12, 1859; Gerrit Smith, *John Brown*, brochure, 1867.

29. Godine, *The Black Woods*, 337; Hadley Krucek-Aaron, "Race and Remembering in the Adirondacks: Accounting for Timbucto in the Past and the Present," in *The Archeology of Race* (University Press of Florida, 2015), 142; Miller, *This Radical Land*, 78–79, 272n122. Daegan Miller, "At Home in the Great Northern Wilderness: African Americans and Freedom's Ecology in the Adirondacks, 1846–1859," *Environmental Humanities* 2 (2013): 121. In explanation for his perspective, Miller said, "I'm not sure there's anything particularly worthwhile in Brown's example [of revolutionary commitment]."

30. Giving Timbucto and Smith's scheme extra import and clout does not rectify the incorrect or racist accounts of the past, it continues to distort the past. *Possession* of a Smith land deed meant nothing in terms of voting. To qualify to vote, black men had to *own* real property valued at $250 or more. To own property, a person had to *register* a land deed with the County where the property resided. (Then, the owner had to pay land taxes each year or the State might confiscate the property and sell it for back taxes.) Although the land lots given to black men were often referred to as farms, the lots that Smith gave away were unimproved and worth about $40. Only by building a house and cultivating the land might the property reach a value of $250. Of the grantees who registered their deeds and paid taxes, fewer than one hundred ever improved their lots and only about twenty of those reached a value to enable them to vote.

31. Redpath, *The Public Life of Captain John Brown*, 59, 63.
32. Du Bois, *John Brown*, 110–11.

Chapter 5

1. *The Conquest of Kansas, by Missouri and Her Allies* (Phillips, Sampson, 1856), 332. Phillips was a special correspondent of the *New York Tribune*.
2. Sanborn, *Life and Letters*, 105. SB to Mother, Brothers, and Sisters, August 16 and August 20, 1855, Stutler.
3. Wealthy Brown to Watson Brown, September 16, 1855, in Villard, *Fifty Years After*, 92.
4. JB to family, August 9, 1855, Stutler; JB to MB, September 4, 1855, in Sanborn, *Life and Letters*, 199–200.
5. JB to MB, September 4, 1855, in Sanborn, *Life and Letters*, 199–200. JB to MB, September 15, 1855, Stutler.
6. JB to MB, October 13–14, November 2 and 23, 1855, in Sanborn, *Life and Letters*, 201–5.
7. JB to MB, November 30, 1855, Stutler; MB to JB, May 20, 1856, Sykes.
8. JB to MB, January 1 and February 1, 1856, Stutler; JB to MB, November 30, 1855, Stutler; JB to MB, February 6, 1856, Gee.
9. MB to JB, May 20, 1856, Sykes. To make some cash, Watson hired out to sow seeds for Henry's brother, Samuel Thompson.
10. HT to RBT, April 16 and May 1856, in Villard, *Fifty Years After*, 133–34.
11. RBT to HT, May 14, 1856, Cotter.
12. Sanborn, *Life and Letters*, 235. Atchison and General Stringfellow came from Missouri to lead proslavery men in making Kansas a slave state.
13. "Song of the Border Ruffian," *Punch* 31 (December 6, 1856): 229; *Gazette* (Montreal, Canada), June 11, 1857.
14. *New-York Tribune*, May 21, 1856.
15. Jason Brown recollections in Villard, *Fifty Years After*, 151.
16. Villard, *Fifty Years After*, 151.
17. JB to MB and children, June 1856, in Villard, *Fifty Years After*, 148.
18. SB, December 27, 1859, in *Liberator*, February 17, 1860; Sanborn, *Life and Letters*, 261–62, 273. The party consisted of John, Owen, Frederick, Salmon, and Oliver Brown; Henry Thompson; Theodore Weiner; and James Townsley.
19. Villard, *Fifty Years After*, 183. The Pottawatomie Creek murders did not become a "Massacre" in 1856. Not until after the Harpers Ferry raid in 1859 did the term appear with any frequency.
20. George W. Martin, ed., *Transactions of the Kansas State Historical Society, 1907–1908* (State Printing Office, 1908), 126; Sanborn, *Life and Letters*, 171–72.
21. "Exciting News from Kansas" and "The Fiends," *Liberator*, September 5, 1856.

22. Sanborn, *Life and Letters*, 336–37. Hearing news of Henry's injury at Black Jack, William Thompson left North Elba to join emigrants on their way to Kansas in early August. John Brown came into their camp in Nebraska and took William to his wounded brother.

23. JB to MB and children, September 7, 1856, in Ruchames, *Reader*, 99.

24. "The Spirit of Black Republicanism—Proof of the Treasonable Purposes of the Sectionalists," *Buffalo Courier*, July 16, 1856.

25. Eleanor Atkinson, "The Soul of John Brown: Recollections of the Great Abolitionist by his Son," *The American Magazine* (October 1909); Oates, *Purge This Land*, 194.

26. Villard, *Fifty Years After*, 248. "Carrying the war into Africa" means retaliating on an enemy by adopting his own tactics, generally attacking the enemy's home turf. The phrase originated from the legend of Roman general Scipio outmaneuvering Hannibal and his army by going into Africa and threatening Carthage.

27. "When Will It Stop?," *Brooklyn Evening Star*, March 5, 1857, includes "To the Friends of Freedom" by John Brown.

28. "Old John Brown's Farewell to the Plymouth Rocks, Bunker Hill Monuments, Charter Oaks, and Uncle Tom's Cabins," Sanborn, *Life and Letters*, 508–9.

29. JB to MB and Children, March 12 and May 27, 1857, in Sanborn, *Life and Letters*, 375 and 410. The stone was probably carved with Frederick's inscription and then placed in James Allen's shop in Westport in 1857.

30. JB to Amos A. Lawrence, March 19, 1857, and Lawrence to JB, March 20, 1857, in Villard, *Fifty Years After*, 279–80. Perhaps it was the letter and $70 Lawrence sent to John "for own personal use" on February 19 that spurred John to write this appeal.

31. JB to William Barnes, April 3, 1857, in Ruchames, *Revolutionary*, 112; Sanborn, *Life and Letters*, 408–14.

32. JB to Sanborn, May 15, 1857, in Sanborn, *Letters and Letters*, 408. Later accounts (such as Donaldson, *History of the Adirondacks*, vol. II, 9) have erroneously stated that this money was used to pay for Lot 95, the John Brown Farm property. This fund had nothing to do with Lot 95; it was about buying Lot 88 for Mary and Ruth.

33. JB to Sanborn, August 13, 1857, in Sanborn, *Life and Letters*, 412–14.

34. Sanborn to Stearns, August 1857, and JB to Sanborn, August 27, 1857, in Sanborn, *Life and Letters*, 111–14; Sanborn, *Recollections of Seventy Years*, 125.

35. Frank Sanborn to George Stearns, August 25, 1857, Stutler; Sanborn, *Life and Letters*, 98–99. The details of the transactions were complicated. Smith received $288.89 (principal and interest owed him on the property), $2.87 (discount on the Thompsons agreement), and $111.66 (principal and interest John Brown owed him). The deed to Ruth was signed August 20, 1857, but not recorded until February 7, 1859. Mary never recorded her deed to the north half of Lot 88. John feared that old creditors (from business lawsuits) might try to recover funds from

these personal property holdings. He did not want anything said about this land transaction, nor did he want any deeds to be recorded at that time. JB to MB, April 16, 1858, Cotter (Stutler, "John Brown's Land at North Elba").

36. Byron Brewster, "Reminiscences of John Brown of North Elba," *Saranac Lake News*, February 4, 1911; John G. Fay, Letter to the Editor, *Lake Placid News*, December 11, 1942.

37. SB, "My Father, John Brown," *The Outlook* (January 25, 1913); JB to MB, November 23, 1855, in Sanborn, *Life and Letters*, 204–5; RBT, in Sanborn, *Life and Letters*, 100.

38. Sanborn, *Life and Letters*, 121.

39. J. Miller McKim, "Mrs. Brown and Her Family," *National Anti-Slavery Standard*, December 3, 1859; JB to MB, November 23, 1855, in Sanborn, *Life and Letters*, 204–5; RBT, in Sanborn, *Life and Letters*, 100.

40. Villard, *Fifty Years After*, 24–25; Laughlin-Schultz, *The Tie That Bound Us*, 4; Higginson, *Contemporaries*, 241.

41. Sanborn, *Recollections of Seventy Years*, 126.

42. "Marriages," *Elizabethtown Post*, October 30, 1857. The couple was married by Rev. Dillon C. Osgood (son of Iddo). Abbie Hinckley Brown, "Across the Plains in the Early 60's," *Lake Placid News*, September 29, 1916.

Chapter 6

1. Reynolds, *John Brown, Abolitionist*, 214–15.

2. Edward W. Emerson, *The Complete Works Of Ralph Waldo Emerson*, vol. XI (Houghton, Mifflin, 1906, original 1878), 281; Ralph Waldo Emerson, *The Journals and Miscellaneous Notebooks of Ralph Waldo Emerson*, vol. 14 (Belknap Press of Harvard University Press, 1978), 394–410.

3. Thoreau, "Slavery in Massachusetts," 1854.

4. William H. Seward, "Freedom in the New Territories (Appeal to a 'Higher Law')," March 11, 1850, in Robert C. Byrd, *The Senate, 1789–1989: Classic Speeches, 1830–1993* (US Government Printing Office, 1988), 308; "Meeting in Jay," *Essex County Republican*, October 26, 1850.

5. Thoreau, "Walking."

6. Thoreau, "A Plea for Captain John Brown," in Thoreau, *Miscellanies*, 197–236.

7. Oates, *To Purge This Land*, 197.

8. Thoreau, "Walking."

9. Joel Tyler Headley, *The Adirondack, Or Life in the Woods* (Baker and Scribner, 1851). In 1848, Headley wrote *The Life of Oliver Cromwell*, a book John Brown kept as close as his Bible. Reynolds, *John Brown, Abolitionist*, 231.

10. Charles Fenno Hoffman, *Wild Scenes in the Forest and Prairie* (London, 1839), 36.

11. Phillip G. Terrie, "Romantic Travelers in the Adirondack Wilderness," *American Studies* 24, no. 2 (Fall 1983): 62. Hoffman's account was published in 1839; McEntee visited in 1851.

12. JB statement quoted in Jason (and Owen) to Brothers, February 15, 1853, in Gibbons, *Extracts of Letters of the John Brown Family*, 12–13.

13. JB to RBT, August 10, 1852, in Sanborn, *Life and Letters*, 151.

14. Villard, *Fifty Years After*, 73.

15. DeCaro, *Fire from the Midst of You*, 210. Jason and Owen wrote these letters in 1853. RBT to Wealthy Brown, August 6, 1850, in *Placid Pioneer* (Spring 1968).

16. AB to JBJr, July 18, 1857, *Placid Pioneer* (Spring 1968). The party included Annie, Salmon, and Watson Brown; William Thompson and Isabelle Thompson Brown; Rudolphus, Alexis, and Abbie Hinckley; Simeon Hasbrook, "a black fellow"; Theodore Calkin; Milton Silsby; and Judson Ware, a motherless nephew who lived with the Hinckleys.

17. "John Brown's Grave," *Des Moines* (Iowa) *Register*, December 12, 1886.

18. Rev. Joel Headley quoted in *The Republican* (Keeseville, NY), January 3, 1852.

19. Henry David Thoreau, August 23, 1858, in Bradford Torrey and Franklin Sanborn, eds., *The Writings of Henry David Thoreau, Journal*, vol. 11 (Houghton Mifflin, 1906), 119–20.

20. Ralph Waldo Emerson, "The Adirondacs: A Journal. Dedicated to My Fellow-Travellers in August, 1858," in *Poems of Ralph Waldo Emerson* (Thomas Y. Crowell Company, 1899), 266–67.

21. Thoreau, "Walking."

22. Gatewood, *Free Man of Color*, 82.

23. "Letter from Elihu Burritt to the Anti-Slavery Convention at Cincinnati. Worcester, May 23, 1845," *Western Citizen*, July 3, 1845.

24. JB, "Declaration of Liberty." Stauffer and Trodd, *Tribunal*, 38–43.

25. JB to Sanborn, February 24, 1858, in Sanborn, *Life and Letters*, 444–45.

26. *Terre Haute Daily Gazette*, September 22, 1870; Nathaniel Bartlett Sylvester, *Historical Sketches of Northern New York and the Adirondack Wilderness* (William H. Young, 1877), 138–40.

27. Robert L. Duffus, "The Grave of Osawatomie," *Nation*, February 14, 1920, 199.

28. Thoreau, "Walking."

Chapter 7

1. Theodore Tilton, "A Personal Interview With Captain Brown's Wife," *New York Independent*, November 17, 1859; *New York Times*, November 18, 1859; *Liberator*, November 25, 1859.

2. JB to Mary, December 30, 1857, Stutler; JB to MB, January 30, 1858, in Ruchames, *Revolutionary*, 117–18.

3. JB to JBJr, February 4–5, 1858, Stutler; JB to MB, March 2, 1858, in Sanborn, *Life and Letters*, 442–43.

4. "Provisional Constitution," Stauffer and Trodd, *Tribunal*, 26–37; R. J. Hinton, "A Defense of the Memory of John Brown," *Liberator*, December 16, 1859.

5. JB to F. B. Sanborn, February 24, 1858, in Sanborn, *Life and Letters*, 444–45.

6. JB to MB, March 18, 1857, in Sanborn, *Life and Letters*, 388.

7. JB to MB, January 30, 1858, in Ruchames, *Revolutionary*, 117–18; RBT to JB, February 20, 1858, in Sanborn, *Life and Letters*, 441–42; HT to JB, April 21, 1858, in Warren F. Broderick, "'No Mortal Eye Can Penetrate': Louis Ramson's Portrait of John Brown," *Hudson River Valley Review* (Autumn 2012), 43.

8. Oliver Brown to JB, April 14, 1858, Stutler. The 1855 census listed Martha Brewster, age twelve, living with her aunt and uncle, Julia Brewster Nash and Timothy Nash, who were opposed to abolition.

9. JB to MB and Children, April 27–28, 1858, Stutler; JB to MB, May 1, 1858, Stutler. As an incentive, John offered to send $200 to provide for the men's families. Sons John Jr., Owen, and Jason of Ohio were also willing to serve as recruits.

10. JB to JBJr, April 8, 1859, Stutler.

11. "Provisional Constitution," in Stauffer and Trodd, *Tribunal*, 26–37. Brown planned to transfer power within the existing system, specifically, to Frederick Douglass, but Douglass refused the position. Two black men, Alfred M. Ellsworth and Osborne Anderson, were elected as members of the congress. Among those present at the Chatham conference, several would join Brown in 1859: Osborne Anderson, W. H. Leeman, John E. Cook, Steward Taylor, J. H. Kagi, Charles P. Tidd, and Owen Brown. "Browns Papers" [91] in *Doc. No. I. Governor's Message and Reports*, 147.

12. JB to MB and children, May 12, 1858, Stutler. Higginson objected to the delay, fearing it would be delayed forever. Privately, he hatched a plan to deploy men to Pennsylvania's southern border to get rumors started. Once the name of John Brown circulated and frightened Virginia, the men could go home. There was no support for the scheme, and it was never attempted. Thomas Wentworth Higginson to JB, May 7, 1858, in Cotter to Gee, March 14, 1970, Stutler.

13. JBJr to RBT and HT, January 12, 1857; JBJr to brother, 1858, in Sanborn, *Life and Letters*, 105.

14. JBJr to brother, 1858, in Sanborn, *Life and Letters*, 105; JBJr Notebook, March 26 and 28, 1858, in Gibbons, *Extracts of Letters of the John Brown Family*, 9; JB to MB, April 6, 1858 (misdated 1856), Cotter; JB to JBJr, June 9, 1858, and November 1, 1858, Ohio.

15. JB to MB and children, June 16, 1858, Stutler.

16. JB to MB, September 13, 1858, Stutler.

17. JB to MB and children, January 11, 1859, Stutler.

18. Sanborn, *Life and Letters*, 491n1.

19. JB to MB, March 25, 1859, Stutler; JB to Mary, May 6, 1859, Ohio.

20. 1860 Census for North Elba, Essex County, NY.

21. Amos Bronson Alcott, in Villard, *Fifty Years After*, 398.

22. Thomas Wentworth Higginson, *Contemporaries* (Houghton, Mifflin, 1899), 238.

23. *Elizabethtown Post*, June 18, 1859.

24. Ella Thompson Towne to Owen Brown Family Reunion, May 27, 1932, in "Recollections of North Elba," Cotter; "Thomas H. Peacock Expires," *Post Standard* (Syracuse, NY), June 15, 1942.

25. "John Brown, His Raiders and Their Last Resting Place," *Elizabethtown Post and Gazette*, August 31, 1899; Robert F. Hall, *John Brown at Elizabethtown* (Private Press of Alvin S. Fick, 1977). Hall's story said that Brown arrived in Elizabethtown in October, but Brown was in Keene on June 9, having left his family in North Elba for the last time. As Hall stated in the Foreword, his story was somewhere between fiction and fact.

26. "Billy Nye," *Plattsburgh Sentinel*, August 8, 1890.

27. "John Brown's Grave," *The Times* (Philadelphia, PA), July 19, 1891; "John Brown's Grave," *Des Moines* (Iowa) *Register*, December 12, 1886.

28. JB to MB, July 27, 1859, in Sanborn, *Life and Letters*, 530. In his earlier years, John Brown had been a postmaster, which perhaps accounted for his distrust of the mail system.

29. HT and RBT to JBJr and Wealthy, February 1, 1853, in Gibbons, *Extracts of Letters of the John Brown Family*, 11–12. Note that this part of the letter was written by Henry.

30. Sanborn, *Life and Letters*, 122.

31. "A Brief Biography," *Lake Placid News*, July 14, 1916, from *Morning Oregonian*; "John Brown's Grave," *The Times* (Philadelphia, PA), July 19, 1891.

32. *Cleveland Daily Leader*, March 27, 1860.

33. JB to MB, June 23, 1859, in Villard, *Fifty Years After*, 404–5. The letter was misdated July 5, probably an intentional error.

34. JB to MB, January 30, 1858, in Sanborn, *Life and Letters*, 441; Robert McGlone, "Rescripting a Troubled Past: John Brown's Family and the Harpers Ferry Conspiracy," *Journal of American History* (1989), 1186; MB to JB, June 29, 1859, Villard, *Fifty Years After*, 404–5. The letter arrived at the Kennedy farm on July 16.

35. Featherstonhaugh, *John Brown's Men*, 13; "Mrs. John Brown and her Family," *National Anti-Slavery Standard*, December 3, 1859; RBT to JBJr, August 17, 1859, "Browns Papers" [54] in *Doc. No. I. Governor's Message and Reports*, 128.

36. AB recollections in Villard, *Fifty Years After*, 416–20.

37. AB Adams in Hinton, *John Brown and His Men*, 265.

38. JB to MB, August 16, 1859, Stutler.

39. Sanborn, *Life and Letters*, 531.

Chapter 8

1. Villard, *Fifty Years After*, 413.
2. John Ball Jr. (James Redpath), "A Letter from the South," *National Anti-Slavery Standard*, December 2, 1854.
3. James Redpath, *The Roving Editor Or, Talks with Slaves in the Southern States* (A. B. Burdick, 1859), iii–vii.
4. JB to J. Henrie, August 11, 1859, "Browns Papers" [82] in *Doc. No. I. Governor's Message and Reports*, 143.
5. Villard, *Fifty Years After*, 409–12. The warning letter contained a reference to an "armory in Maryland," but no armory existed there. The secretary concluded the entire letter was nonsense.
6. Gerrit Smith, "Peterboro, August 27, 1859," *Liberator*, September 16, 1859. Interestingly, the federal government would also argue that it was not an insurrection, but an invasion.
7. "From Rev. A. L. Post," September 30, 1859, in *National Anti-Slavery Standard*, October 15, 1859.
8. Oliver Brown to Martha, September 9, 1859, in Sanborn, *Life and Letters*, 547; Watson Brown to Belle, September 3, 1859, in Sanborn, *Life and Letters*, 542–43.
9. Belle Thompson Brown to Watson, September 14, 1859, "Browns Papers" [9] in *Doc. No. I. Governor's Message and Reports*, 102.
10. JB to MB and children, October 1, 1859, in Sanborn, *Life and Letters*, 550. On September 30, the girls and Oliver reached Harrisburg, Pennsylvania, and met with John. "Pinch them" means reduce the animals' food.
11. JB to MB, October 8, 1859, Stutler.
12. Oliver to Martha, October 9, 1859, in Hinton, *John Brown and His Men*, 579–80.
13. Watson to Belle, October 14, 1859, in Sanborn, *Life and Letters*, 549.
14. SB to Byron R. Brewster, *Lake Placid News*, July 24, 1914.
15. Hinton, *John Brown and His Men*, 445. Although this is the oft-repeated narrative, no single newspaper edition gave the full details. Most likely, the family pieced the story together from multiple sources over a period of days. For accounts of the Harpers Ferry raid, see the Bibliography.
16. "The Latest News," *New-York Tribune*, October 18, 1859.
17. *New-York Tribune*, October 19, 1859.
18. "Great Insurrection at Harper's Ferry, Va.," *Elizabethtown Post*, October 22, 1859; *New-York Tribune*, October 20, 1859.
19. Drew, *John Brown Invasion*, 12; *New York Times*, October 20, 1859; "Great Insurrection at Harper's Ferry, Va."; *New-York Tribune*, October 20, 1859.
20. Lou V. Chapin, "The Last Days of Old John Brown," *Overland Monthly* (April 1899), 331.

21. Hinton, *John Brown and His Men*, 445.

22. Chapin, "The Last Days of Old John Brown."

23. Thomas Wentworth Higginson, "A Visit to John Brown's Household in 1859," in Ruchames, *Reader*, 219–23. The narrative was beautifully written and extensive, full of fascinating details about the Brown family, their farm, and wild scenery. However, as a member of the Secret Six, Higginson was not an unbiased observer; he tended to employ some exaggeration.

24. RBT to Mary Stearns, January 17, 1860, Stutler.

25. Higginson to Editor of *Tribune*, "The Family of John Brown," November 13, 1859, in *National Anti-Slavery Standard*, November 19, 1859.

26. Higginson, "A Visit," 219–23.

27. JB to family, October 31, 1859, in Sanborn, *Life and Letters*, 579–80.

28. "The Insurrection," *Charleston (SC) Mercury*, October 31, 1859, in *New York Herald*, November 5, 1859; "From Harpers Ferry," *Weekly Leavenworth Herald*, October 29, 1859.

29. "By Telegraph for the Baltimore Sun," *Baltimore Sun*, December 6, 1859.

30. "So Perish All the Enemies," *Fayetteville (NC) Semi-Weekly Observer*, October 20, 1859.

31. "The Virginia Insurrection," *Liberator*, October 21, 1859.

32. Frederick Douglass, "Capt. John Brown Not Insane," *Douglass' Monthly* (November 1, 1859).

33. "Gerrit Smith's Insanity, Attempt to Commit Suicide," *National Era* (Washington, DC), November 17, 1859; *Cazenovia (NY) Republican*, February 29, 1860; John R. McKivigan and Madeleine Leveille, "The 'Black Dream' of Gerrit Smith, New York Abolitionist," *Syracuse University Library Associates Courier* 20 (Fall 1985), 51–76; "Letter of Gerrit Smith," *Liberator*, June 8, 1860.

34. Gerrit Smith, "Peterboro, August 27, 1859," *Liberator*, September 16, 1859; Stauffer, *Black Hearts of Men*, 44.

35. Reynolds, *John Brown, Abolitionist*, 347.

36. Thoreau, "A Plea for Captain John Brown," in Thoreau, *Miscellanies*, 197–236.

37. Letter to editor of *Cleveland Plain Deale*r, November 18, 1859, in Stauffer and Trodd, *Tribunal*, 128–31.

38. Thoreau, "A Plea for Captain John Brown."

39. Carolyn L. Karcher, *The First Woman in the Republic: A Cultural Biography of Lydia Maria Child* (Duke University Press, 1994), 419.

40. Mrs. Child to JB, October 26, 1859; "Emerson on Courage," *Liberator*, November 18, 1859. Emerson gave his "Courage" lecture on November 8 in Boston.

41. Frances E. Watkins (Harper) to JB, November 25, 1859, in Redpath, *Public Life*, 345.

42. "The Character of the Harper's Ferry Affair and Its Authors," *Brooklyn Daily Eagle*, October 21, 1859, quoting *Albany Evening Journal*; "Confessions of an Abolitionist," *New York Times*, October 20, 1859, from *Philadelphia Press*.

43. J. Miller McKim, "Mrs. Brown and her Family," *National Anti-Slavery Standard*, December 3, 1859; Higginson, "A Visit," 229.
44. Villard, *Fifty Years After*, 455.
45. Higginson, "A Visit," 224.
46. JB to MB, November 10, 1859, in Villard, *Fifty Years After*, 540–41.
47. Redpath, *Echoes*, 427.
48. RBT to JB, November 27, 1859, *Magazine of History* (August 1908), 99–100.
49. JB to sisters Mary A. and Martha, November 27, 1859, in Ruchames, *Reader*, 152–53.
50. JBJr to JB, November 28, 1859, in Redpath, *Echoes*, 429.

Chapter 9

1. Finkelman, "Manufacturing Martyrdom," in Finkelman, *His Soul Goes Marching On*, 46–47.
2. "John Brown's Body," *Republican Democrat* (Ravenna, OH), November 30, 1859; "Speech of Hon. M. B. Lowry, State Senator from Erie County, Delivered at the Colored Ladies' Festival," *Harrisburg* (PA) *Telegraph*, April 5, 1869; "Sensation Writing—A Virginia Requiem," *Anti-Slavery Bugle*, December 24, 1859, in *Richmond News* of December 3, 1859.
3. "To Arms!," *New York Times*, November 4, 1859; M. E. Bickle, M.D. to Governor Wise, November 25, 1859, Historical Society of Pennsylvania, Philadelphia.
4. "The Programme of Brown's Execution," *Sunbury* (PA) *Gazette*, December 3, 1859; Wilson, *John Brown, Soldier of Fortune*, 380.
5. JB to MB, November 10, 1859, in Villard, *Fifty Years After*, 540–41.
6. Redpath, *Public Life*, 405.
7. Higginson to Friends (AB and Sarah Brown), November 4, 1859, Stutler.
8. JB to Higginson, November 4, 1859, in Redpath, *Public Life*, 272.
9. JB to Higginson, November 9, 1859, in Villard, *Fifty Years After*, 513.
10. Hinton, *John Brown and His Men*, 374–75.
11. JB to MB and children, November 8, 1859, Stutler; JB to MB, November 10, 1859, in Villard, *Fifty Years After*, 540–41.
12. MB to Gov. Wise, November 21, 1859, Historical Society of PA, Philadelphia. Quite likely, Furness prevented any mention of the Thompsons's bodies since sympathy for family members wielded a stronger appeal.
13. Gov. Wise to MB, November 26, 1859, Stutler.
14. M. (James Miller McKim), "Mrs. Brown and her Family," *National Anti-Slavery Standard*, December 3, 1859; J. Miller McKim to JB, November 29, 1859, Cotter.
15. "What Is the Chivalry of the South," *Liberator*, November 25, 1859, from *Independent Democrat* (Charles Town, VA); John M. McLaughlin, *A Memoir of Hector Tyndale* (Collins, printer, 1882), 118.

16. *Anti-Slavery History of John Brown Year* (American Anti-Slavery Society, 1861), 125.

17. "Arrival of the Major General of the Virginia Militia," *The Democrat* (Ravenna, OH), November 30, 1859; "The Execution and Its Incidents," *National Anti-Slavery Standard*, December 10, 1859.

18. John M. McLaughlin, *A Memoir of Hector Tyndale* (1882), 118. Twenty-six months later, on February 7, 1862, Tyndale walked into Harpers Ferry as a Major in the Twenty-eighth Pennsylvania Infantry and "put the first torch to the hotel in which he was insulted!" His soldiers burned all the buildings, except for the engine-house, "the Gibraltar from which the brave old man fired his first gun at Virginia slavery." Wendell Phillips called it "poetic justice" that Tyndale saved the one building "which Brown himself made historical and immortal." The building would soon be known as John Brown's Fort. "Speech of Wendell Phillips, Esq., in Boston, At the Society Meeting of the Massachusetts Anti-Slavery Society, Thursday Evening, January 29, 1863," *Liberator*, February 13, 1863.

19. "Mrs. Brown's Opinions," *Harper's Weekly*, December 10, 1859; "Personal," *New York Tribune*, December 10, 1859.

20. "Account of Congressman J. M. Ashley," *Toledo Blade*, December 6, 1859; Letter from A. Hinckley, *Elizabethtown Post*, December 24, 1859.

21. "Preparations for the Execution of John Brown," *National Era* (Washington, DC), December 8, 1859. "His Wishes About His Property," *Harper's Weekly*, December 10, 1859.

22. David Barker, "To John Brown," *Liberator*, December 2, 1859.

23. *Albany Evening Journal*, quoted in *National Era* (Washington, DC), December 8, 1859; "The Harper's Ferry Tragedy," *Burlington Free Press*, December 16, 1859; "Various Particulars," *National Anti-Slavery Standard*, December 10, 1859.

24. Stonewall Jackson, December 2, 1859, in Mary Anna Jackson, *Memoirs of Stonewall Jackson by his Widow* (Prentice Press, 1895), 130. Sanborn, *Life and Letters*, 622.

25. "Sensation Writing—A Virginia Requiem."

26. Capt. John H. Zittle, *A Correct History of the John Brown Invasion* (Maii, 1905), 143–44; "The Body of John Brown," *Brooklyn Evening Star*, December 5, 1859.

27. "Sensation Writing—A Virginia Requiem."

28. "'Tis Done," *National Anti-Slavery Standard*, December 10, 1859, from "The Spirit of Virginia," *Richmond Enquirer*.

29. G. W. Light, "John Brown's Final Victory," in Redpath, *Echoes of Harper's Ferry*, 332.

30. Thoreau, "A Plea for Captain John Brown," in Thoreau, *Miscellanies*, 197–236.

31. Stauffer and Trodd, *Tribunal*, 131–33.

32. "Meeting at New Bedford," *Liberator*, December 16, 1859.

33. "John Brown Hung To-day," *New York Reformer*, December 8, 1859, from *Utica Herald*, December 2, 1859.

34. "John Brown's last letter to his family," JB to family, November 30, 1859, in Redpath, *The Public Life*, 365–37. Mary said that John did not leave any final public statement or address. She thinks his final letter to his family, justifying his enterprise and motives, was all the record he cared to leave. "Personal," *New York Tribune*, December 10, 1859.

35. AB Adams to Higginson, December 4, 1859, BPL.

36. *Highland (OH) Weekly News*, November 14, 1861.

37. *New York Tribune*, December 17, 1859.

38. "The Remains of John Brown in New York," *Brooklyn Evening Star*, December 5, 1859.

39. *New York Daily Tribune*, December 6, 1859; Finkelman, "Manufacturing Martyrdom," in Finkelman, *His Soul Goes Marching On*, 49.

40. "The Burial of John Brown. The Passage of the Body to North Elba. The Funeral. From Our Special Reporter. Troy, December 10, 1859," *New York Tribune*, December 12, 1859.

41. "The Burial of John Brown," *National Anti-Slavery Standard*, December 17, 1859, revised report from *Tribune*.

42. Caroline Halstead Barton Royce, *Bessboro: A History of Westport, Essex County, New York* (1902), 485.

43. Marie-Jeanette Brookings Tuttle, *Three Centuries in Champlain Valley* (1909), 405. David Turner, "Historical Reminiscences, Essex County, its Shire Town, Court House and Prominent Men," *Elizabethtown Post*, March 2, 1899. The guards of honor are generally given as O. Abel Jr., J. Q. Dickinson, Richard L. Hand, and Henry J. Adams. Other accounts have included Mr. Haskell and A. C. H. Livingston. "The Burial of John Brown," *New York Tribune*, December 12, 1859.

44. "The Burial of John Brown," *New York Tribune*, December 12, 1859.

45. David Turner, "Historical Reminiscences," *Elizabethtown Post*, March 2, 1899.

46. "The Burial of John Brown," *New York Tribune*, December 12, 1859. In 1852, Norton was elected Town Supervisor for Keene. He had recently changed from the Whig Party to the "Abolition or Liberty Party." *Essex County Republican*, March 13, 1852.

47. Lou V. Chapin, "The Last Days of Old John Brown," *Overland Monthly* (April 1899), 331.

48. "The Burial of John Brown," *New York Tribune*, December 12, 1859.

49. Rev. Joshua Young, "The Funeral of John Brown," *New England Magazine* (April 1904), 229–43.

50. Joshua Young, *God Greater Than Man: A Sermon Preached June 11th After the Rendition of Anthony Burns* (Samuel B. Nichols, 1854).

Chapter 10

1. "The Burial of John Brown," *New York Tribune*, December 12, 1859.

2. "Improvements at the John Brown Farm," *Lake Placid News*, August 5, 1921. Another account claimed the alto singer was Amelia (age 5), not Albertine (age 9), but that is unlikely, and there are many errors in this account. Mary Lee, "John Brown Rests amid the Mountains," *New York Times*, October 20, 1929. RBT to Thomas Wentworth Higginson, December 27, 1859, BPL.

3. This and seceding quotes about the funeral in this section are from "The Burial of John Brown," *New York Tribune*, December 12, 1859.

4. "John Brown's Funeral, Another Account of the Burial of the Famous Old Man," *Plattsburgh Sentinel*, September 8, 1899.

5. Ellen Brown Fablinger to McDonald, November 20, 1909, McDonald Papers at Harpers Ferry National Park.

6. "Billy Nye," *Plattsburgh Sentinel*, August 8, 1890. Bill Nye became famous in Stoddard's tale of Hitch-Up Matilda.

7. *Elizabethtown Post*, December 10, 1859; "The Death of John Brown," *Reveille*, Elizabethtown, NY (vol. 5, no. 17, December 1959).

8. *Elizabethtown Post*, June 18, 1859; E. H. Sears, "Random Readings: John Brown's Grave," *Religious Magazine and Monthly Review* (July 1871), 94–95.

9. S. (Samuel) C. Dwyer to Hon. A. R. Boteler, October 21, 1859, "Browns Papers" [93], in *Doc. No. I. Governor's Message and Reports*, 148. Dwyer made a few errors regarding date and place of residence of Browns.

10. *Elizabethtown Post*, November 19, 1859.

11. *Elizabethtown Post*, October 22, 1859. Editor and proprietor, David Turner.

12. (Winslow Watson), "John Brown as a Farmer," *New York Daily Herald*, November 3, 1859.

13. "The Old Guard for Douglas," *Plattsburgh Republican*, July 28, 1860.

14. *Elizabethtown Post*, November 12, 1859. Governor Wise received many appeals for a pardon of Brown.

15. K, "Communications," *Elizabethtown Post*, November 26, 1859.

16. "Treason in the United States" and "John Brown," *Elizabethtown Post*, December 3, 1859. The word *moulder* was used in reference to dead bodies quite frequently prior to the "John Brown Song" in 1861. *Elizabethtown Post*, December 24, 1859. The Keene meeting was led by Phineas Norton and T. S. Nash.

17. "Brooklyn. Colored Peoples' Funeral Services—Honors to John Brown in Essex County," *Evening Post*, December 12, 1859. Rev. Hodges ended the service most appropriately, with the hymn "Blow Ye the Trumpet, Blow."

18. "The John Brown Fund," *New-York Tribune*, December 8, 1859.

19. *Elizabethtown Post*, November 12, 1859.

20. Editorial, *Elizabethtown Post*, November 26, 1859.

21. "Mr. Lincoln's Reply," *Chicago Tribune*, August 23, 1858.

22. "A Clergyman on John Brown," *Berkshire County Eagle* (Pittsfield, Massachusetts), December 1, 1859.

23. Victor Hugo, "Victor Hugo on John Brown," *Liberator*, December 31, 1859. Hugo's letter to the *London News* was written on December 2, 1859.

24. F. A. Mitchel, "John Brown's Grave," *Wilkes Barre Times*, October 5, 1901; "A Clergyman on John Brown."

25. "By Telegraph for the Baltimore Sun," *Baltimore Sun*, December 6, 1859. Opinion of Governor Wise.

26. Redpath, *Public Life*, 406.

27. Young, "The Funeral of John Brown;" Editorial, *Burlington Sentinel*, December 16, 1859.

28. "Letter of Joshua Young" to Anti-Slavery Society, March 13, 1860, in *Liberator*, May 18, 1860. With the loss of angry parishioners, financial support dwindled, and officers of the Burlington Unitarian Church forced Young to resign as pastor in 1862. He moved on to a ministry in Massachusetts, and did not hesitate to make visits to the John Brown Farm. In 1899, he had the courage to conduct another burial service at the farm for John Brown's son and comrades. After Rev. Young retired from pastoral duties, he decided to explain his part in the John Brown burial. In early 1904, at the age of eighty-one, he completed his manuscript of "The Funeral of John Brown," which contributed valuable personal insight to the historic event. It was the last piece of literary work written by Rev. Young. He died a week or two after submitting the article to *New England Magazine*.

29. Thoreau, "A Plea for Captain John Brown," in Thoreau, *Miscellanies*, 197–236. The essay was first read to an audience on October 30, 1859. Henry David Thoreau, "The Last Days of John Brown," written from his journal notes for July 4, 1860.

30. A Countryman, "John Brown's Invasion," *New-York Tribune*, December 10, 1859.

31. "The President's Message," *Harper's Weekly*, January 7, 1860.

32. "Speech at Leavenworth, Kansas," December 3, 1859.

33. "John Brown," *Elizabethtown Post*, December 3, 1859. David Turner (editor and proprietor), *Elizabethtown Post*, October 22, 1859; "The Final Disposition of the Remains of John Brown," *Elizabethtown Post*, December 10, 1859.

34. *Elizabethtown Post*, December 24, 1859.

35. Speech of Charles O'Conor, Esq., "At the Union-Saving Meeting, in the Academy of Music, New York, December 19, 1859," *National Anti-Slavery Standard*, December 30, 1859.

36. "The Final Disposition of the Remains of John Brown," *Elizabethtown Post*, December 10, 1859.

37. "The Shriek of a Kansas Republican," *Plattsburgh Republican*, March 24, 1860. According to "Correspondence of the Post," *Elizabethtown Post*, March 10, 1860, this was the largest vote ever polled in North Elba (by seven votes). "Slung

shot" refers to a hard object (small metal ball or rock) attached by a strap to the wrist and swung to strike an opponent. They were widely used as weapons in the 1800s, since they were easy to make, silent, and effective.

38. "North Elba—Essex Co.," *Plattsburgh Republican*, March 17, 1860; "Correspondence of the Post," *Elizabethtown Post*, March 10, 1860. Regarding bullying, the Democrats accused their opponents of "some hard swearing" and threats. "We don't wonder that it was considered best for all concerned that the villain [who wrote the letter] should withhold his name." "The Shriek of a Kansas Republican." The letter must have been authored by Salmon Brown or Henry Thompson, the only remaining North Elba men who fought in Kansas.

39. "Clinton County Democratic," *Plattsburgh Republican*, March 17, 1860; "Town Meetings," *Elizabethtown Post*, March 10, 1860; "The Home of John Brown," *Pointe Coupee Democrat*, April 7, 1860; *Daily Delta* (New Orleans, LA), March 31, 1860; *Evening Post* (Cleveland, OH), April 2, 1860.

40. "Another Expose," *Banner of Liberty*, May 2, 1860. The paper published an extract of a private letter written by "a near neighbor of Mrs. John Brown" to a friend in Alexandria, Virginia. The letter lacks a date and name, gives the incorrect names of the Browns as "Lamon" and "Hugh," and appears in only one newspaper (a pro-Democrat paper with many Southern subscribers). However, the letter also contains correct and precise details about the Browns, which makes its authenticity most probable.

Chapter 11

1. RBT to Higginson, December 27, 1859, BPL.

2. *Woodstock Sentinel*, December 28, 1859. AB Adams to A. M. Ross, December 28, 1887, Gilder Lehman Collection.

3. Higginson to Brown family, November 4, 1859, Stutler; AB to Higginson, December 21, 1859; RBT to Higginson, December 27, 1859; SB to Higginson, December 21, 1859; RBT to Mary Stearns, January 17, 1860. BPL.

4. *Weekly Anglo-African*, January 7, 1860; New Haven people to Mrs. Brown and from her in return, *Weekly Anglo-African*, March 10, 1860; Detroit people to Mrs. Brown and from Mrs. Brown in return, *Weekly Anglo-African*, February 11, 1860; "Contributions in Aid of the Family of Capt. John Brown," *Liberator*, February 10, 1860.

5. William Still, *The Underground Railroad* (1871; reprinted, Johnson Publishing, 1970), 791.

6. *Weekly Anglo-African*, February 11, 1860; MB to Herman L. Vaill, December 27, 1859, Stutler; MB to Mr. and Mrs. George Stearns, December 27, 1859, Stutler. Although McKim lacked confidence in Redpath's "veracity" and recommended Lydia Maria Child be allowed to author the book, Mary Brown chose

Redpath. The Brown family hosted Mrs. Redpath at the farm when she came to collect the materials and hand-carry them back to Boston.

7. AB Adams to Higginson, December 28, 1859, and December 21, 1859, BPL

8. *Anti-Slavery History of John Brown Year*, 135.

9. "The Will of John Brown," *National Era*, December 8, 1859; Clarence Gee, "The Stone on John Brown's Grave," *New York History* (April 1961), 157–68.

10. JB to MB and children, March 12 and May 27, 1857, in Sanborn, *Life and Letters*, 375, 410; JB to MB, June 16, 1858, Stutler; JB to MB, May 6, 1859, Ohio.

11. Higginson, "A Visit."

12. *Elizabethtown Post*, December 24, 1859. Rev. Young spoke at an oyster supper held for the benefit of the Brown family. Cyrenus Payne attended the benefit, too. "The John Brown Tombstone," *Kansas City Journal*, May 9, 1897.

13. JB to MB, November 16, 1859.

14. RBT to Higginson, December 27, 1859, BPL; MB to Bullard, January 24, 1860, Cornell University Library; MB to McKim, March 6, 1860; AB Adams to Higginson, January 17, 1860, BPL. Annie Brown Adams wrote about Martha in a letter to Dr. Alexander Ross, December 18, 1887, in Hinton, *John Brown and His Men*, 445.

15. Those who knew Martha mourned the loss of one so kind, benevolent, and noble. *Weekly Anglo-African*, April 14, 1860; RBT to Mary Stearns, April 22, 1860, Stutler; AB Adams to A. M. Ross, December 28, 1887, Gilder Lehman Collection.

16. RBT to Stearns, April 22, 1860.

17. Joel Myerson and Daniel Shealy, eds., *The Selected Letters of Louisa May Alcott* (Little, Brown, 1995), 55.

18. Higginson, "A Visit."

19. JB to MB, March 7, 1844, in Sanborn, *Life and Letters*, 60–61; Douglass, *John Brown, An Address by Frederick Douglass*, 1881.

20. "New England Anti-Slavery Convention," *Liberator*, June 8, 1860.

21. David Karsner, *John Brown: Terrible Saint* (Dodd, Mead, 1934), 213.

22. Luther Lee, "Fourth of July Oration," *Liberator*, August 3, 1860.

23. RBT to Mary Stearns, April 22, 1860, Stutler. Ruth said "a grand trip to the summit of Whiteface Mountain" was planned for July 5, but nothing more was said about the hike. "Fourth of July Celebration at North Elba," *Frontier Palladium* (Malone, NY), June 14, 1860.

24. *Oration, Delivered in Corinthian Hall, Rochester, By Frederick Douglass, July 5th, 1852* (Lee, Mann, 1852).

25. Douglass letter read at farm, "Celebration at North Elba, the Fourth of July Among the Adirondacks, The Journey to John Brown's House," *Liberator*, July 27, 1860.

26. Hinton, *John Brown and His Men*, 505–7; Osborne P. Anderson, *A Voice from Harper's Ferry* (Printed for the author, 1861). Anderson was the only survivor

among those who went into the town. The other four surviving raiders (white men) had not actually gone into the town on October 16 and 17. Anderson's book recalled the incidents before, after, and during the raid from his unique perspective: a black man who was "an actor in the scene." Anderson also tried to correct the record about things that never happened and actions that had been omitted from other accounts. In 1864, he enlisted as a Union soldier.

Chapter 12

1. RBT to Mary Stearns, April 22, 1860, Stutler.
2. J.C., "North Elba and the Fourth of July Next," *Burlington* (VT) *Weekly Free Press*, June 1, 1860; "The Fund for the John Brown Family—How It Was Distributed," *Anti-Slavery Bugle*, August 11, 1860.
3. "Celebration at North Elba," *Liberator*, July 27, 1860; J.C., "North Elba and the Fourth of July Next." Rev. Nathan Wardner of Jay later served as chaplain of the Ninety-Sixth Regiment Infantry N.Y. Volunteers.
4. Luther Lee, *Autobiography of the Rev. Luther Lee* (Phillips & Hunt, 1882), 295; L. C. Patridge, "The Fourth at North Elba," *Anti-Slavery Bugle*, August 4, 1860, from *Wesleyan*, letter dated July 16, 1860, Waitsfield, Vermont.
5. Luther Lee, "Fourth of July Oration," *Liberator*, August 3, 1860. Kansas was officially admitted to the Union as a free state on January 29, 1861.
6. Luther Lee, *Autobiography*.
7. "Celebration at North Elba," *Liberator*, July 27, 1860.
8. "The Fourth at North Elba," *Anti-Slavery Bugle*, August 4, 1860.
9. "Celebration at North Elba, *Liberator*, July 27, 1860; *Douglass' Monthly*, September 1860.
10. L. C. Patridge, "The Fourth at North Elba."
11. Henry D. Thoreau, *Anti-Slavery and Reform Papers* (Swan Sonnenschein, 1890), 34 and 60. In a similar vein, Brown said, "A few men in the right, and knowing they are right, can overturn a mighty king. Fifty men, twenty men, in the Alleghenies, could break slavery to pieces in two years." Sanborn, *Life and Letters*, 122.
12. "Celebration at North Elba," *Liberator*, July 27, 1860. It has been erroneously reported that Thoreau spoke at the John Brown Farm, but he did not attend the July 4 celebration. Hinton read the address that Thoreau had prepared from his journal entries starting in December 1859.
13. *Anti-Slavery Bugle*, December 8, 1860; Thaddeus Hyatt, letter of July 16, 1860, in "To the Friends of John Brown," *New-York Daily Tribune*, July 26, 1860.
14. "The Fanatics at Their Orgies," *National Anti-Slavery Standard*, August 4, 1860; "Abolitionism," *Topeka Tribune* (KS), August 18, 1860.

15. "The Old Guard for Douglas," *Plattsburgh Republican*, July 28, 1860. Winslow Watson wrote, "While Republicans are gathering about the grave of a traitor and murderer to commemorate and endorse his deeds, let Democrats rally around the Constitution and preserve and perpetuate the Union."

16. "The Insurrectionary Party," *Buffalo Courier*, June 27, 1860; "The News," *New York Daily Herald*, June 23, 1860.

17. "Abolitionism," *Topeka Tribune* (KS), August 18, 1860; "The Presidential Nominees," *Alexandria Gazette*, June 25, 1860; "Candidates," *Evansville* [IN] *Daily Journal*, June 30, 1860; "The News," *New York Daily Herald*, June 23, 1860.

18. J.H.C., "All Compromises Useless," *Liberator*, December 28, 1860.

19. Stauffer, *Black Hearts of Men*, 33.

20. Paul Finkelman, "John Brown: America's First Terrorist," *Prologue Magazine* 43, no. 1 (Spring 2011); "Harper's Ferry and Its Lessons," *New York Times*, November 29, 1859.

21. Iddo Osgood, Robert G. Scott, and Timothy (T. S.) Nash presided at the first meeting of the newly formed Town of North Elba. Timothy Nash lived on Lot 101 and ran a sawmill for a few years. He married Julia Burdick of Keeseville in 1846. Timothy was the brother of Joseph V. Nash, who started Nash's hotel and married Harriet C. Brewster (the aunt of Martha). Lydia Alzada Nash, sister to Timothy and Joseph, was Martha's mother. The 1855 census lists Martha living with Timothy and Julia. Timothy Nash was Superintendent of Schools in North Elba, 1850; Supervisor of North Elba, 1851 to 1852, 1864 to 1865; and North Elba Postmaster from May 2, 1859 to March 21, 1861.

22. T. S. (Timothy) Nash to Brother(-in-law) and Sister, April 17, 1861. Author's collection.

23. T. S. (Timothy) Nash, "Personal Recollections of John Brown," *Essex County Republican*, April 27, 1900.

24. Bowditch, *Life and Correspondence of Henry Ingersoll Bowditch*, 101; "Letter from Henry C. Wright," *Liberator*, October 3, 1862. Seventy men may have enlisted but it is improbable that they were all North Elba residents.

25. Villard, *Fifty Years After*, 465–66. After Virginia's secession, the slave states of Arkansas, North Carolina, and Tennessee soon joined the Confederacy. Meanwhile, citizens in northwestern areas of Virginia resisted joining the Confederacy and began pursuing statehood. In 1863, Lincoln accepted the new state of West Virginia into the Union.

Chapter 13

1. "An Excursion to the Adirondack Mountains, in the Summer of 1861," *Friends' Intelligencer*, vol. XVIII (T. Ellwood Zell, 1862), 665–67. When Company

K of the Thirty-Eighth New York Volunteers headed south, they carried a flag presented by the ladies of the town. The flag was returned to Elizabethtown in 1862, tattered and wrapped about the body of Captain Dwyer, who was wounded in the battle of Williamsburg and died a few days later. The flag is in the collections of the Adirondack History Museum in Elizabethtown, New York.

2. Ednah D. Cheney, ed., *Louisa May Alcott, Her Life, Letters, and Journals* (Roberts Brothers, 1890), 127. Louisa had sold only a few pieces of writing to *Atlantic Monthly* by 1861.

3. A. B. Adams, "[Louisa May Alcott in the Early 1860s]," in Daniel Shealy, ed., *Alcott in Her Own Time* (University of Iowa Press, 2005), 7–11.

4. A. B. Adams, "[Louisa May Alcott in the Early 1860s]"; Laughlin-Schultz, *The Tie That Bound Us*, 93.

5. Higginson, *Cheerful Yesterdays*, 208–9; White, *Poetry, Lyrical, Narrative and Satirical, of the Civil War*, 6.

6. Boyd B. Stutler, "Glory, Glory Hallelujah/The Story of 'John Brown's Body' and 'Battle Hymn of the Republic'" (1960), 14–31, Stutler; George Kimball, "Origin of the John Brown Song," *New England Magazine* (1890), 371–76.

7. "The Progress of Events," *Weekly Vincennes* (IN) *Western Sun*, September 7, 1861, from *New York Independent*.

8. "How to End the War," *Douglass' Monthly*, May 1861.

9. Stutler, "Glory, Glory," 25.

10. Andrew Ward, *Dark Midnight when I Rise* (Amistad, 2001), 216.

11. Julia Ward Howe, *Reminiscences: 1819–1899* (Houghton, Mifflin, 1900), 275.

12. White, *Poetry, Lyrical, Narrative and Satirical, of the Civil War*, viii; Gail Hamilton, "Glory, Hallelujah!" *Liberator*, April 4, 1862.

13. Eleanor Atkinson, "The Soul of John Brown, Recollections of the Great Abolitionist by his Son," *American Magazine* (October 1909).

14. RBT to Mary Stearns, April 22, 1860, Stutler; Salmon Brown, "My Father, John Brown," in Ruchames, *Reader*, 189.

15. Henry C. Wright, *Liberator*, August 31, 1860.

16. "The Remains of John Brown," *National Anti-Slavery Standard*, September 8, 1860.

17. Rev. Joshua Young, "The Funeral of John Brown," *New England Magazine* (April 1904).

18. MB to Sarah Brown, November 11, 1860, Sykes; "Distribution of the John Brown Fund," *Douglass' Monthly* (October 1860).

19. "Letter from Mrs. John Brown," *Richmond (VA) Times-Dispatch*, August 7, 1860. Letter written July 25, 1860.

20. "Distribution of the John Brown Fund," *Douglass' Monthly*, October 1860.

21. MB to Stearns, October 31 and November 21, 1860, June 23 and August 13, 1861, and May 14, 1862, Cotter; MB to Sarah Brown, November 11,

1860; "Celebration at North Elba," *Liberator*, July 25, 1860; "An Excursion to the Adirondack Mountains," *Friends' Intelligencer*. Mary said they were more successful at growing crops in 1861.

22. SB to Fred Lockley, August 14, 1914, Stutler; "An Incident for History," *Liberator*, March 28, 1862.

23. "An Incident for History." The letter writer, L.G.B., was probably Lawrence Goodhue Bigelow, father of Lucius who attended John Brown's funeral with Rev. Joshua Young.

24. "A Small Potato Affair," *Sandusky (OH) Daily Commercial Register*, March 20, 1862.

25. *The United States Army and Navy Journal and Gazette, Volume 2, 1864–65* (Publication Office No. 39 Park Row), 154 (October 29, 1864).

26. The Ninety-Sixth Regiment Infantry New York Volunteers, Civil War Newspaper Clippings, New York State Military Museum and Veterans Research Center. In *The Black Woods* (261), Amy Godine says Wardner "*would* see to it that the child did not look the part," that is, he *chose* this slave girl because she was light-skinned. Based on this motive, which is pure conjecture, Godine dismisses Wardner's commitment to radical abolition and equalitarianism. That logic implies that dark-skinned people (not light-skinned people) should be rescued from slavery.

27. For more details on black Civil War soldiers of the region, see chapter 3 of Svenson, *Blacks in the Adirondacks*, and chapter 23 of Manchester, *The Plains of Abraham*.

28. Shane Facteau, "John Brown not the Only One to Die in Fight Against Slavery," *Lake Placid News*, November 28, 1997. Article includes letter from Willard Thompson in Washington, DC, November 13, 1862.

29. "John Brown-ism," *Liberator*, April 4, 1862, from *New York Journal of Commerce*.

30. Abraham Lincoln, "A Letter from President Lincoln, Reply to Horace Greeley," *New York Times*, August 24, 1862.

31. "Letter from Henry C. Wright" (to William Lloyd Garrison, September 26, 1862), *Liberator*, October 3, 1862; "God Bless Abraham Lincoln!" *Liberator*, October 10, 1862.

32. Edna Dean Proctor, "The President's Proclamation," in Frank Moore, ed., *Personal and Political Ballads* (George P. Putnam, 1864), 341–43.

33. MB to Mrs. Stearns, January 7 and March 3, 1863, Stutler; "An Agreeable Entertainment," *Liberator*, January 23, 1863.

34. MB to Mrs. Stearns, March 3, 1863, Stutler.

35. Donn Piatt, *Memories of the Men Who Saved the Union* (Belford, Clarke, 1887), 150.

36. JBJr to Franklin Sanborn, February 17, 1864, Stutler.

37. MB to Mrs. Stearns, August 4, 1863, Stutler.

Chapter 14

1. Vincent Y. Bowditch, *Life and Correspondence of Henry Ingersoll Bowditch* (Houghton, Mifflin, 1902), 83.
2. "John Brown's Daughter-in-Law Recalls a Simple Life in the 1800s," *Lake Placid News*, July 16, 1987; Abbie Hinckley Brown, "Across the Plains in the Early 60's."
3. Fred Lockley, "In Earlier Days," *Oregon Daily Journal*, August 17, 1914.
4. MB to Mrs. Stearns, January 7 and March 3, 1863, Stutler.
5. MB to Mrs. Stearns, August 4, 1863, Stutler; "A Visit to the Adirondacks," *Friends Intelligencer* (October 10, 1868), 489 (extract from a letter dated August 3, 1863).
6. AB to William Lloyd Garrison, June 9, 1863, Stutler.
7. David Turner, "Historical Reminiscences," *Elizabethtown Post*, March 2, 1899. David Turner, a resident of Essex County and previous editor of *Elizabethtown Post*, later moved to Virginia and met ex-governor Wise.
8. Abbie Hinckley Brown, "Across the Plains in the Early 60's." Some people in the small wagon train "were tinctured with colored blood," recalled Abbie. "They seemed to know who we were and were very friendly."
9. *New York Tribune*, September 22, 1864.
10. Abbie Hinckley Brown, "Across the Plains in the Early 60's."
11. SB, in Keith Lingenfelter, "John Brown Family of Red Bluff," *Wagon Wheels* (Spring 1981), 22.
12. AB to JBJr, October 9, 1864, in *Liberator*, November 25, 1864.
13. Aurelius W. Brodt to Mrs. Daniel B. Brodt, April 24, 1865, Stutler; Abbie Hinckley Brown, "Across the Plains in the Early 60's."
14. Henry Ward Beecher, "The Nation's Duty to Slavery," October 30, 1859, in Henry Ward Beecher, *Patriotic Addresses* (Fords, Howard & Hulbert, 1887), 206–7.
15. Henry Ingersoll Bowditch, "Letter to Mrs. H., July 27, 1865," in Von Holst, *John Brown*.
16. "The Will of John Brown," *National Era*, December 8, 1859; Clarence Gee, "The Stone on John Brown's Grave," *New York History* (April 1961), 157–68.
17. "The Mission of the War, A Lecture by Frederick Douglass," *New-York Tribune*, January 14, 1864. Frederick Douglass delivered this speech before the Woman's Loyal League at the Cooper Institute in New York City.
18. Henry Ingersoll Bowditch, "Letter to Mrs. H., July 27, 1865," in Von Holst, *John Brown*; Vincent Y. Bowditch, *Life and Correspondence of Henry Ingersoll Bowditch* (Houghton, Mifflin, 1902), 83.
19. Louisa May Alcott, "With a Rose, That Bloomed on the Day of John Brown's Martyrdom," *Liberator*, January 20, 1860. Alcott read the poem at a Concord meeting on December 2, 1859.

20. Thoreau met John Brown in life, whereas Bowditch and Richards did not. Ironically, the two latter men came to know Brown through recollections provided by the same Essex County citizen, lawyer Robert S. Hale of Elizabethtown (House of Representatives, 1865 to 1866, 1873 to 1874). Bowditch and Richards were both friends of the Hale family and made several visits to the Hale home.

21. Douglass, *John Brown, An Address by Frederick Douglass*, 1881.

22. Henry D. Thoreau, *Anti-Slavery and Reform Papers* (Swan Sonnenschein, 1890), 34 and 60. In a similar vein, Brown said, "A few men in the right, and knowing they are right, can overturn a mighty king. Fifty men, twenty men, in the Alleghanies, could break slavery to pieces in two years." Sanborn, *Life and Letters*, 122.

23. MB to son Owen, January 31, 1864, Cotter.

24. Indenture, Mary A. Brown to Alexis Hinckley, April 20,1866, for $700, conveyed parcel of land Lot 95, containing 244 acres more or less, excepting and reserving land enclosed as a burying place on which the remains of John Brown were interred, with the right to pass to and from said reserved tract, being about one quarter of an acre.

25. Henry C. Lyon in "An Historic Incident," *Kate Field's Washington*, September 26, 1894. Colonel Lee of Boston spent the summer months at his country home, Stony Sides, on Lake Champlain near Westport, New York.

26. Alexis Hinckley, "The Truth About John Brown's Farm," *Essex County Republican*, March 5, 1896.

27. Frederick Douglass, "Capt. John Brown Not Insane," *Douglass' Monthly* (November 1, 1859), 1.

Selected Bibliography

Books About John Brown and Family

Anderson, Osborne P. *A Voice from Harper's Ferry*. Printed for the author, 1861.
Anti-Slavery History of John Brown Year. American Anti-Slavery Society, 1861.
Benet, Stephen Vincent. *John Brown's Body*. Doubleday, Doran, 1928.
Boyer, Richard O. *The Legend of John Brown: A Biography and a History*. Alfred A. Knopf, 1973.
Brands, H. W. *The Zealot and the Emancipator*. Anchor Books, 2020.
Carton, Evan, *Patriotic Treason: John Brown and the Soul of America*. Free Press, 2006.
Chamberlin, Joseph Edgar. *John Brown*. Small Maynard, 1899.
Connelley, William Elsey. *John Brown*. Crane, 1900.
DeCaro, Louis A., Jr. *Fire from the Midst of You: A Religious Life of John Brown*. New York University Press, 2002.
DeCaro, Louis A., Jr. *John Brown: The Cost of Freedom*. International Publishers, 2007.
DeWitt, Robert M. *The Life, Trial and Execution of Capt. John Brown*. Robert M. DeWitt, 1860.
Doc. No. 1. Governor's Message and Reports of the Public Officers of the State of the Board of Directors and the Visitors, Superintendents, and Other Agents of Public Institutions or Interests of Virginia. William F. Ritchie, 1859.
Douglass, Frederick. *John Brown: An Address by Frederick Douglass at the Fourteenth Anniversary of Storer College, Harper's Ferry, WV, May 30, 1881*. Morning Star Job Printing House, 1881.
Drew, Thomas, ed. *The John Brown Invasion: An Authentic History of the Harper's Ferry Tragedy*. James Campbell, 1860.
Du Bois, W. E. Burghardt. *John Brown*. George W. Jacobs, 1909.
Featherstonhaugh, Thomas. *John Brown's Men: The Lives of Those Killed at Harper's Ferry*. Harrisburg, 1899.
Finkelman, Paul, ed. *His Soul Goes Marching On: Responses to John Brown and the Harpers Ferry Raid*. University Press of Virginia, 1995.

Hinton, Richard J. *John Brown and His Men.* Funk & Wagnalls, 1894.
Horwitz, Tony. *Midnight Rising: John Brown and the Raid that Sparked the Civil War.* Henry Holt, 2011.
Karsner, David. *John Brown: Terrible Saint.* Dodd, Mead, 1934.
Laughlin-Schultz, Bonnie. *The Tie That Bound Us: The Women of John Brown's Family and the Legacy of Radical Abolitionism.* Cornell University Press, 2013.
Libby, Jean, ed. *John Brown's Family in California.* Allies for Freedom, 2006.
Lucid, Robert F., ed., *The Journal of Richard Henry Dana, Jr.* Belknap Press of Harvard University Press, 1968.
Malin, James C. *John Brown and the Legend of Fifty-Six.* The American Philosophical Society, 1942.
McClellan, Katherine Elizabeth, *A Hero's Grave in the Adirondacks.* Published by author, 1896.
Oates, Stephen B. *To Purge This Land with Blood: A Biography of John Brown.* Harper & Row, 1970.
Peterson, Merrill D. *John Brown: The Legend Revisited.* University Press of Virginia, 2004.
Quarles, Benjamin. *Allies for Freedom: Blacks and John Brown.* Oxford University Press, 1974.
Quarles, Benjamin. *Blacks on John Brown.* Board of Trustees of the University of Illinois, 1972.
Redpath, James. *The Public Life of Capt. John Brown.* Thayer and Eldridge, 1860.
Redpath, James. *Echoes of Harpers Ferry.* Thayer and Eldridge, 1860.
Reynolds, David S. *John Brown, Abolitionist: The Man Who Killed Slavery, Sparked the Civil War, and Seeded Civil Rights.* Vintage Books, 2006.
Ruchames, Louis, ed. *A John Brown Reader.* Abelard-Schuman, 1959.
Ruchames, Louis, ed. *John Brown, The Making of a Revolutionary.* Grosset and Dunlap, 1969.
Sanborn, Franklin. *Life and Letters of John Brown: Liberator of Kansas, and Martyr of Virginia.* Roberts Brothers, 1891.
Sanborn, Franklin. *Recollections of Seventy Years, Volume I.* Gorham Press, 1909.
Stauffer, John. *The Black Hearts of Men: Radical Abolitionists and the Transformation of Race.* Harvard University Press, 2002.
Stauffer, John, and Zoe Trodd, eds. *The Tribunal, Responses to John Brown and the Harpers Ferry Raid.* Belknap Press of Harvard University Press, 2012.
Villard, Oswald Garrison. *John Brown 1800–1859: A Biography Fifty Years After.* Houghton Mifflin, 1910, 465–66.
Von Holst, Dr. Hermann, with Frank Preston Stearns, ed. *John Brown.* Cupples and Hurd, 1888.
Warren, Robert Penn. *John Brown: The Making of a Martyr.* Payson & Clarke, 1929.
Wilson, Hill Peebles. *John Brown, Soldier of Fortune.* H. P. Wilson, 1913.
Zittle, Capt. John H. *A Correct History of the John Brown Invasion.* Maii, 1905.

Other Books

Annual Report of the Regents of the University of the State of New York, Volume 79. C. Wendell, Printer, 1866.
Blight, David. *Race and Reunion.* Belknap Press of Harvard University, 2001.
Bowditch, Vincent Y. *Life and Correspondence of Henry Ingersoll Bowditch.* Houghton, Mifflin, 1902.
Brown, George Levi. *Pleasant Valley: A History of Elizabethtown, Essex County, New York.* Post and Gazette Print, 1905.
Cheney, Ednah D., ed. *Louisa May Alcott, Her Life, Letters, and Journals.* Roberts Brothers, 1890.
Donaldson, Alfred Lee. *A History of the Adirondacks, Volume 1 and Volume 2.* Century, 1921.
Douglass, Frederick. *The Life and Times of Frederick Douglass.* De Wolfe, Fiske, 1895.
Emerson, Edward W. *The Complete Works of Ralph Waldo Emerson, Volume XI.* Houghton, Mifflin, 1906, original 1878.
Emerson, Ralph Waldo. *Poems of Ralph Waldo Emerson.* Thomas Y. Crowell, 1899.
Emerson, Ralph Waldo. *The Journals and Miscellaneous Notebooks of Ralph Waldo Emerson, Volume 14.* Belknap Press of Harvard University Press, 1978.
Frothingham, Octavius Brooks. *Gerrit Smith: A Biography.* G. P. Putnam's Sons, 1878.
Gatewood, Willard B., Jr., ed. *Free Man of Color: The Autobiography of Willis Augustus Hodges.* University of Tennessee Press, 1982.
Godine, Amy. *The Black Woods: Pursuing Racial Justice on the Adirondack Frontier.* Three Hills, an Imprint of Cornell University Press, 2023.
Headley, Joel Tyler. *The Adirondack, Or Life in the Woods.* Baker and Scribner, 1851.
Higginson, Thomas Wentworth. *Cheerful Yesterdays.* Houghton, Mifflin, 1898.
Higginson, Thomas Wentworth. *Contemporaries.* Houghton, Mifflin, 1899.
A History of California . . . Biographical, Volume III. Historic Record, 1915.
Howe, Julia Ward. *Reminiscences: 1819–1899.* Houghton, Mifflin, 1900.
Jackson, Mary Anna. *Memoirs of Stonewall Jackson by his Widow.* Prentice, 1895.
Johnson, Clifton. *Highways and Byways from the St. Lawrence to Virginia.* Macmillan, 1913.
Lee, Luther. *Autobiography of the Rev. Luther Lee.* Phillips & Hunt, 1882.
Lethaby, W. R. *Architecture, Mysticism and Myth.* Macmillan, 1892.
Longstreth, Thomas Morris. *The Adirondacks.* Century, 1917.
Lundy, Rev. Dr. John Patterson. *The Saranac Exiles: A Winter's Tale of the Adirondacks.* J. P. Lundy, 1880.
MacKenzie, Mary. *Lake Placid and North Elba, A History 1800–2000.* Bookstore Plus, 2002.
Manchester, Lee, ed. *The Plains of Abraham: A History of North Elba and Lake Placid (Collected Writings of Mary MacKenzie).* Nicholas K. Burns, 2007.

Manchester, Lee. *Adirondack Heritage, Travels Through Time in New York's North Country.* Lulu.com, 2007.
Martin, George W., ed. *Transactions of the Kansas State Historical Society, 1907–1908.* State Printing Office, 1908.
McLaughlin, John M. *A Memoir of Hector Tyndale.* Collins, printer, 1882.
Moore, Frank, ed., *Personal and Political Ballads.* George P. Putnam, 1864.
Moore, John Jamison, DD. *History of the A. M. E. Zion Church in America.* Teachers' Journal Office, 1884.
Murray, Rev. William H. H. *Adventures in the Wilderness; or Camp-Life in the Adirondacks.* De Wolfe, Fiske, 1869.
Myerson, Joel, and Daniel Shealy, eds. *The Selected Letters of Louisa May Alcott.* Little, Brown, 1995.
Otis, Melissa. *Rural Indigenousness.* Syracuse University Press, 2018.
Perry, Mark. *Lift Up Thy Voice.* Viking Penguin, 2001.
Piatt, Donn. *Memories of the Men Who Saved the Union.* Belford, Clarke, 1887.
Proceedings of the Colored National Convention, Held in Rochester, July 6th, 7th and 8th, 1853. printed at the Office of Frederick Douglass's Paper, 1853.
Proceedings of the National Convention of Colored People, and Their Friends, Held in Troy, NY on the 6th, 7th, 8th and 9th October, 1847. Steam Press of J. C. Kneeland, 1847.
Proctor, Edna Dean. *Poems.* Hurd and Houghton, 1867.
Richards, Thomas Addison. *The Romance of American Landscape.* Leavitt and Allen, 1855.
Ripley, C. Peter, ed. *The Black Abolitionist Papers, Vol. IV: The United States, 1847–1858.* University of North Carolina Press, 2015.
Royce, Caroline Halstead Barton. *Bessboro, A History of Westport, Essex County, New York.* n.p., 1902.
Sernett, Milton C. *North Star Country.* Syracuse University Press, 2002.
Shealy, Daniel, ed. *Alcott in Her Own Time.* University of Iowa Press, 2005.
Still, William. *The Underground Railroad.* Porter & Coates, 1872.
Stoddard, Seneca Ray. *The Adirondacks Illustrated.* Weed, Parsons, 1874.
Street, Alfred B. *Woods and Waters, or the Saranacs and Racket.* M. Doolady, 1860.
Stutler, Boyd B., "Glory, Glory Hallelujah/The Story of 'John Brown's Body' and 'Battle Hymn of the Republic.'" C. J. Krehbiel, 1960.
Svenson, Sally E. *Blacks in the Adirondacks.* Syracuse University Press, 2017.
Sylvester, Nathaniel Bartlett. *Historical Sketches of Northern New York and the Adirondack Wilderness.* William H. Young, 1877.
Terrie, Phillip G. *Forever Wild: A Cultural History of Wilderness in the Adirondacks.* Syracuse University Press, 1994.
Thoreau, Henry David. *Anti-Slavery and Reform Papers.* Swan Sonnenschein, 1890.
Thoreau, Henry David. *Miscellanies.* Houghton Mifflin, 1893.

Torrey, Bradford, and Sanborn, Franklin, eds. *The Writings of Henry David Thoreau, Journal, Volume 11.* Houghton Mifflin, 1906.
Tuttle, Mrs. George Fuller. *Three Centuries in Champlain Valley.* Saranac Chapter, D.A.R., 1909.
United States Army and Navy Journal and Gazette, Volume 2, 1864–65. Publication Office No. 39 Park Row, October 29, 1864.
A Virginian (William McDonald). *The Two Rebellions; or, Treason Unmasked.* Smith, Bailey, 1865.
Ward, Andrew. *Dark Midnight When I Rise.* Amistad, 2001.
Watson, Winslow C. *A General View and Agricultural Survey of the County of Essex, 1852.* New York State Agricultural Society, 1853.
Watson, Winslow C. *The Military and Civil History of the County of Essex, New York.* J. Munsell, 1869.
Watson, Winslow C. "Supplement to Survey of Essex County." In *Transactions of the NY State Agricultural Society, 1853.* C. Van Benthuysen, 1854, 699–741.
White, Richard Grant. *Poetry, Lyrical, Narrative and Satirical, of the Civil War.* American News Company, 1866.
Wright, Theodore S., Charles B. Ray, and James McCune Smith. *An Address to the Three Thousand Colored Citizens of New York Who Are the Owners of 120,000 Acres of Land . . . Given to Them by Gerrit Smith Esq.,* 1846.
Young, Joshua. *God Greater Than Man: A Sermon Preached June 11th After the Rendition of Anthony Burns.* Samuel B. Nichols, 1854.

Magazine and Journal Articles

"Address of the New York State Convention to Their Colored Fellow Citizens." *Colored American,* November 21, 1840.
Atkinson, Eleanor. "The Soul of John Brown: Recollections of the Great Abolitionist by His Son." *American Magazine,* October 1909.
Brown, Salmon. "My Father, John Brown." *The Outlook,* January 25, 1913.
Chapin, Lou V. "The Last Days of Old John Brown." *Overland Monthly,* April 1899.
Dana, Richard Henry, Jr., "How We Met John Brown." *Atlantic Monthly,* July 1871.
Duffus, Robert L. "The Grave of Osawatomie." *Nation,* February 14, 1920.
"An Excursion to the Adirondack Mountains, in the Summer of 1861." *Friends' Intelligencer* XVIII. T. Ellwood Zell, 1862, 665–67.
Featherstonhaugh, Thomas. "The Final Burial of the Followers of John Brown." *New England Magazine,* April 1901.
Field, Kate. "In and Out of the Woods." *The Atlantic Almanac for 1870,* Field, Osgood, 1869.
Gee, Clarence. "The Stone on John Brown's Grave." *New York History,* April 1961.

Kimball, George. "Origin of the John Brown Song." *New England Magazine*, 1890.
Logsdon, Gene. "Why the Midwest Is Square." *The Old Farmer's Almanac*, 1987.
McGlone, Robert. "Rescripting a Troubled Past: John Brown's Family and the Harpers Ferry Conspiracy." *Journal of American History*, 1989.
Miller, Ernest C. "John Brown's Ten Years in Northwestern Pennsylvania." *Pennsylvania History*, January 1948.
NYS Report of Commissioners of Fisheries, Game, and Forests. 1896.
Thoreau, Henry David. "Walking." *The Atlantic*, June 1862.
"A Visit to the Adirondacks." *Friends Intelligencer*, October 10, 1868, 489. Extract from a letter dated August 3, 1863.
Young, Rev. Joshua. "The Funeral of John Brown." *New England Magazine*, April 1904.

Index

Page numbers in *italics* refer to illustrations

abolition/abolitionists: acceptance of violence, 52, 66, 82, 116, 128, 129, 156, 189, 191, 195–96, 207, 223; assaults on (hatred, threats, and violence toward), 13–14, 51, 61, 62, 66, 79, 80, 81, 125, 137, 152, 168, 194; black activism in, 19, 21, 27–28, 35, 38–39, 40, 41–42, 44, 67, 103, 128, 158; blamed for Civil War, 213; blamed for continuance of slavery, 89, 164, 166; blamed for JB's actions in Harpers Ferry, 162, 196; Essex County activism in, 37, 51–52, 90, 108, 162, 196; JB and Brown family dedication to, 11, 12, 35–36, 91, 103, 182; moral suasion, 66, 82, 101, 108–109, 126, 128; politics/Liberty Party, 38, 40, 41, 162, 194–95; prejudice of, (social equality with black people), 35–36; vying for JB's body, 134, 144, 145, 209, 218

Adair, Samuel and Florilla (Brown), 62, 78

Adams, Elijah (Elizabethtown sheriff), 147, 201

Adirondack Mountains (Adirondack Park), *10*; appeal to JB as home, 9, 29–30, 65; connection to freedom, 4, 6, 19, 29–30, 91–92, 96–97, 190, 193, 225; naming, xi, 237n1; scenery, 1, 5, 29, 30, 37, 91–92, *94*, 96–97, 153, 188, 209. *See also* wilderness; names of individual counties, towns, and mountains

Agassiz, Louis, 95, 96

Alcott, Amos Bronson, 106–107, 178, 202–204, 215, 235

Alcott, Louisa May, 178–80, 202–204, *203*, 208, 223–24, 266n2, 268n19

Algonquin Peak, 92, 93

Allegheny Mountains: in JB's initial plan, 17–18, 29–30, 64, 67, 82, 99–100, 247n8; in JB's Virginia plan, 101–11, 115, 183

American Revolution: compared with JB's actions, 90–91, 128, 143, 167–68, 183, 187, 189–90,

American Revolution *(continued)*
  195, 221, 222; JB's grandfather's service in, 174–75, 222. *See also* Declaration of Independence; July Fourth
Anderson, Jeremiah, 111, 121
Anderson, Osborne Perry, 121, 184–86, *185*, 191–93, 194, 235, 253n11, 263n26
Appo, William, 55–57, 73, 107, 122, 246n32
Appo, William Jr., 212
Atchison, David R., 79, 249n12
Ausable River, xii, 57, 60, 62

"Battle Hymn of the Republic," 207
Beecher, Henry Ward, 221
Benet, Stephen Vincent (*John Brown's Body*), 30–31, 49, 164–65, 221–22
Bible: on Golden Rule, 111, 130, 164; on slavery, 43, 97, 128, 130, 162, 164, 191; on sowing, reaping, and harvesting, 43, 101, 192, 224–25; on wilderness, 91–92, 93, 97; passages referenced by JB, 30, 64, 78, 92–93, 105, 107, 126, 128, 133, 181, 202, 227, 244n1
Bigelow, Lucius H., 150–51
Bigelow, Lawrence Goodhue, 267n23
Blacksville: founding of, 19–20, 233; JB's aid of, 24–25, 36; voters in, 40–41, 72, 163. *See also* Hodges, Willis
"Blow Ye the Trumpet Blow," 82, 153, 188, 260n17
Boston, Massachusetts: abolitionists of 35, 95, 118, 152, 164, 190, 194; aid/support for JB and family from, 84, 123, 172, 177; JB visits, 83, 101; "John Brown Song," 204–205, 207; MB visits, 135, 181; vying for Brown's body, 134, 144, 145, 209, 218
boulder (big rock) at John Brown Farm graveyard: as JB monument, *64*, 209, 221, 226; as JB's place to read Bible, 133, 221; as podium, 182, *183*, 188, 190–91
Bowditch, Henry Ingersoll, 198, 217, 223, 269n20
Brands, H. W., 6
Brewster, Byron Remembrance, 57, 86, 119
Brewster, O. Byron, 71
Brown, Abbie (Hinckley), 57, 64, 87–88, *88*, 94, 109, 118, 177, 217–18, 220–21, 230, 236, 252n16, 268n8
Brown, Annie (daughter of John and Mary), *46*, *112*, 231; Alcott, Louisa May, and, 202, 203; Anderson, Osborne, reunion with, 185–86, 193; childhood in North Elba, 30, 45, 62, 82; climbing Whiteface, 93–94, 252n16; father's hair, 159; at Fort Edward Institute, 218; at Kennedy farm, 109–10, 111–13, 117; move to California, 219–21; reaction to Harpers Ferry news, 119, 121–22, 171–72, 173–74; reaction to father's hanging, 143, 148; at Sanborn's school, 176–78, 180, 202–204; teaching at freedmen's school, 218–19
Brown, Dianthe (Lusk), 11–12, 15, 229
Brown, Ellen (1) (daughter of John and Mary), 24, 26, 231
Brown, Ellen (2) (daughter of John and Mary), 62, 78, 82, 110, 117, 148, 159, 202, 218, 221, 231

Brown, Frederick (son of John and Dianthe), 15, 62, 81–82, 84, 175, 222, 230, 250n29
Brown, Frederick "Freddy" (son of Watson and Isabelle), 110–11, 117, 178–80, *179*, 186, 218, 230
Brown, Isabelle "Belle" (Thompson), 82, 110, 117–18, 121, 173, 178–80, *179*, 210, 230, 252n16
Brown, Jason (son of John and Dianthe), 229; criticism of North Elba, 61, 93; in Kansas, 62, 81; land deeds in North Elba, 36, 47, 245n9; mentioned, 15, 182, 210, 253n9
Brown, John, xii, 2–3, *13*, *130*
—action, not talk, 15, 36, 40, 80, 99, 101, 223
—advice sent to MB and family, 48, 77, 99, 104, 105, 106, 108, 110, 118, 124, 176
—aliases: Nelson Hawkins, 101, 108; Shubel Morgan, 108, Isaac Smith, 108
—appearance, 16, 32, 96; with beard, *100*
—body: abolitionist plans for, 134–35, 144–46, 209, 218; in Elizabethtown, 147; in New York City, 145; in North Elba, 148–49, *149*; in Philadelphia, 144–45; in Vermont, 146; substitute of fake, 144; Southerners plans for, 134–35; at undertaker, 145
—bounty for, 84, 99, 106
—business difficulties (bankruptcy, lawsuits), 6, 15, 43, 46, 52, 53, 250n35
—character of, 6, 16–18, 106–107, 129, 161–63; adhering to smallest details, 53, 106; delay, propensity for, 24–26, 61, 62, 104, 106, 240n39; lack of guilt, 80, 124, 131, 227; moral heroism of, 6, 8, 83, 128, 143, 208, 209, 223, 225, 226–27; noninvolvement in organizations and political parties, 40; penmanship, 161, 166; speaking words of truth, 1, 17, 131, 161, 166; square with the world, 63–65
—childhood and youth, 12
—deaths of children, 12, 15, 26, 53, 229–31, 246n27
—education, views on, 12, 28, 41, 176
—ending slavery as his Godly mission, 7, 66, 99, 106, 107, 115, 124, 139, 197
—funeral, 153–59, *154*, *157*, 163, 165
—grave. *See* grave of JB; tombstone.
—hanging. *See* hanging of JB
—in jail. *See* jail
—locks of hair, 158–59
—mail service, distrust of, 80, 101, 105, 110
—North Elba as home: Essex fever, 6–7, 59, 82; missing home, 47, 48, 82, 85, 86; move to Flanders farm, 7, 11, 29–30, 240n39; move to John Brown Farm, 60–61, 62–63
—in Ohio (JB and family residence from 1851 to 1855), 53, 59–62
—plan for liberating slaves: initial Allegheny plan, 17–18, 29–30, 64, 67, 82, 99, 247n8; later Virginia plan, 101, 102, 104, 105–106, 109
—principles. *See* Bible; duty; Declaration of Independence; Golden Rule; sacrifice
—relationship with: black settlers, 7, 18, 24–26, 28–37, 47, 59, 62,

Index | 279

Brown, John *(continued)*
71–72, 73, 240n35, 247n8; his
children, 16–17, 26, 41, 48, 53,
59–62, 65, 75, 77, 79–81, 84–85,
87, 93, 101–102, 104–105,
113, 116–17, 121–22, 131–32,
143, 238n12; his grandchildren,
102, 131, 193; his wife MB, 12,
15–16, 43–44, 77, 78, 80, 84–87,
99, 105–106, 109–10, 117, 124,
129, 131, 135–39
—violence of. *See* violence
Brown, Sergeant John (Civil War
soldier), 204–205, 207, 214
Brown, Capt. John (JB's grandfather),
174–75, 222
Brown, John Jr. (son of John and
Dianthe): about JB, 132, 208;
Flanders farm visit, 46; as Harpers
Ferry recruit, 253n9; at July 4,
1860 meeting, 182, 187, 191,
210; in Kansas, 62, 65–66,
75–77, 81; on Lincoln and Civil
War, 215; on moving to North
Elba, 59–60, 61, 104–105;
relationship with Timbucto, xii,
18, 41, 46, 241n5
Brown, Martha (Brewster): baby
Olive, 177–78; death of, 178,
263n15; as heroine of Harpers
Ferry tragedy, 178; at Kennedy
farm, 109–10, 111, 113, 117;
as part of family at John Brown
Farm, 102, *103*, 109, 117–18,
171; pregnancy of, 113, 117–18,
171; reaction to Harpers Ferry
news, 119, 121, 124, 171–72;
mentioned, 57, 105, 173, 196,
230, 253n8, 265n21
Brown, Mary Ann (Day), *14, 46,*
230–31; aid after raid, 171,
172–74, 187, 209–10; in Boston
for New England Anti-Slavery
Convention, 181; character of,
86, 87, 124, 145–46, 169, 171,
172–73, 176, 179, 181–82, 209–
10; childhood and youth, 11–12,
238n5; on Civil War, 214–15;
commitment to cause, 12, 14,
18, 99, 107, 110, 124, 129, 131,
182, 196; in Concord for tea
party, 178–80; on Emancipation
Proclamation, 214; at Flanders
farm, 31, 43, 46, 48, 50; in
Harpers Ferry and Charles Town,
137, 139, 137–40, 259n34; JB's
affection for (sympathy with), 12,
15, 77, 84–87, 105–106, 136,
139–40; at John Brown Farm,
64, 65, 75, 77–78, 84–85, 86,
87, 106, 110, 192, 210, 246n32,
262n6, 267n21; journey to
California, 219, 221; journey to
farm with JB's body, 133, 135,
144–49, *149;* journey to Virginia,
123, 124, 135–37; Kennedy
farm, not going to, 109–10;
letters with Wise about JB's body,
136–37, 257n12; Lot 88, 57,
84–86, 250n35; marriage to JB,
early years of, 12–16, 238n7;
as mother, 12, 16, 24, 26, 45,
53, 62, 86, 110, 124, 148, 182,
246n27; move from North Elba,
218; renting/selling farm, 226,
269n24; retrieving son's bodies in
Virginia, 135–37, 144; schooling
for daughters, 176–77, 218;
tombstone for JB and family, 133,
174, 175–76; water cure, 43–46,
73, 218, 244n4
Brown, Oliver (son of John and
Mary), 230; death, 121, 124,
135, 137, 144, 222; grave, *2,*

280 | Index

4; as Harpers Ferry recruit/
soldier, 101–102, *103*, 109–11,
117–19, 255n10; inscription on
tombstone, 174–76; in Kansas,
75, 77–78, 81, 234, 249n18; at
Kennedy farm, 109, 111, 117–19;
as martyr/hero, 155, 156; in
North Elba, 30, 45, 62, 105,
109–10, 118
Brown, Owen (JB's father), 12, 77, 78
Brown, Owen (son of John and
Dianthe), 229; escaped from
Kennedy farm, 172; at Flanders
farm, 30, 45, 47–48, 61, 93; as
Harpers Ferry recruit/soldier, 111,
121, 172, 253n9, 253n11; at
John Brown Farm, 191, 193, 210,
245n9; in Kansas and Iowa, 62,
78, 99, 249n18; at Kennedy farm,
111, 117–19; in Ohio, 218
Brown (Thompson), Ruth (daughter
of John and Dianthe), 229;
about JB, 30, 53, 86, 93, 102,
121, 149, 154; at Flanders farm,
30, 32, 45, 47–48, *49*, 49–50,
52, 54; July 4, 1860 meeting,
182, 187, 210, 263n23; at
Lot 88 home, 57, 59–60, 62,
65, 77–79, 84–87, 105–106,
250n35; move from North Elba,
217–18; reactions after Harpers
Ferry, 121, 123, 131, 172, 178;
relationship with husband Henry,
49–50, 78–79; relationship with
Timbucto settlers, xii, 18, 29, 45,
241n5
Brown, Salmon (son of John and
Mary), 230; at Flanders farm,
30, 45; at John Brown farm, 64,
81, 82, 86, *87*, 93–94, 118–19,
124, 177, 208, 210, 262n38; as
Harpers Ferry recruit, 101–102,

109; in Kansas, 62, 65, 75, 78,
80, 81, 82, 249n18; move from
North Elba, 217, 218–21, 236;
at new home in North Elba (near
Hinckleys), 57, 88, 210; recruiting
Union soldiers, 211, 217
Brown, Sarah (daughter of John and
Mary), 231; in California, 221;
childhood in North Elba, 30,
45, *46*, 62, 64, 110, 148, 159;
at Fort Edward Institute, 218; at
Sanborn's school, 176–78, 180,
202, 204
Brown, Watson (son of John and
Mary), 230; death of, 121, 124,
135, 137, 144, 222; at Flanders
farm, 30, 45; grave, *2*, 4; as
Harpers Ferry recruit/soldier,
101–102, 119; inscription on
tombstone, 174–76; at John
Brown Farm, 62, 75, *76*, 76–78,
82, 93, 110–11, 249n9; in
Kansas, 82; at Kennedy farm,
111, 117–19; as martyr/hero, 155,
156
Brown, Wealthy (Hotchkiss) (wife of
John Jr.), 46, 59–60, 76, 218,
229
Burlington, Vermont, 11, 135,
151–52, 165, 188, 261n28

California, Brown family's move to,
217–21, 229–31, 236
Canada: Chatham, Ontario, 103–104,
117, 184, 234, 253n11; JB in,
102–104, 105–106, 107, 234;
mentioned, 11, 20, 34, 36, 54,
111, 116, 117, 163, 177, 184,
244n31
Carasaw, William 45, 67, 73, 212
Cascade Pass and Cascadeville, 71,
104, 240n34

celebrity of Brown family, 7, 159, 178–80, 181, 208–10, 211–12, 220
Charles Town, Virginia (West Virginia), xi, 119, 137–42; mentioned, 2, 3, 123, 145, 194, 229. *See also* jail
Child, Lydia Maria, 128, 181, 262n39
Civil War: black troops in, 207, 212, 213, 214, 222, 264n26; ending slavery, as goal of, 197, 201, 207, 213, 222; Essex County and, 197–98, 201, 202, 211–13, 226, 255n1; Harpers Ferry and, 198; JB (Harpers Ferry raid) as trigger for, 195–96, 203, 207, 213, 222–25; "John Brown Song," role in, 204–207, *206*, 224; Northern aggression as cause of, 125, 195, 197, 213; outbreak of, 197–98, 235; preserving Union, as goal of, 197, 213, 222; rebirth of nation, 222–23, 225; states' rights and slavery as causes of, 125, 161, 194, 196–97, 207
Clarke, Rev. James Freeman, 164
class prejudice, 7, 35, 40, 67, 83, 86, 143, 180, 223
Clinton County, 48, 193
colorphobia. *See* racism
Compromise of 1820, 61, 90, 195, 234
Connecticut, 12, 174–75
Concord, Massachusetts: abolitionists in, 89–90, 127; Brown girls going to Sanborn's School, 177–78, 180, 202–204; Brown family visits, 178–80; Civil War excitement in, 204; JB visits, 91–92, 106–107; mentioned 181, 192, 208, 234–35, 268n19. *See also* Alcott; Emerson; Thoreau

Confederate States of America (Confederacy): formation of, 167, 195, 197, 198, 265n25; mentioned, 204, 205, 213, 215, 220
Constitution, US: Declaration of Independence versus, 184, 265n15; as model for JB's "Provisional Constitution," 103–104, 253n11; slavery and, 13, 51, 89, 90, 100, 125, 152, 167, 184, 196–97, 213
Cook, John E., 111, 121, 126, 174, 209, 253n11
Copeland, John Anthony, 118, 121, 174, 191
Coppoc, Barclay, xi, 111, 121, 174, 193
Coppoc, Edwin, xi, 111, 121, 174
Cummin, Mrs., 45

Dana, Richard Henry, 31–35, 233, 242n13, 242n14, 242n17
Davis, Jefferson, 195, 205, 213
Day, Charles and Mary Ann, 11, 238n5
Day, Orson, 11, 24, 48, 78, 238n5
DeCaro, Louis, 6, 8
Declaration of Independence: equality and, 143, 183–84, 222, 225; as explanation for JB's actions, 126, 143, 187–91; inalienable truths of, 5, 183, 187–91; as JB's principles, 5, 18, 90–91, 101–102, 183–84, 187, 189–91, 227; as model for JB's "Declaration of Liberty," 97–98, 99; slavery and, 18, 183–84, 188–91, 195–96
"Declaration of Liberty," 97–98, 99, 183
Delamater, George B., 24, 41, 172, 238n5, 238n7, 241n7, 244n31

Delamater, Thomas and Martha (Day), 11–12
Delany, Dr. Martin R., 103
Democratic (Democracy) Party/Democrats, 38, 161–62, 168, 188, 194, 196, 262n38, 265n15
Dickson, Mr. and Mrs., xi, 46, 54, 57, 67, 245n8
disunion, 104, 147, 152, 161, 164, 166, 167, 194, 195–98
Donaldson, Alfred, 70–71, 242n9, 242n17, 250n32
Douglass, Frederick, *17*; on Brown family household, 16–17, 181; on Civil War's mission, 201, 222–23, 268n17; on JB, 4, 16–18, 30, 115, 126, 184, 190–91, 225, 227–28; on JB's Allegheny (Harpers Ferry) plan, 17–18, 30, 99–100, 115, 184; JB's opinion of, 43, 99, 115, 225, 227–28, 253n11; on July 4 meaning for black people, 184; on Smith land giveaway, 19, 23–24, 68, 69, 240n33, 247n19; on slavery, 68, 126, 184, 207, 225; on use of violence, 184, 191, 201, 207
Dred Scott Decision, 100–101, 103
Drummond, 37, 45
Du Bois, W. E. B., 6, 73
Duffus, Robert L., 27
Durand, Milo, 159
duty, as principle of JB and Brown family, 4, 8, 15, 66, 67, 78, 98, 181, 197, 227
Dwyer, Samuel, 160, 201, 260n9, 265n1

egalitarianism/equality: of abolitionists, 18, 35–36, 97, 183–84, 222, 267n26; of JB and Brown family, 6, 7, 18, 33, 35, 36, 65, 98, 103, 115, 143, 163, 172, 191, 227

Elizabethtown, New York: Civil War enlistments, 201, 265n1; county fair in, 48–49; funeral party in, 147; Underground Railroad in, 34; mentioned, 24, 30, 47, 53, 62, 108, 151, 159, 254n25
Emancipation Proclamation, 214–15, 236
Emerson, Ralph Waldo, 15, 60, 89–91, 95–96, 98, 128, 178, 208, 215, 256n40
enslaved black people. *See* slavery
Epps (Appo), Albertine, 55, 56, 155, 246n32, 260n2
Epps, Lyman (and Ann), xi, 45–46, *55*, 55–56, 57, 67–68, 73, 95, 102, 104, 217, 245n8, 246n31; on JB, 108, 109; singing at funeral and events, 153–54, 159, 188, 190
Epps, Lyman Jr., 55, 71, 154, 243n17, 246n31, 246n32
equality. *See* egalitarianism
Erhardt, Joel Benedict, 158, 159
Essex County, New York, xii, 2, 6, 9, *10*, 48–49; antislavery activity, 51–52, 108–109, 191, 193; Civil War, 197–98, 201, 202, 211–13, 226, 255n1; fair, 48–49. *See also* Harpers Ferry raid; neighbors; North Elba
Essex County Courthouse, 130, 147, *148*, 259n43
Essex fever, 7, 59, 104

Fairman, Col. James, 211
Field, Kate, 226
Finkelman, Paul, 196
Flanders, Chapin and Caroline, 25, 31, 57, 242n9
Flanders farm (Lot 110), 10, 29, 31–34, 52, 57, 241n5; Browns at,

Index | 283

Flanders farm (Lot 110) *(continued)* 31–34, 43, 45–53; crops, 47, 52; house, 31, 52, 242n9, 242n14; JB's rental of, 25, 31, 33, 52; livestock, 47, 48
Forbes, Hugh, 104
Fort Edward Institute, 218, 236
Fort Sumter, firing on, 197–98, 203, 235
Frazier, Silas, 57, 67, 212
free black people: as citizens, 222; as Civil War soldiers, 207; critical of July 4 celebrations, 184; disagreements among, 28; education, 41–42; elevating conditions of, 24, 27–28, 98; exclusion from Civil War service, 212–13; as Harpers Ferry recruits/soldiers, 184–85; prejudice/discrimination towards, 18, 27, 35–36; land ownership (of farms), 18, 28; slave catchers' pursuit of, 27, 241n1; voting property requirement, 28, 41
Free Soil Party, 40, 81, 97, 243n26
free states, 2, 13, 61–62, 65–66, 79–81, 111, 115, 264n5
freedom: in the Adirondacks, 4, 6, 19, 29–30, 91–92, 95–97, 190, 193, 217, 225; JB as symbol of, 4, 126, 128–29, 182, 190, 195, 214; mountains as home of, 97; mountains as pathway to, 17–18, 29–30, 117; nation based on, 195–96, 222–23; from slavery, 116–17, 124, 128–30, 155–56, 174, 190, 193, 196, 213–14; tombstone inscription "for adherence to the cause of freedom," 7, 174, 188; Universal Freedom, 129, 193, 195
Fugitive Slave Act (Law) of 1793, 51

Fugitive Slave Act (Law) of 1850, 51–52, 54, 66, 90, 152, 233
fugitive slaves, 14, 35, 51, 52, 105, 116, 127–28, 152, 163, 164, 197, 212, 213, 241n1; myth of, in North Elba, 33–34, 70–71, 242n17; Thomas, Cyrus, 31, 34

Garnet, Henry Highland, 19, 21, 23, 27–28, 41
Garrison, William Lloyd, 27, 45, 125, 165, 181, 219
Golden Rule, 5, 91, 111, 130, 164, 181, 227
grave of JB, 1–3, *2*, *183*, *224*; as Calvary/Mecca/shrine, 1, 5, 129, 133, 167–68, 182, 187, 188, 195, 223; JB's choice of, 133, 221; moving of, 209, 218
graves of raiders, 2, 4, *122*, 124, 144, 175
Green, Shields, 115, 121, 174, 191
Gregory, Dick, xv, 1–5, 227
Grimke, Angelina, 27, 176
Grimke, Sarah M., 35–36, 176

Hale, Robert Spafford, 53, 147, 159, 269n20
Hall, Robert, 254n25
Hand, Augustus C., 147
hanging of JB, 140–41, *142*, 145; as death knell of slavery, 143, 196; reactions by black communities, 143, 146; reactions by Brown family, 131–32, 137–38, 143, 147; reactions of JB to prospect of, 120, 131, 133, 139, 141, 222; reactions by North Elba (Essex County) townspeople, 107, 147–48, 159–64, 167–69, 194, 196; reactions by Northerners, 3, 125–27, 142–43, 144–46,

155–57, 164–65, 166–68, 189, 196–97, 221, 225; reactions by Southerners, 141–42, 164–65, 167–68, 196; ropes for, 140–41
hanging of Harpers Ferry raiders, 174
Harpers Ferry, Virginia, xi, 1, 2; Civil War, 198, 258n18; MB's visit to, 137, 144, 149
Harpers Ferry raid, 119–21, *120*, 255n15
—capture of JB and raiders, 126
—deaths, 119, 120–21, 122, 124, 222
—engine house (John Brown's Fort), 119–20, *120*, 258n18
—escapes from, 126, 158, 172, 184, 191, 193
—failure/success of, 121, 124, 127, 155–57, 189, 196, 208, 221
—JB's mistakes at, 221
—JB's plans for, 101–11, 115, 183; initial Allegheny plan, 17–18, 29–30, 64, 67, 82, 99–100, 247n8
—JB's recruitment for, 101–103, 108, 109, 110, 115
—postponement of, 104, 253n12
—raiders (recruits, soldiers), 111, 117–21, 122, 126, 172, 174, 184–85, 191, 193, 209
—reactions by: Brown family, 119, 121–24, 138, 178; JB, 124–25, 129–31, 135–36, 138, 180; North Elba (Essex County) townspeople, 107, 151, 160–64, 167–69, 194; Northerners, 125–29, 147, 155–56, 164–65, 166–67, 189, 223; Southerners, 119–20, 125–27, 129, 164–65, 167–68
—skepticism prior to, 109, 115–16, 184
—warnings about, 115–17

—mentioned, 3–8, 33, 106, 147, 177, 187, 189, 203, 205, 207, 227
Hasbrook, Josiah and Susan, xi, 55–57, 67, 73
Hasbrook, Josiah Jr., 56–57, 212
Hasbrook, Simeon, 56, 94, 252n16
Hazlett, Albert, 111, 121, 174
Headley, Joel, 91–92, 95, 251n9
Henderson, James, xii, 20–21, 24, 28–29, 36–37, 54, 57, 241n5, 243n20, 246n29
Higginson, Thomas Wentworth: aid for raiders' families and prisoners, 173–74; on black settlers, 73; on character of Brown family, 7, 123–24, 180–81; on "John Brown Song," 204; with MB to Boston, 135, 235; as Secret Six member, 83, 123, 129, 253n12; visit to John Brown Farm, 123–24, 175, 180–81, 256n23
higher law, 89–90, 97–98, 152, 166
Hinckley, Alexis, 64, 88, 102, 109, 211, 226, 230, 252n16, 269n24
Hinckley, Horatio, xi, 57, 105, 210, 230, 245n8
Hinckley, Abbie. *See* Brown, Abbie (Hinckley)
Hinton, Richard, 6, 190–92, 264n12
Hodges, Willis, 5, 19–21, *20*, 24–29, 36, 40–41, 71, 97, 240n33, 240n35, 241n1, 243n19
Howe, Samuel Gridley, 83, 126
Howe, Julia Ward, 207, 215
Hudson River, 34, 92
Huffmaster, Mrs., 112
Hugo, Victor, 164
Hyatt, Thaddeus, 145, 193–94, 210

Indian Pass, *29*, 32, 92, 95, 151, 242n16

Iowa, 77, 82, 85, 99, 105, 111, 217, 236; Brown family in, 218–20

jail, Charles Town, *138*, *139*; escape of Stevens and Hazlett from, 174; letters from JB in, 131, 135–36; letters to JB in, 131–32; plan to rescue JB from, 123, 124; visit by MB to, 135–40
Jay, Town of, 31, 51–52, 71, 135, 158–59, 211–12, 245n21
Jefferson, Samuel, 36, 48, 57, 67
Jefferson, Thomas, 30, 36, 48, 57, 67
John Brown Farm (Lot 95): Browns leave, 217–19; Browns move to, 62–63; crops grown at, 62, 78, 86, 98, 105, 106, 107, 117, 118–19, 180, 210; graveyard, *3*, *5*, 226, 229–30; house, *5*, 33, 60–64, *64*, *65*, 76–77, 85, 209, 210, *227*, 242n14; livestock at, 77, 78, 86, 106, 180; location (maps) of, *10*, *57*; ownership of, 47, 226, 233, 250n32; as Site of Conscience, 8, 193; as State Historic Site, 1–4, 226; visitors to 85–86, 123–24, 149, 152, 153, 175, 177, 180–81, 185–86, 187–88, 226–27, 261n28, 264n12
"John Brown Song," 198–99, 204–208, *206*, 213–14, 224, 260n16
July Fourth (Independence Day): abolition, significance of, 183–84, 187, 188; as Adirondack summer, 182; JB scheduled raid on, 101, 106, 183; on Whiteface Mountain summit, 94
July Fourth Meeting of 1860, 182–86, 187–94; Brown family reunion, 187; Kennedy farm housemates reunite, 193; letters read at, 190–91, 192–93; resolutions of, 193; speeches at, 188–91

Kagi, John H., 108, 111, 121, 253n11
Kansas Territory: antislavery settlers in, 61, 62, 66, 75, 79–81; Black Jack battle, 81, 85, 234, 250n22; climate, 75, 77, 78; JB in, 77–84, 86–87; JB's appeal for aid for, 66, 82–83; JB's decision to go to, 61–63, 65–67, 72, 75, 247n8; JB's sons as new settlers in, 62, 65–66; Lawrence attacks, 79–81; Osawatomie battle, 81; Pottawatomie killings, 80–81, 249n19; proslavery border ruffians in, 61–62, 65, 66, 75, 78–81, 249n12; statehood, 264n5; violent conditions in, 65–67, 75–76, 78–82, 91, 101, 111, 234; as war, 61, 76, 79, 80; mentioned, 2–3, 6–8, 105, 107, 133, 140, 160, 163, 168–69, 175, 189, 193, 211, 218, 227, 229–30, 250n22
Kansas-Nebraska Act of 1854, 61, 66, 234
Keene, Town of, xi, 10, 23, 41. *See also* neighbors; North Elba
Keeseville, New York (Essex County), 34, 51, 123, 188, 193
Kellogg, Orlando, 53, 147
Kennedy farm (in Maryland), 109–13, 117–18, 122, 171, 185, 193, 231, 235

Lake Champlain, xii, 9, 11, 34, 68, 93, 146–47, 151, 187, 269n25
Lake Placid (lake), xii, 4, 93, *94*, 104
Lake Placid (village), xii, 1, 2, 3, 5, 71
Land purchases by JB. *See* North Elba properties associated with JB

Land giveaway (experiment) of 1846. *See* Smith land giveaway (of 1846) to black men
Landrine, Mr., 37
Lansing, Wendell, 51, 193, 245n21
Langston, Charles H., 128, 143
Lawrence, Amos, 84, 250n30
League of Gileadites, 52
Leary, Lewis Sheridan, 118, 121, 191
Lee, Col. Francis, 226, 269n25
Lee, Rev. Dr. Luther, 182, 188–90
Lee, Robert E., 120
Leeman, William Henry, 111, 121, 253n11
Lewis, Wait J., 23, 239n30
Liberty Party, 38, 40, 259n45
Lincoln, Abraham: calls for Union troops, 198; elected President, 194–95; emancipation policy of, 164, 213, 215; Emancipation Proclamation, 213–15; on JB, 166–67; on rebirth of nation, 222–23; on slavery, 164, 167, 207, 213–14; on saving the Union, 207, 213
Loguen, J. W. (Jermain Wesley), 23, 240n30, 244n32
Lovejoy, Elijah, 13–14
Lowell, James Russell, 95

Martin, John Sella, 190
martyrdom of JB: by Alcott, Louisa May, 223–24; by Beecher, 221; by Emerson, 128; by Hodges, 163; by Hyatt, 193; by Lee, Luther, 187, 189–90; by MB, 138; by McKim, 155; by Phillips, 197; South's fear of, 142; by Thoreau, 143; by Turner, 162; by Watkins, 128–29; by Young, 155
Maryland. *See* Kennedy farm

Massachusetts. *See* Boston; Concord; Northampton; Springfield
May, Samuel (Jr.), 179, 181
McKim, James Miller and Mary, 134–37, 144–45, 149, 155–56, 163, 173, 262n6
Meriam, Francis Jackson, 118, 121, 193
Missouri: JB's rescue of slaves from, 105–106, 107, 111, 160; mentioned 7, 8, 77, 79–82, 140, 163, 220, 249n12
Missouri Compromise of 1820, 61, 90, 195, 234
monument for JB, 134, 168, 175–76, 209, 221–23, 226
Morehouse, Stephen Warren, 212
Mount Auburn Cemetery, 144–45, 209
Mount Marcy (Tahawus), 1, 4, 32, *92*, 94

Nash, T. S. (Timothy), 57, 196–97, 253n8, 260n16, 265n21
native (indigenous) people, xi, 24, 56, 83, 96, 127, 220
neighbors of John Brown, 87; antislavery activity of, 51–52, 108–109, 191, 193; appeal for mercy for JB, 162; criticism of JB, 102, 151, 160–63, 168–69, 194, 196–97, 262n40; at funeral, 153, 158–59; politics, 51–52, 161–63, 168, 188, 194, 261n37, 262n38, 265n15; recollections as unreliable, 159–60, 242n17; support for JB, 36, 48–49, 102, 107 147, 159–63, 193, 197, 213, 217. *See also* North Elba; Timbucto
Newby, Dangerfield, 111, 121, 173–74, 191

North Elba Cemetery, 26, 56–57, 63, 177–78, 212, 218, 230–31
North Elba properties associated with JB: Lot 88, 56, *57*, 84, 85, 106, 234, 250n32, 250n35; Lot 93, 36, 47, *57*, 243n20, 245n9; Lot 95, *10*, 33, 36, 46–47, 52, *57*, 60–64, *64*, 84, 223, 224, 241n5, 243n20, 245n9, 250n32, 269n24; Lot 110, *10*, 31, 33 *57*, 233; maps of, *10*, *57*. See also Flanders farm (Lot 110); John Brown Farm (Lot 95)
North Elba, Town of, xi–xii, 2–7, 10; as West Keene, 28–29, 241n5; character of townspeople, 11, 48–49, 238n4; climate, harsh, 9, 11, 24, 25, 54, 60, 68, 73, 93, 117, 177, 180, 182, 217, 218; farming, 9–11, 47–48, 86, 104, 105, 106, 237n2; healthfulness of, 46, 47; livestock, 10, 11, 30, 32, 47–49, 53, 56, 67, 78, 86, 93, 106, 161; maps of, *10*, *57*; population, 7, 11, 22; remoteness of, 6, 7, 28, 29, 37, 46. See also Flanders farm; John Brown Farm; neighbors; Timbucto
Northampton, Massachusetts, 43–46, 73
Norton, Phineas, 108, 148, 151, 159, 259n46, 260n16

Oates, Stephen, 6, 16
Oberlin College, 12, 118, 184
Ohio: aid to MB from, 172; JB and family in, 2, 7, 12, 24, 53–54, 59, 61–62, 71, 105, 171, 208, 218, 229–31, 234, 236; recruits from, 118, 121, 253n9
Osgood, Iddo, 32, 37, 52, 57, 242n13, 243n21, 245n21, 265n21

Osgood, Dillon, 104, 251n42

Parker, Theodore, 83
Pennsylvania: Chambersburg, 107, 108, 111, 115; Crawford County, 11–12, 172; mentioned 7, 41, 56, 101, 126, 158–60, 184, 229–30, 236, 255n10, 258n18. See also Philadelphia
Perkins, Simon, 16, 53
Peterboro, New York: Garnet moves to, 23; home of Gerrit Smith, 18, 126; JB visits, 24, 84, 101; Sanborn visits, 85; Secret Six meet in, 101
Philadelphia, Pennsylvania, 7, 56, 101, 129, 134–36, 144–45, 158, 172–73, 195, 201, 221
Phillips, Wendell, 9, 11, 71, 75, 145, 147, 149, 152, 156–58, 163, 165, 167, 173, 177, 181, 197, 215, 258n18
Philosophers' Camp, *95*, 95–96
Pitchoff (Keene) Mountain, 24, 30, 62, 148, 151
poetic justice, 208, 258n18
Pond, Byron, 147
poverty of Brown family: cheerful/content with plain, simple life, 6, 85–86, 87–88, 132, 172, 180–81; compared to North Elba neighbors, 86; compared to societal norm, 16–17, 86, 180–81; JB on, 15, 181; JB sends supplies and cash to family, 6, 48, 77, 78, 82, 86, 105, 106, 117–18; lack of cash, 76–77, 85–86, 180–81; pioneer life, 3, 6, 7, 9, 11, 180; upon reaching California, 221
Providence/omen, 5, 53, 100, 113, 118, 135, 124, 152, 178, 193, 204, 219

"Provisional Constitution and Ordinance for the Proscribed and Oppressed People of the United States," 99, 103–104, 183–84, 253n11

Quakers, 73, 111, 126, 201–202, 218

race, as a social construct, xii
racism, 27–28, 35–36, 39, 68–70, 126; fear of freeing slaves, 167; white supremacy, 100–101, 165, 184, 196
Ray, Rev. Charles B., 21, 68
rebirth, 91, 104, 225; of JB (his soul marches on), 4, 132, 182, 192–93, 194, 207, 208, 221, 224–25; of nation, 183–84, 195–96, 222, 225
Redpath, James, 6, 73, 115–16, 135, 173, 187, 191, 262n6
Reed, Mrs., 31, 45
religion. *See* Bible
Republican Party/Republicans, 125, 161, 167–68, 194–95, 243n26, 265n15
Reynolds, David, 6, 127, 247n8
Rice, Mr., 45
Richards, Thomas Addison, 68
Richards, William Trost, 224–25, 269n20
Ruggles, David, 44, 44–46, 73
Rush Academy, 41–42, 57, 244n32

sacrifice for the cause: JB willing to die as, 82, 101, 108, 115, 124, 131, 139, 157, 164, 192, 208, 209; as principle of Brown family, 75, 78, 83, 84–87, 117, 123–24, 131, 157, 180–81, 192, 192
Sanborn's School, 177–78, 202, 204
Sanborn, Franklin, 6, 83–85, 101, 115, 126, 190, 208; visits Brown family, 85–87, 177, 234–35

Scott, Robert, 29, 31, 57, 93, 160, 242n13, 265n21
Secret Six, 83, 101, 104, 106, 108, 123, 126, 256n23
Seward, William H., 90, 215
Shepherd, Heyward, 119, 120
slave owners, 19, 38, 89, 101, 116–17, 126, 129, 152, 160, 165, 167, 191, 195, 197, 207
slave states, 13, 61, 105, 166, 195, 213–15, 249n12, 265n25
slavery: abolitionists blamed for continuance of, 35, 89, 164, 166, 213; clergymen's views on, 21, 62, 83, 98, 141, 152, 164–65, 223; as dehumanizing and debasing, 8, 27, 40, 68; ending of, by Civil War, 201, 207, 212, 213–15, 222–23; ending of, by raid/JB execution, 129, 143, 156, 164, 166, 184, 196, 215, 223, 225; expansion of, 40, 61, 164; foreign importation of slaves, 164, 225; gradual emancipation of, 164, 213, 215; as injustice, 8, 27, 97–98, 100–101, 143, 184, 196; JB and Brown family views, and empathy for enslaved people, 12–14, 34–36, 43, 75, 97–98, 99–102, 103, 106, 107, 130–32, 143, 215; as legal and constitutional, 8, 100–101, 125, 167, 184, 213; myth of enslaved people as happy and content, 35, 163, 165; as national wrong (guilty nation), 35–36, 51, 141, 164, 184, 195–96, 208, 215, 223, 226–27; as sin (immoral), 8, 51–52, 65, 125, 129, 152, 162, 164, 213, 223; support of, in North, 89, 125, 164, 167, 197; in violation of Declaration of Independence, 18, 183–84,

slavery *(continued)*
  188–91, 195–96; as violent, 8, 18, 126, 128, 164, 184, 196, 241n1; as war on black people, 18, 195, 196, 223
Smith, Gerrit, 18, *39*; disassociated with JB, 226; hypocrisy of 38–39, 40; involvement with Harpers Ferry, 101, 116, 126; land monopoly, 40; land sales, 41, 47, 56, 84–85, 87, 160, 244n32, 245n9, 250n35; mental breakdown, 126, 194; as politician (for Liberty Party), 38, 40, 194–95; racism of, 69–70, 126; support of JB, 62, 66, 71, 82–83
Smith land giveaway (of 1846) to black men, 18–24; black abolitionists views on, 19–20, 25, 36–37, 38–39, 68; as blessing or curse, 23–24, 69; deeds, 21, 23, 36, 40, 70, 239n19, 248n30; failure blamed on character of black people, 38, 54, 68–71, 126; farming (as Jeffersonian notion), 18, 39; fugitives as grantees, 242n17; goals/motives, 18–19, 21, 23, 28, 30, 38–40, 69–70, 239n16; grantee requirements, 21; idealism/romanticism of, 18–19, 22, 69; impact on existing residents, 22–23; JB's offer to help, 11, 24, 240n33; land agents, 18, 21–23, 39, 68, 97; location of, 18, 241n5; obstacles deterring grantees from moving north, 21–23, 54, 67, 68, 70, 73, 239n19; positive results of, 20, 21, 61, 72–73, 97; praise for Gerrit Smith, 19–21; quality of land, 22, 25, 36, 240n30, 243n20; voting aspect of, 19,
28, 38–39, 40–41, 72, 248n30. *See also* Blacksville; Timbucto; wilderness
Smith land giveaway (of 1849) to white men and women, 70
Smith, James, McCune, 21, 36–40, 68, 243n21, 243n22
Springfield, Massachusetts, 16–18, 24, 31, 43, 46–47, 52, 181, 231, 233
Spring, Rebecca, 176–77, 180
St. Armand, 10, 51–52, 245n21
Stauffer, John, 6, 126, 195, 238n12
Stearns, George and Mary, 83, 177–78, 215, 235
Stevens, Aaron Dwight, 111, 120, 174
Stevens, Dr. George T., 159
Still, William, 158, 159
Stoddard, Seneca Ray, 54, 246n29, 260n6
Stone, Lucy, 46
Street, Alfred Billings, 94–95
Stringfellow, Gen. Benjamin F., 81, 249n12
Sumner, Charles, 80

Taylor, Stewart, 111, 121, 253n11
Thomas, Cyrus, 31, 34, 36, 45, 52
Thompson, Dauphin, 4, 94–95, 109–11, 121, 124, 135, 155–56, 235
Thompson, Ella Jane, 79, 107–108, 229, 254n24
Thompson, Archibald, 57
Thompson, Franklin, 84–85
Thompson, Henry: building house at John Brown Farm, 60–61, 62, 63; as carpenter, 50, 61; as guide, 94; as husband to Ruth Brown, 49–50, 50, 78–79, 229; on JB's actions, 131; as JB's son-in-law, 47, 53, 60, 93; in Kansas, 75, 77, 78, 80, 81, 85, 229, 249n18; on moral suasion, 108–109; moving

from North Elba, 217, 218;
in North Elba, 54, 56, 57, 59,
65, 81, 85, 93, 104, 105, 106,
168, 262n38; possible recruit for
Harpers Ferry, 101–102, 109
Thompson, Isabelle "Belle." *See* Brown,
Isabelle "Belle" (Thompson)
Thompson, Jane, 159
Thompson, John, 57, 76, 168
Thompson, Mary Brown (wife of
William Thompson), 121, 173
Thompson, Roswell, 50, 52, 57, 159,
245n21
Thompson, Samuel, 57, 84–85, 249n9
Thompson, Willard, 213–14
Thompson, William, 4, 81, 109–11,
124, 135, 155–56, 210, 235,
250n22, 252n16
Thoreau, Henry David, 1, 89–91, 96,
98, 127–28, 143, 164, 166, 178,
192, 203, 208, 223, 225, 261n29,
264n12
Tidd, Charles Plummer, 111, 121,
172, 253n11
Timbucto (black community in North
Elba), xii, 7, 28–29, 72, 241n5
—Brown family interactions with,
7, 11, 18, 31, 36–37, 45–46,
48, 56, 94, 102, 104, 107, 122,
246n12
—criticism of black settlers in, 33,
35, 36–37, 38, 45, 54, 68, 72
—decline/demise of, 54, 67–73
—farm crops and livestock, 21, 56,
67
—difficulties at, 36–38, 45, 54, 67
—Freeman's Home and, 71, 248n26
—impact on existing North Elba
residents, 22, 41–42
—JB's aid of, 24–26, 28–30, 31,
36–37, 47, 59, 62, 71–72, 73,
240n35

—land deeds (and ownership), 36,
67, 93, 248n3
—myth of: black men's character
as cause of demise, 69–71;
fugitives, 32–35, 70–71, 242n17;
JB as cause of demise, 71–72;
overblown success, 72–73,
248n30; Underground Railroad,
32–35, 70–71; voting as major
goal, 72, 248n30
—naming of, xii, 28–29, 70–71,
241n5
—as political theater, 38–40, 41,
42
—population of, 37, 54, 59, 67,
243n22
—positive experiences at (promise
of), 28, 37, 45, 54–56, 67, 68,
72, 73
—as recruits for JB's Allegheny plan,
30, 102
—Smith's role in causing demise of,
69–70, 72, 73
tombstone: inscriptions, 7, 174–77,
188, 250n29; JB's affection
for, 133, 174; as memorial to
grandfather, 84, 174–75, 222;
shipped to Westport, New York,
84, 175; as tombstone/memorial
at farm graveyard, 133, *157*, 175,
176, *183*, 7, 222, *224*
Torrington, Connecticut, 2, 12, 229
tourists/visitors: to Adirondacks, xii,
31–32, 36–37, 91–92, 95–96,
98, 201–202, 209, 240n30,
269n20; to John Brown Farm,
85–86, 123–24, 149, 152, 153,
177, 185–86, 187–88, 226–27,
261n28, 264n12
traitor (committed treason): JB as 125,
129, 134, 161, 162, 166–67, 189,
194; Henry Wise as 198–99

Index | 291

trial of JB: insanity plea, 129; JB speech to Court, 129–31, *130*; sentencing, 131
Troy, New York, 20, 24–25, 34, 41, 53, 55–56, 106, 117, 146, 239n16
Truth, Sojourner, 45
Tubman, Harriet, 30, 102, 106
Turner, David, 159, 161–64, 167–68, 196, 268n7
Tyndale, Hector, 137, 144, 258n18

Uncle Tom's Cabin, 108
Underground Railroad: in Essex County, 34, 242n16; myth of, in North Elba, 30, 33–34, 71, 242n16, 242n17; mentioned 11, 15, 21, 51, 54, 102, 150, 152, 158, 188
utopia experiments, 45, 72

Vermont, 11, 34, 38, 68, 93, 135, 146–47, 150–51, 165, 178, 192, 211
Villard, Oswald Garrison, 6
violence:
—abolitionists gradual acceptance of, 52, 66, 82, 116, 128, 129, 156, 189, 191, 195–96, 207, 223
—everyday use of, (sanctioned by government), 127–28
—JB's sons rebuke of, 101
—JB's view of: to combat/end slavery, 18, 36, 66, 80, 91, 98, 101, 116–17, 223; to prevent further bloodshed (save lives), 80, 106, 107, 141; in self-defense, 18, 66, 80; as threat to proslavery forces (strike terror), 80, 82
—in Kansas, 65–67, 75–76, 78–82, 91, 101, 111, 234
—in nature, 91, 93, 98
—reactions to JB's use of, 8, 82, 125–28; by Douglass, 191, 207; by Emerson and Thoreau, 91, 127–28; by Essex County neighbors, 161–63; by Lee, Luther, 189–90; by Lincoln, 161–63, 167; by Phillips, 156, 258n18; by Redpath, 116
—right of slave to use, 36, 189
—of slavery, 8, 18, 126, 128, 164, 184, 196
—unsanctioned by government, 81, 125, 127–28, 167, 223
Virginia: secession from Union, 198, 265n25; slavery in, 163, 174, 184, 241n1; West Virginia split from, 265n25; mentioned, xi, 2, 6–7, 18–19, 27, 101, 107–37, 140–46, 156, 162, 167, 169, 187–91, 194, 207, 219, 222, 253n12. *See also* Harpers Ferry; Harpers Ferry raid; Charles Town
voting (suffrage) of black men in New York: grantees as voters, 40–41, 67, 72, 244n28; JB's view on, 40; Negro Suffrage referendum (1846), 38–39, 243n24; Smith land giveaway (and Timbucto) connection to, 19, 28, 38–39, 40–41, 72, 248n30

Wallface Mountain, 92
Wardner, Rev. Nathan, 188, 211–12, 264n3, 267n26
Ware, Judson, 211, 252n16
Washington, George, 167–68, 189
Washington County, New York, 11
Washington, DC, 193, 195, 213, 221
water cure, 43–46, 73, 218, 233, 244n4
Watkins (Harper), Frances Ellen, 128, 133, 171–73, *173*

Watson, Winslow, 9, 11, 41–42, 161–62, 238n4, 265n15
Weld, Theodore, 2, 176
West Virginia, xi, 2, 159, 265n25
Westport, New York, 24, 30, 34, 47, 51, 84, 105–106, 123, 146–47, 151, 159, 175, 212, 234, 242n16, 250n29
Whig Party, 38
Whiteface Mountain, 1, 4, 32, 64, 93–95, *94*, 153, 263n23
Whitehall, New York, 11, 24, 26, 48, 50, 78, 238n5, 241n7
Wilmington, New York, 51–52, 123, 188, 245n21
wilderness (wild lands), xi, xii; in Bible, 90–91, 93, 97; as an ideal, 19, 95, 96, 97; JB's actions motivated by, 5, 90, 97–98, 217; JB's affection for, 24, 29, 30, 65, 92–93, 96; as land of promise for black settlers, 18–19, 21–23, 30, 37, 54, 69, 97; as place of closeness to God (Omnipotence), 30, 91–93, 93, 97; as place of freedom, 9, 19, 91, 95–96, 97, 117; as place of hardship/danger, 8, 9, 22, 68, 69, 91, 93, 97, 98; as place of healing, 46, 47, 91–92, 96; as place to produce character, 8, 90, 96, 98; as place of romantic (wild) scenes of Nature, 29, 69, 91–92, 95–96, 104, 123, 188, 256n23; as place "of slavery and injustice," 97. *See also* Adirondack Mountains; higher law
wildness, 91–92
Wise, Henry: Annie Brown at mansion of, 219; on disposal of JB's body, 134–35; on JB's character, 129; letters with MB, 136–37; secession of Virginia, 198–99; mentioned 125, 146, 162, 169, 198, 213, 260n14, 268n7
women: excluded from Smith land giveaway to black men, 70; excluded from antislavery societies, 35; excluded as soldiers, 204; judged on appearance, 176, 180; as vital to cause of freedom, 4, 52, 84–85, 87, 109–10, 111–13. *See also* individual names of women
Wright, Henry C., 134, 181, 209
Wright, Theodore S., 21

Young, Rev. Joshua, *150*, 150–52, 154–55, 157–58, 165, 209, 261n28, 263n12

www.ingramcontent.com/pod-product-compliance
Lightning Source LLC
Chambersburg PA
CBHW031723230426
43669CB00007B/226